Advocacy in the magistrates' cour

A guide for the defence

CU00918539

JOHN MACKENZIE is a solicitor and partner at Mackenzie Persaud in West London. He is a specialist in criminal law and an experienced author and lecturer. He is a Higher Courts advocate in civil and criminal proceedings.

Advocacy in the magistrates' court
A guide for the defence

John Mackenzie, SOLICITOR

LAG Legal Action Group
1994

This edition published in Great Britain 1994
by LAG Education and Service Trust Limited
242 Pentonville Road, London N1 9UN

© John Mackenzie 1994

All rights reserved. No part of this publication may be reproduced, stored in a retrieval system or transmitted in any form or by any means, without permission from the publisher.

British Library Cataloguing in Publication Data
A CIP catalogue record for this book is available from the British Library.

ISBN 0 905099 51 6

Phototypeset by J&L Composition Ltd, Filey, North Yorkshire
Printed in Great Britain by BPC-Wheatons Ltd, Exeter

Contents

Introduction

There is no art to compare with the art of the advocate. It is exhilarating, unpredictable, nerve-wracking. The advocate writes his own lines, delivers them and manipulates his audience. The successes take the advocate to pinnacles of satisfaction, the failures to the depths of gloom and despair. The opportunities for variety are endless and unpredictable. In few fields of human endeavour can results depend to such an extent upon the capabilities and energies of the participant.

Summary advocacy, that is advocacy in the magistrates' courts, is probably as demanding a form of criminal advocacy as any. It is far from being the poor relation of that practised in the higher criminal courts. It may seem heresy to the aficionados of the senior courts, but there are several features that make summary advocacy a higher art form. Some magistrates tend not to apply the burden of proof correctly. It can seem that the prosecution in a summary trial does not have to prove its case beyond a reasonable doubt; it is the defendant who has to prove his innocence. The defence advocate rarely has the luxury of relying upon the strength of the defence evidence to achieve an acquittal. The defence advocate has to demolish the prosecution evidence in cross-examination and ensure that his closing speech exploits every weakness in the prosecution case. There is no judge in a summary trial to 'sweep up' for the defence advocate who fails to prepare and present his case in full. If the defence advocate does not make a point to the justices, it remains unmade. On the other hand, where the defence advocate is well prepared and thorough, there is no judge to blunt his efforts. For these and other reasons the magistrates' court is the most demanding of tribunals.

This book contains two parts. Part I presents techniques for use by the summary advocate. These techniques are not definitive. They are designed to assist the advocate in developing a personal style of advocacy. Nothing that is said is intended as a 'rule'. This part of the book is intended to generate thought and to help advocates devise and develop their own style. Many features of advocacy are learnt in the school of hard knocks. The advice may not prevent the advocate suffering the hard knocks, but it will enable the advocate to recognise the knock when it comes and learn as much as possible from it. Hard knocks are an inevitable feature of advocacy and the advocate who manages to avoid them cannot be taking the risks essential to the art.

Part I ends with a chapter containing contrasting examples of cross-examination by an experienced and an inexperienced advocate.

Part II is an extended case study. It presents a fictionalised account of a summary trial from the moment the defendants emerge from the police station with charge sheets in their hands to the end of their hard-fought trial. The pitfalls and techniques explained and discussed in Part I are illustrated in action in the account in Part II. This account contrasts a novice advocate with an experienced advocate, both acting for the defence. It illustrates effective and ineffective speeches, examination-in-chief and cross-examination. Again the account is not intended to be definitive. It is designed to warn and inspire. Where points in Part I are illustrated in Part II, this will be indicated by cross-references to the appropriate page or section in the fictionalised account.

Views expressed in this book are sometimes controversial. They are presented to stimulate thought rather than as the official line or received wisdom of the legal profession or the Legal Action Group.

'He' includes 'she'. What is written of male advocates or defendants applies equally to female and usually vice-versa.

Part I

The Summary Advocate

CHAPTER 1

The make-up of the advocate

Advocacy is a diffuse and subjective art. Advocates develop styles from their professional experience and other features in their make-up, their education, social antecedents and personalities. The advocacy of an extrovert will be different from that of an introvert; that of an eccentric different from a conventional personality. The advocacy of a barrister will be different from the advocacy of a solicitor.

An individual's style will develop during the course of a career. Changes in the content of an advocate's practice will change the advocate's approach and presentation. Change of political affiliation will change the style. Increased age and status may give the advocate greater authority; on the other hand, it may also cause complacency and slackness.

The advocate appearing regularly in the magistrates' court will have a style suited to that form of litigation. It would be less well suited to an action before a High Court judge. A Queen's Counsel used to appearing in the Court of Appeal may not attract a lay bench with his presentation. Each develops a style suited to his usual forum.

It is essential that an advocate has a full working knowledge of the rules of evidence and procedure. These are not covered in this book. The rules are set out in textbooks on evidence and the statutory provisions are in any practitioner's handbook. It is not realistic to expect to master this complex subject in a single drive. Whenever a case raises an issue relating to a feature of evidence or procedure the advocate should take the opportunity to research this aspect thoroughly. Over a period of time the advocate will in that way build up a good working knowledge of the important rules. It is a failing of many advocates that they assume that because they are experienced advocates they know the rules of evidence and procedure. This is, unfortunately, rarely the case.

CHAPTER 2

The summary trial

The primary feature of the summary trial is that it is usually held before a tribunal of lay persons. Advocacy before a lay tribunal is probably more demanding than advocacy before a professional tribunal and offers more scope for the advocate's skills. A professional tribunal is less receptive to the skills of the advocate and has a higher level of legal and procedural knowledge. The advocate in a higher court does not need to be so scrupulous in covering every feature of a case and less depends upon his persuasive skills. Justices in a magistrates' court react more to the advocacy to which they are subjected. They comment and question.

A jury in a Crown Court trial is unable to react to the case it is hearing and is little more than a row of blank eyes. The advocate can have little idea of the impact he is making. In the Crown Court the judge takes much of the conduct of the case out of the hands of the advocates. The judge's summing up to the jury is a great leveller between the parties. In the magistrates' court the advocates operate without an overseeing judge. The defence advocate has great influence over the justices, if he is able and willing to exercise that influence. No one speaks after the defence advocate in a summary trial; his closing speech can have a decisive impact. If there are difficult points of law, it is frequently the advocates who provide the justices with significant legal advice.

Summary trials are quicker than a Crown Court jury trial. A day-long summary trial in the magistrates' court might take three days in its equivalent form in the Crown Court.

In the Crown Court, the defence advocate is served with the prosecution statements in advance and has the opportunity to analyse them at leisure. It is rare for the Crown Prosecution Service to serve the prosecution witness statements in advance for a summary trial. Much of the prosecution evidence comes unannounced to the defence advocate, who has to absorb it as he goes along during the trial. He will hear evidence for the first time from a witness immediately before having to cross-examine that witness on this very evidence. Once he has learnt to cope with these difficulties, the experienced and competent summary advocate is as skilled as any advocate in the system.

1. The dynamics of a trial

The sequence of a contested summary criminal trial is similar to that of a Crown Court criminal trial.

1 The charges are put to the defendant and the pleas are taken.
2 Any preliminary matters are dealt with, such as objections to charges being tried together. This sort of matter is best dealt with at an earlier preliminary hearing so that the magistrates trying the case are not aware that there are other charges against the defendant if the decision is to hold separate trials.
3 The prosecutor then opens the prosecution case to the magistrates.
4 The prosecutor calls the first prosecution witness, who gives evidence-in-chief under questioning from the prosecutor.
5 The defence advocate cross-examines the witness.
6 The prosecutor is entitled to re-examine the witness on matters that have arisen in cross-examination.
7 The prosecutor calls each of his witnesses in this fashion.
8 If there are any prosecution witnesses whose statements can be read because their evidence is not contested by the defence, this can be done at any stage.
9 If it seems appropriate to the defence advocate, he can submit to the justices at the end of the prosecution case that there is no case for the defendant to answer on any of the charges against him.
10 The defence advocate may address the magistrates in opening his case before calling any evidence. If he does this and wishes to make a closing speech, he gives the prosecutor the opportunity for a closing speech. It is rare in any criminal trial for the defence to make an address in opening.
11 The defence advocate calls the defendant to give evidence if he wishes to call him. The defendant is subjected to examination-in-chief, cross-examination and re-examination in the same way as the prosecution witnesses.
12 The defence advocate calls any other witnesses or reads uncontroversial evidence from statements.

13 At the end of the defence case the defence advocate addresses the magistrates.
14 The magistrates retire to consider their verdict. They can if they wish ask the clerk to join them in their private room and advise them on the law. He must not take part in their deliberations on the facts and verdict. Some clerks insist on advising the magistrates in open court.
15 The magistrates return to court and deliver their verdict.
16 If the verdict is guilty, the prosecutor will give the defendant's criminal record and any antecedents known to the prosecution.
17 The defence advocate addresses the justices in mitigation of sentence.
18 The magistrates retire again and on return deliver sentence. In practice, in a case of any seriousness they will be likely to adjourn sentence for reports to be prepared.

The defence advocate should expect the defence case to be at its highest at the end of the prosecution case. The defence advocate's cross-examination, if properly done, will have reduced the prosecution evidence to its lowest point. As the defence case gets under way, the same diminishing effect is brought about in reverse by the prosecutor's cross-examination. The defence evidence loses its strength under cross-examination and the defence case subsides from its high point at the end of the prosecution case. This is a common phenomenon and should be recognised and accepted. A good closing speech may then restore the defence case to its high point as all the effective points made in cross-examination are reviewed before the magistrates. It would be hard to over-estimate the importance of the defence closing speech. A high proportion of summary trials are won or lost through the quality of this address to the magistrates by the defence advocate.

2. Strategy in a summary trial

The defence strategy in most summary trials will be substantially opportunistic. Too many features of the case are incapable of prediction for it to be otherwise. However, generally speaking the defence advocate's strategy should follow this course:

1 Observe the prosecution case closely to see if any essential component of the offence alleged is omitted, either due to inadvertence or lack of evidence.

2 Undermine the cohesion of the prosecution evidence by cross-examination.

3 Undermine the credibility of the prosecution evidence by cross-examination.

4 Present as strong a case as possible in the defence evidence.

5 Exploit in full the weaknesses of the prosecution case and the strengths of the defence case in the defence closing speech.

There is a simple but devastating technique that tends to be used in most criminal trials. It arises from the somewhat bludgeon-like approach that is inevitable in the adversarial system. The defence will turn the trial away from the issue of whether the defendant committed the offence onto one of whether the prosecution witnesses have been truthful on some side issue. Sometimes the side issue is one of complete triviality. Nevertheless such an issue can quite easily become the most important feature of the case and the yardstick against which the prosecution case is judged. For example, in a summary public order offence in which the defendant is alleged by two police officers to have thrown a brick at a meeting, it may become an issue as to whether the defendant was taken to the police station in a police van or a police car. One officer says it was a van and another officer says it was a car. The case may then be decided with a verdict of not guilty because the justices feel that if the officers cannot be relied upon on this side issue, it cannot be said that their evidence is without a doubt in relation to the central issue of the throwing of the brick. A high proportion of cases turning on police evidence are affected in this way. The defence advocate should be constantly searching for side issues of this sort which may destroy the credibility of the prosecution case. (See sections 13, 17 and 18 in Part II on the use of spelling mistakes in the officers' notebooks.)

CHAPTER 3

Style and content

1. Use of language

Skill in the use of language is everything for the advocate. The advocate needs to think clearly and present his argument and questions in an easily understandable form. This is not necessarily a matter of natural flair. An advocate can train himself to think clearly and express those thoughts succinctly. It is easier to control an argument if it is delivered in short sentences. Where the argument needs to be qualified, the advocate should do so in separate sentences avoiding the use of conditional clauses. By constantly monitoring the way he speaks, the advocate will come to speak in this manner as a matter of course.

When selecting his or her words, the advocate should opt for the simplest and shortest. In this way he will habitually speak in a manner that is clear and easily understood. As well as ensuring that the court understands what he is saying, this will have a corresponding effect on clarifying the arguments in the advocate's own mind. A well thought out and easily understood argument will stimulate further ideas in the advocate's own mind as he speaks and listens to him or herself speaking. An advocate needs to develop the habit of thinking intensively about the current case even when not in court so that the mind constantly reviews and sorts the possible arguments.

The use of short sentences and simple words reduces the danger of a witness or the defendant misunderstanding the advocate. A person who misunderstands does not always make this known. He may be too shy to admit that a long word is unfamiliar and guess at its meaning. If a misunderstanding occurs during important evidence, the consequences can be devastating for the defence case.

2. The voice

A loud, confident voice conveys the impression that the advocate is convinced by his own arguments. A soft voice may give the reverse impression. Some judges and magistrates are hard of hearing. The advocate who can always be easily heard is a welcome relief to them and perhaps they consider the argument more sympathetically. It is certainly more likely to be heard.

A defendant in the dock is reassured by hearing his advocate speaking up in an assertive manner. If there are people in the public gallery, they will be impressed by the advocate they can easily hear. They may be the advocate's next clients.

3. Signals and body lanuage

An advocate gives signals to the listener in a number of ways. These signals may convey meanings the advocate does not intend or wish. The advocate may be completely unaware of the existence of many of these signals. The advocate should monitor his advocacy to ensure that he delivers only the intended meaning.

The primary signal is in the words the advocate uses. The words may contain secondary meanings of which the advocate is unaware and which he does not intend. This is particularly so when jargon is used. Lawyers are particularly prone to incorporating jargon in their speech, often without appreciating its implications. A common example of jargon is the expression 'I am instructed'. This expression can have the effect of distancing the advocate from the information he is giving. For example:

MAGISTRATE: Is the defendant in employment?
ADVOCATE: He instructs me that he is.

The signal to the magistrates may be that the advocate does not commit himself to the truth of the information. Many an advocate uses this piece of jargon as a matter of course, perhaps because it sounds like the type of expression that advocates should use. He will probably be unaware that he is signalling that he dissociates himself from the information he is giving and consequently casting doubts on its reliability.

A feature of this sort of signal is that it is not apparent on the face of the words spoken other than to persons in the court who are familiar with the jargon. In other words, it is a technique for passing additional information to the court, perhaps without the defendant being aware that this is being done. This is a very dangerous practice and should be carefully controlled. An advocate should only give such a signal if he has genuine doubts as to the reliability of the information and wishes to warn the court of these doubts. Otherwise the exchange should go:

MAGISTRATE: Is the defendant in employment?
ADVOCATE: Yes. He is.

An advocate should as a matter of routine check his delivery to make sure that his speech contains no signals other than his precise intended meaning.

Signals can be given by the advocate's voice and manner. If an advocate stands full square to the court and speaks loudly and clearly, looking the magistrates in the eye, the signal will be that the advocate has confidence in his case and expects the court to accept the points he makes. Speaking softly or failing to look at the magistrates when addressing them can be read as signals of lack of confidence in the arguments or facts being deployed.

The advocate may undermine his advocacy by physical mannerisms which distract the magistrates' concentration or irritate them. These might be putting hands in the pockets or moving pens around on the desk or putting a foot on the seat. The advocate is unlikely to discover the effect of any idiosyncratic behaviour on his advocacy in the eyes of the court. It is therefore important for the advocate to ensure that there is nothing idiosyncratic in his style that might detract from his advocacy.

It may be appropriate to use gestures when they are intended to convey a specific meaning. For example, it might be that an advocate waves his pen at a witness when making a telling point in cross-examination. If the magistrates know the advocate and recognise the gesture, it may help indicate to them that the point is a significant one. It is important that the advocate has such control of his delivery that these features are seen to be used intentionally and to a purpose and not as unconscious and perhaps ludicrous quirks.

CHAPTER 4

Preparation for the summary trial

The key to effective advocacy is thorough preparation. Preparation gives the advocate a complete grasp of the facts of the case and the law that may be important in the case. In addition, preparing the foreseeable parts of the case will leave the advocate's mind free to cope with the unforeseen. Proper preparation does not mean rigidly deciding the format of the case by, for example, writing out a speech or a cross-examination. There are a number of reasons why this is undesirable. The very nature of the summary trial and its inbuilt difficulties mean that the information available to the advocate in advance of the trial is insufficient to plan fully for the trial. The Crown Prosecution Service does not usually serve the statements of its witnesses, so the advocate cannot know what the prosecution witnesses are going to say in detail. Even in cases where the prosecution statements are served, they are only a general guide to the evidence the witnesses are going to give and can be highly misleading.

Careful preparation means having a complete grasp of the facts that are available to the advocate and thinking about the case extensively so that every possible idea on the conduct of the case is considered. It means having such a grasp of the case that the speech or cross-examination springs spontaneously from the material assembled in the mind. The advocate thereby retains the qualities of flexibility and spontaneity, the qualities that spring from complete understanding of the case and bring a case to life.

Thorough preparation also requires familiarity with all the law and procedure that may be needed during the case. The stages of preparation will be broadly:

1 Assembling all the documentation that is available.
2 Taking comprehensive statements or proofs of evidence from the witnesses available.

3 Viewing the scene if at all possible.
4 Researching the relevant law and procedure.
5 Ensuring that the defendant and defence witnesses are prepared for the ordeal of giving evidence.
6 In certain cases there may be expert evidence to assemble and sift through.
7 Devising a broad but flexible strategy for the case.
8 Ensuring that the advocate has all the information in the case in a readily accessible form.

1. Documents

The defence advocate should as a matter of course write to the Crown Prosecution Service (CPS) requesting the following documents:

1 The custody records.
2 The tapes of interviews of the defendant.
3 Copies of all charge sheets.
4 Copies of the prosecution witness statements.

Items 1 to 3 must be served if requested, although it may be necessary (depending on the area) to obtain them from the police and not the CPS. The CPS may also serve the prosecution witness statements on request or may refuse. This is entirely within the CPS' discretion. If the CPS refuses, it can be pointed out to it in correspondence that the defence will be forced to take instructions frequently during the trial as the prosecution witnesses produce unexpected points in their evidence and that service of the statements will assist the defence to speed up the trial. Applications can be made to the magistrates for pressure to be brought on the CPS to serve the statements.

The CPS may try to serve certain prosecution witness statements under the Criminal Justice Act 1967 s9 so as to avoid the trouble of calling those witnesses. The defence will then be in a position to point out that no proper assessment of whether a witness can be accepted under s9 can be made unless *all* the prosecution statements are served and that consequently those witnesses will be required to attend court and give evidence orally unless the CPS can see their way to serving all the prosecution statements.

It may be appropriate to write and ask the CPS to disclose the identities of all witnesses to the alleged offence known to the police or CPS that are not going to be called as witnesses in the prosecution case.

Equally it may be appropriate to ask for written confirmation that there are no photographs or video evidence available of the alleged offence. If there is such evidence and it is favourable to the defence, it may well not find its way as far as the CPS.

Custody records

A close analysis of the prosecution documents available to the defence will often give a useful insight into the way the prosecution case has been assembled and provide material for cross-examination. It is rarely possible to assess what a document may reveal in advance. It is often a matter of the advocate making himself as familiar as possible with the document so that on the umpteenth reading patterns will be discerned and features of interest begin to appear.

The custody record contains a considerable amount of information that will usually have been recorded at the time of the defendant's arrival at the police station under arrest. This generally is before the police witnesses compile their notes or statements are taken from witnesses. If, therefore, the prosecution case changes as the witnesses decide what to say, the change may be apparent from the wording in the custody record. For example, a police officer may claim to have written his notes at a particular time but have written into his notes a detail that reference to the custody record shows was not available for the officer to have adopted at the time he claims for the writing of his notes. The officer may claim to have arrested the defendant for one offence but the custody officer has recorded in the custody record the reason for the arrest as a different offence.

It will be useful if the advocate has methodically broken down this sort of information from the custody record into a readily accessible schedule before the hearing. In the hectic rush of the trial it may not otherwise be possible to identify such an opportunity. Where there are a number of defendants in a trial, it may well be particularly helpful to create a schedule of information available in all the custody records in a form that enables comparisons to be made quickly during the trial.

Careful examination of the custody records may reveal other useful features that the defence advocate might never have expected. For example, a careful analysis of the sergeants acting as custody officers to a group of defendants might reveal that this function was performed illegally by one of the officers involved in the incident for which the prosecution has been brought. The advocate needs to examine the custody records thoroughly and with an open mind, ready to identify any useful point, and not limited to looking for the usual features.

Records of interview

Careful analysis of interviews may well reveal information useful in the conduct of the case. It will in any case be necessary to know what the defendant has said in answer to the allegations put by the interviewing officer. If the answers are damaging to the defence, the prosecutor is likely to use them in his case and cross-examine the defendant on them. It is essential for the defence advocate to check the answers thoroughly and ensure that there is no unnoticed answer that contradicts the defence case. It is surprisingly easy to overlook sections of an interview or to assume an interpretation favourable to the defence which is not justified. This may happen when the advocate fails to look closely at the true meaning of what has been said. Where there are awkward parts, the defendant must be questioned closely about them. At the very least he will be prepared for the cross-examination and at best may have some explanation which reduces the damage caused to his case in cross-examination.

A further important consideration is that in a summary trial, where information on the prosecution case is likely to be scarce, the content of the interviewing officer's questions may give valuable insights into the prosecutor's case. It may be that the evidence that is called at trial by the prosecution is inconsistent with the interviewing officer's questions. This may be a source of useful cross-examination. For example, an officer may make an allegation in his evidence against the defendant that was not raised during the interview or was raised in a different form. These may be telling points when put to the officer in cross-examination. (In sections 13 and 17 of Part II Rachel Red investigates the discrepancies between what the arresting officers told the custody officer and their evidence to the court.)

The charge sheets

Although strictly part of the custody record, the charge sheet is worth considering as a separate category of document. In many cases, particularly public order cases where the main evidence is from the police, the history of charges can be of considerable significance. This is particularly so where there are changes of charge during the life of the case. Changes in the offence charged, or the date or place of the alleged offence may show a fundamental change in the allegations being made which cries out for vigourous exploration in cross-examination. The offences on the charge sheets should be compared with the reasons for arrest given on the custody record. In the Gorringe case at the end of this Part (pp 71 *et seq.*) the defendant was alleged to have been arrested under the Public Order Act 1986 s5 and then charged with assault on the police. This sort of contradiction needs to be ruthlessly examined.

The prosecution witness statements

The prosecution may be prepared to serve their witness statements on the defence in advance of a summary trial, particularly if the trial is likely to be a long one. These statements are likely to reward careful analysis.

It is important to remember the nature of a witness statement. It is unlikely to be an objective account of an incident. The statement will reflect not only the recollection but also the attitudes of the witness whose evidence it purports to record. The statement is unlikely to reveal on its face the forces that influence the witness to say what he has said in the statement. It requires careful thought and analysis on the part of the advocate before these forces reveal themselves and can be understood, if they do reveal themselves at all. A witness statement taken from a member of the public will be written out in almost every instance by an investigating police officer. The content of a witness statement may be affected by the attitude of the police officer who recorded it. This will be particularly so in cases where the officer recording the statement feels a strong commitment to a conviction. It is important for the advocate to try to identify these forces and to establish the effect they have had on the evidence presented for the prosecution. This may be the only way to challenge an apparently incontrovertible piece of evidence. The advocate may know little about the witnesses before the hearing of the case and be unable otherwise to put before the justices any reason why the witness might be untruthful or unreliable or just wrong.

The advocate needs to carry out a painstaking dissection of the statements and all the information given on the statement forms. Such a dissection may for example reveal collusion between the witnesses. Witnesses in a prosecution may deny collusion in compiling their statements but have written into those statements common features that show a high probability of collusion.

To take a fictionalised example, in a case of disorderly conduct against a hunt saboteur the prosecution intend, in addition to the police evidence, to call two lay witnesses, Mr ABC and Mr DEF. The prosecution make their witness statements available to the defence. Mr ABC's statement reads:

> On 15th August 1990 at about 3.35pm I was riding my bay mare along *the sandy track which bounds the land of Mr Oatgrower,* farmer, when I saw an anti run out of the woods on the left and run on up the path in front of me. He was shouting and waving his arms about. As I saw him pass Mr DEF the anti *slowed down and, turning his head to his right, I saw him spit at Mr DEF.* I know this anti to be called *Murvin.* I only know him by his first name. I have seen him on two or three previous occasions and have heard the other antis using his name.
> Signed: ABC. Dated: 15th September 1990
> Witnessed by PC UVW.

Mr DEF's statement reads:

> I was out hunting at about three o'clock on 15th August 1990 with the Middlemarch dormouse hounds. I was riding down *the sandy track which bounds Mr Oatgrower's land.* An anti I know to be *Murvin* Foxperson ran past me on my left. I saw him *slow down, turn his head to his right and spit at me.* He then shouted at me and called me a blood-sucking dormouse murderer and ran on. My horse does not like loud noises and it reared, nearly knocking me to the ground.
> Signed: DEF. Dated: 15th August 1990.
> Witnessed by PC XYZ.

The sequence of events given in each statement is similar, although the statements are too short for this to be significant. Had there been in each statement a sequence of perhaps five or more features and those features were given in the same order in each statement, this might have been a significant indication of collusion. However there are two phrases used in each statement that can only be there through some form of collusion. These phrases are in italics. It is inconceivable that the two witnesses would have used these expressions and words unless one had been able to refer to the description given by the other. Furthermore the name Murvin is spelt in an unusual manner. The wide difference in the dates of the statements makes it unlikely that the two witnesses devised their accounts together. What these similarities suggest is that Mr ABC was shown the witness statement of Mr DEF and dictated his statement largely from Mr DEF's statement.

The spelling of Murvin may be explained by PC XYZ having knowledge of how to spell the name in that way from other documents and having automatically written it with that spelling as he wrote out the witness statement to the dictation of DEF.

This analysis shows that at least two of the parties to the prosecution case, Mr ABC and PC UVW, were prepared to behave improperly in the preparation of witness statements by referring to another witness statement. This statement is likely to have been in PC UVW's possession when he interviewed Mr ABC. This will give the defence advocate valuable material with which to attack in cross-examination the conduct and good faith of both these witnesses and the conduct of the police officers. Although the likelihood is that only Mr ABC behaved improperly in giving his statement, his conduct gives the defence advocate the material to attack Mr DEF as well. It may well be that PCs UVW and XYZ are key prosecution witnesses and that the whole of the prosecution case is thrown into doubt by the manner in which the statement of Mr ABC was taken.

The analysis of these statements will enable the defence advocate to cross examine both Messrs ABC and DEF on the basis that there must have been collusion between them of some sort. It is likely that PC UVW will add to the confusion by denying that he showed Mr DEF's statement to Mr ABC, thereby making it that much more difficult for the prosecutor to sort out the muddle. Muddle leads to doubt which may lead to acquittal. (Rachel Red exploits the collusion allegation in section 18 in Part II when cross-examining PC Pink after careful consideration of the officers' notebooks.)

2. Proofs from the defendant and his witnesses

The taking of the proof of evidence from the defendant will usually be the starting-point for the preparation of the defence case after the acquisition of such documentation as the prosecution will disgorge. When taking the defendant's proof the advocate should observe the following routine:

1 Find out from the defendant what his account is of the allegations made against him, his description of the arrest and the police investigation of the allegations and a full account of his background.

2 Seek to identify defences and loopholes in the prosecution case which might be exploited.

3 Make an analysis of how well the defendant will give evidence.

4 Make a fundamental analysis of the defence case and decide what evidence the defence needs to support the contentions made by the defendant and to defeat the contentions made by the prosecution.

5 Be constantly on the lookout for material for cross-examination of prosecution witnesses.

6 Look for ambiguities or contradictions in what the defendant is saying and compel the defendant to appreciate that they are there and to sort them out.

7 By questioning the defendant about features of the case that he has overlooked or considers unimportant, make him less vulnerable to cross-examination.

8 Discipline the defendant to listen to the questions that are put to him and to answer the questions concisely and to the point. In this respect the advocate needs to explain to the defendant the danger of rambling answers in that he may a) contradict himself in the course of an answer or series of answers and b) provide information to the opposition that his own advocate was deliberately not eliciting.

The discipline of taking the defendant's proof of evidence causes the advocate to concentrate on the issues in the case to an intensity that may not be repeated, so that this occasion is usually the best opportunity to develop ideas on how the defence can be conducted.

During the taking of the proof of evidence the defendant has the best opportunity to get to know his advocate, to find out how he is thinking about the case and to develop confidence in him and his ability to understand and conduct the case.

The sensation of being questioned by his advocate and having suspect areas of the defence vigorously probed will be similar to the experience of being questioned at trial and will prepare the defendant for it.

It is very important that the advocate does not treat the proof as just an aide-memoire for his own use. A proof of evidence should be prepared so that it stands alone and can be fully understood by another advocate (solicitor or barrister) who has not been involved in the detailed preparation. The proof is a detailed record of the defendant's case to be used in preparing and conducting the case at trial. Every feature of the case that is worth putting into the proof must be explained so that the reader can immediately grasp the full implication of what is being said.

It is wholly inadequate for a defendant to write his own proof. The reasons for this are:

1 The defendant is bound to have views of what is of importance in the case that are coloured by his own involvement.
2 The defendant will not probe his own comments to see if they are realistic.
3 None of the other important experiences that arise in the taking of a proof of evidence occur.

Sometimes it is difficult to extract information from a defendant in a logical sequence. The process of taking a detailed statement will cause the defendant's memory to come to life and revive the stored recollection of an incident. This may take some time or may occur in an erratic manner, so that the defendant remembers features after the proof has moved to a different subject.

Each feature of the case must be explained in full. If, after lengthy discussion with the defendant the advocate records a feature in a shortened form on the assumption that both parties know what is meant, it may turn out to be entirely obscure to another advocate or even to the recording advocate after a lapse of time.

Layout of the proof

Most proofs in a criminal case can be broken into four sections:

1 The defendant's antecedents.
2 Narrative of the incident that is the subject of the charge.
3 Narrative of the police investigation.
4 The defendant's comments on such prosecution statements as are available.

For the narrative sections the advocate should choose a suitable point before the significant action and then require the defendant to describe the narrative in as much detail as possible until a suitable finishing point is reached.

Style of the proof

The way in which the proof is written is important.

1 The proof should contain regular and frequent landmarks of time, day, date and place. This should be done bearing in mind that the proof may be referred to in a moment of crisis during the

trial. A page turned to at random should show time, day, date and place of the action, even if it has been set out several times before on a previous page.

2 Routes should be described in detail and supported by sketch plans.

3 Events such as conversations and journeys should be given time estimates. Estimated distances and dimensions should be included as often as possible.

4 Where subjects arise that might give rise to cross-examination of the defendant or anyone else, they should be dealt with in detail.

5 The proof should be expressed in short sentences avoiding conditional clauses.

6 Wherever possible conversations should be recorded fully and in direct speech, so that 'He arrested me' would properly be recorded as 'PC Groggins then said to me, "You're nicked".'

7 The advocate should take considerable care to avoid ambiguity. Individuals should not be referred to as 'he' or 'she' at any time. On each occasion the name or a unique description should be used so that the reader of the proof is never in the slightest doubt who is being referred to. Similarly with vehicles and addresses. So 'He went home in his car' becomes 'The bald man with the limp got in the green Mini and drove to 74 Acacia Avenue...'

8 The defendant's own usage should be adopted in the proof so far as it is consistent with unambiguity and clarity. In this way the proof will be more likely to reflect the defendant's views of the case.

9 The proof should not contain long words or complicated expressions unless it is certain that the defendant understands them. Otherwise misunderstandings may arise during the trial between the advocate and the defendant.

10 The advocate should be on the lookout for inaccurate verbal usage by the defendant, particularly where the defendant's first language is not English. Where the defendant appears to misunderstand and misuse a particular word or expression, the advocate should note this carefully and brief the defendant on the error.

In starting the proof with the defendant's antecedents, the advocate has the best opportunity of getting to know the defendant. Features of the defendant's make-up may emerge which shed light on the case. If it is at the front of the proof, this information is also readily available for emergency bail applications.

In the narrative sections the advocate should require from the defendant as much detail as possible while progressing through the narrative. Often the defendant will skip lumps of narrative on the assumption that they are of no significance. In that event the advocate should take the defendant back and require him to deal with them. Until the incident has been described it is impossible to say whether it is significant. It may turn out that what seems of little significance at the time it was recorded becomes of importance in the light of matters described later. There is consequently no short cut. Often valuable cross-examination points are hidden away unsuspected in the recesses of the defendant's account.

Where there are documents to be considered, such as custody records, it is good practice to require the defendant to describe the events the document covers without reference to the document. If the document is referred to from the start, there is a tendency to assume the document is correct. This may not be so. Once the defendant's recollection has been recorded, the document should be examined in detail with the defendant and his comments sought on each section.

With a proof of evidence put together with care in this way, the advocate has a powerful tool with which to mould the case. With an inadequate proof few cases will be more than superficial. Knowledge that he has a first class proof of evidence to work from raises the advocate's confidence immeasurably. (See the contrast between the positions of Rachel and Beryl in Part II, chapter 15.)

3. Site views

There may be compelling reasons that make a view an essential step. If the case contains claims by prosecution witnesses of having been able to see some event from a particular position, the advocate will need to test these claims for himself. However, a view is an important step in the preparation of the case even if there is no apparent geographical inconsistency that needs to be sorted out. A view gives the advocate a mental picture of the scene and its dimensions based on reality and not on speculation or written descriptions.

There is another intangible but important advantage in a view. Successful cross-examination depends on the opinion the witness holds of the advocate. If the witness has the impression that the advocate is cross-examining from a position of knowledge rather than one of speculation, the witness will be that much more unsettled. A witness is disconcerted by the 'advocate who knows' and the witness is likely to be impressed in spite of himself by the advocate who has taken the trouble to examine the scene. The witness is less likely to be tempted to lie about the geography of the incident in his evidence.

The act of viewing the scene of an incident makes the advocate consider the various features of the case. It is likely that this will lead the advocate to have a greater understanding of the case and produce points for cross-examination.

4. Preparation on the law

An advocate should make a practice of looking up the law that immediately affects the case as an automatic part of his preparation, even if it is an area of the law that the advocate considers to be one he knows well. Every case is different and the law needs to be considered in the light of the facts of the particular case under preparation. If there is a novel point to be made in the case, a diligent advocate will find it. For example, an advocate might assume that he knows the constituents of theft. Nevertheless he reads over the definitive sections in the Theft Act and finds that he had overlooked the possibility of a defence on the basis of there being 'no intention permanently to deprive'. Although he knew the ingredients, it was only the re-reading that caused the advocate to consider each ingredient as he read it and to consider its specific application to his case, thereby perhaps discovering a defence that he might otherwise have overlooked.

Other more general areas of practice and law should be examined as a matter of routine from time to time to make sure that the advocate has an up-to-date understanding of practice and procedure. Constant familiarisation with sections of statutes and important cases gives the advocate a greater fluency in explaining them to the justices he has to address.

5. Preparation of essential data

It is useful in a case of any complexity to have a schedule of information such as the names of the persons involved, details of the charges they face, information such as car makes and numbers, dates and addresses and a list of the defence witnesses to be called. The preparation of such a list tends to fix the information in the advocate's mind and gives him an immediate crib of the important detail for use during the trial. It is important for an advocate not to fluff names during the trial, particularly the names of the defendant he represents or his own witnesses.

The final preparation

It is said that one of the strengths of a divided legal profession is that the barrister brings a thorough and dispassionate mind to the case once the solicitor has finished preparing it. This is simply a technique and it is one that every advocate should apply before trial. This is particularly so if the advocate prepared the case in the usual manner of progressing from one feature to another without much opportunity to take stock of the whole case. The advocate should collect all the paperwork in the case and organise it so that the documentation needed during the trial is accessible. He should research all the relevant law. He should consider the issues and make dispassionate decisions as to the strengths of the various features of the defence case and decide which to use and in what form. Possible moves by the prosecution should be considered and provisional counter-moves worked out. In this way the defence advocate will have a full assessment of the case and have a strategic view as to how it should be presented.

The charges

The defence advocate should examine each of the charges or the information carefully to see if it has been correctly worded to cover the offences intended by the prosecution and the facts that the evidence will disclose. It may well be that the prosecution has been careless in the wording and that there are points to be made on the charges. This is particularly important in summary proceedings, as the time-limits on commencing summary proceedings may make it impossible to cure faults that are disclosed at trial.

6. Preparation of defence witnesses

There are few people able to go into a witness box and do full justice to the facts they are trying to describe in their evidence-in-chief. Care must be taken to ensure that the witness knows how to deliver his evidence to best effect. Inexperienced witnesses are even less likely to be able to cope with cross-examination. They will be inclined not to listen to the question properly. There is a considerable difference between answering a question in social conversation and in answering the question of a vengeful cross-examiner. One example will show the difficulty:

QUESTION: Did you talk to anyone at the bus stop?
ANSWER: No. I just asked someone whether it was the right stop.

In social discourse this is a perfectly reasonable answer. In cross-examination the witness would be held to have contradicted himself.

Training the witness to answer questions correctly

In a well prepared case each witness should have been given an experience of what it is like to be cross-examined and how to present his evidence by the defence advocate before the trial. That is, not what to say, just how to present it.

A major difficulty with the divided legal profession and the inherent division of responsibilities is that barristers are largely unaware of the difficulties witnesses have because they do not talk to them at the crucial stage of the preparation of the case. Solicitors are equally unaware of these difficulties because they do not frequently have to steer the witness through giving evidence in court and tend not to bother with that part of the case preparation. Consequently neither profession has historically developed the skill of making balanced judgements as to whether to call particular witnesses. In one case a witness will be called when he should not have been, because no one has made a judgement as to whether the witness is capable of giving evidence to a sufficient standard. In another case a witness may not be called because no proper judgement has been made of his ability to give evidence and the barrister fears to call a witness unseen.

It is important for the advocate in a summary trial to avoid this trap. The solicitor as a summary advocate has no professional barriers to making sure that his witnesses are ones that he can rely upon, and that he is aware of their weaknesses and finally that they are sufficiently instructed to ensure that they give their evidence at its strongest.

Drilling the witness

The witness must be warned that his answers to questions must be fully disciplined. He must follow the drill of listening to the question asked, working out in his mind what his answer is and then answering that question and only that question. He must avoid the temptation to answer the question that he thinks should have been asked (as in the above example where the witness thought the question was 'Did you talk to anyone at the bus stop about anything important?'). These principles apply both to examination-in-chief and to cross-examination.

Preparation of the witness

This drilling of a witness in giving evidence is best done when the witness is providing his proof of evidence. During the taking of the witness's proof of evidence the advocate will be asking the witness questions about the case. If the witness fails to answer the question put and gives information that the question does not ask for, the advocate points this out and repeats the question until the witness understands the process and adopts the sometimes alien technique of listening to the question and analysing what is asked before answering. Interspersed with this criticism the advocate will need to explain the reasons for answering precisely the questions asked, so that the witness appreciates that the training is being carried out as much for his benefit as for the advocate's case and that the advocate is not being gratuitously critical. These reasons are primarily that the advocate may wish to introduce into evidence certain specific facts and not other features and that by failing to address the precise point of the question the witness may defeat this aim, and that the longer the answer the witness gives and the more extraneous subjects he introduces into the answer the more likely the witness is to give the prosecution material for cross-examination. It is unlikely that the witness will object to this discipline. Few people like to appear foolish when giving evidence and most will adopt gratefully techniques that will show them at their best in the witness box.

Preparation for cross-examination

Further principles apply to cross-examination. The witness must be drilled to think carefully what his answer is to be before he begins to speak and only to begin to speak when he has decided upon his full answer. The tendency in social discourse is to begin to speak as soon as there is a slight gap in the conversation, before anyone else can occupy it, and to manoeuvre the comment being made while speaking. For example: 'I got to the bus stop at eight thirty. . . I tell a lie I got there at nine . . . the bus was just coming . . . it was coming around the corner . . . No it was by the garage because I saw Jim sprinting out of the shop. . . .'

Such an answer leaves the witness vulnerable in cross-examination and gives the court an adverse impression of his powers of recollection. The mental process of working out what happened that is revealed by this answer must take place in silence in the witness's head so that when he speaks it seems that he has a reliable and consistent recollection of what happened. This may be an illusion, but of course to some extent the whole process of a criminal trial is illusion.

The witness must keep his answer as concise and to the point as he can. It must be explained to the witness that the longer his answer, the more likely it will be that he will provide material for effective cross-examination. He may even contradict himself in the same answer as the speaker did in the example immediately above. The advocate in preparing his case must drill the witness so that he fully understands and applies these principles. The occasion for doing this will be when taking the proof of evidence, with a reminder at court before the witness gives evidence.

CHAPTER 5

The prosecutor's opening speech

From the moment the prosecutor begins his opening address to the magistrates the defence advocate must be keenly aware of everything that is being said and done in the case. The defence advocate should note the prosecutor's opening in detail. The advocate never knows but that some barely noticed trifle may turn out to be a deciding feature in the case. The prosecutor may make some ill-judged comment or statement of fact that can be used to damage the prosecution case or to attack a prosecution witness in cross-examination. For example, the prosecutor may make a comment on the defence case in his opening such as, 'I would be very surprised if this is what happened . . .' Such an ill-judged comment could be used to considerable effect in a closing defence speech to show that even the prosecutor does not believe that the burden of proof has been fully discharged.

In many summary trials the prosecutor's opening is cursory. Some prosecutors do not bother to work out a proper opening for their case and may open with a remark such as, 'There is no need to open this case, the facts will be clear from the first officer's evidence . . .'

The defence case can suffer from this form of slackness. The magistrates hear the first witness without being given an overall view of the facts and circumstances of the case and it may be some way into the evidence before they grasp what the case is about. In the fictionalised account in Part II the prosecutor opens his case with a comprehensive opening speech (see pp 151–154). The defence benefits from this thoroughness (as Rachel Red does at p 195).

CHAPTER 6

The handling of witnesses

1. Conducting the examination-in-chief

Giving evidence is an unnerving experience for the average witness. The witness is substantially re-assured if the advocate who questions him at the trial is known to the witness. It is consequentially of considerable advantage if the preparation of the case has been carried out by the advocate who conducts the trial. Many witnesses in trials conducted by barristers have never spoken to the barrister who questions them and do not really grasp by which side they are being questioned. Where the advocate is the lawyer who has taken the witness statement and discussed his evidence with him in the calm of an office, the witness is more likely to understand the line of questioning and the advocate will have a better understanding of how to put questions to the particular witness to best advantage.

Settling the witness

The advocate should start his examination-in-chief with a series of questions that are of little significance to the case to enable the witness to settle down and become accustomed to giving evidence in court. It is essential that the advocate does not plunge straight into areas of evidence of importance to the case. The witness must be run in and allowed to recover his composure. The advocate can use this introduction to remind the witness that he must remember the drills on giving evidence that were explained to him but that he may have forgotten, that he must listen to the question, decide what his answer is before speaking and then direct his answers to the question asked.

It has to be remembered that strange forces take hold of witnesses, often in wholly unpredictable ways. The star witness goes to pieces and gives evidence in a disastrous manner, while the apparently indifferent witness gives spectacularly successful evidence.

Leading questions

It is not permissible generally to examine a witness-in-chief by way of leading questions. A leading question is one that suggests the answer. As a matter of logic there have to be leading questions in an examination-in-chief. It would otherwise be difficult to take a witness to the beginning of his relevant evidence. In many instances advocates will agree among themselves that a witness can be lead on certain uncontroversial features. On occasions the use of an improper leading question can cause the offending advocate substantial difficulties. (See the end of section 15 and the first questions of section 16 in Part II, pp 179–180.)

2. Cross-examination

Cross-examination of a witness is permitted on any topic that is relevant to the case and on matters that affect the credibility of the witness. This is an area of some complexity and needs to be studied in the textbooks on evidence and procedure. Of particular use are the older editions of Archbold (particularly the 40th and 41st editions).

Cross-examination is not capable of being rigidly categorised other than to say that its purpose is either to discredit the other side's evidence or to establish features of the cross-examiner's case. The advocate's approach to cross-examination will inevitably depend on what he hopes to obtain from the witness and the degree of hostility the witness shows to the advocate's case. If the advocate wishes to obtain information that the witness is ready to give or cannot realistically avoid giving, there will be little need for the advocate to cross-examine vigorously. At the other extreme there will be the antagonistic witness who intends to avoid giving the advocate's case any assistance. It is for this sort of witness that most of the techniques set out in this section are appropriate.

Cross-examination requires of the advocate a combination of a realistic sense of direction coupled with a ruthless opportunism. The advocate's style must be such as to give the witness every opportunity to make mistakes and provide material for further cross-examination with the alertness to take full advantage of the witness when he does make the mistake.

Putting the advocate's case

There tends to be a feeling in the defence advocate that his own case is something of an embarrassment. The essence of advocacy is tearing the other side's evidence apart. The weak link is the advocate's own witnesses who are themselves torn apart by the prosecuting advocate. The necessity to put the defence case in cross-examination is consequently a somewhat irksome part of the task.

In the Crown Court there is a legal obligation to put the salient facts of the defence to the key prosecution witnesses. It is sufficient if the questioning makes it clear to the witness that his assertions are not accepted. This obligation does not apply to summary proceedings (*O'Connell v Adams* [1973] Crim LR 113). The rationale is that in many summary trials the defendant is not represented and the technical difficulty for a defendant in person to put his case to a witness makes this too great an imposition. It is nevertheless good practice for the defence advocate in a summary trial to put his case to the prosecution witnesses. Cross-examination of the first prosecution witness takes place at a time when the magistrates are not likely to have much idea of the nature of the defence case. Putting the defence case in cross-examination to the prosecution witnesses is an excellent opportunity to set out the defence case for the magistrates so that they appreciate the significance of the points made on behalf of the defence.

Where the court is pedantic in requiring advocates to stick to the 'questions only – no comment' rule in examining witnesses, the advocate needs to make sure this is done by way of questions and not in the form 'I put it to you that . . .'

Permissible questions

Leading questions are specifically permitted in cross-examination. However there is authority that this should not go to the extreme of feeding the witness with propositions that he simply echoes (*R v Hardy* (1794) 24 St Tr 199, 755). Cross-examination should be designed to elicit evidence and not be argumentative or comment in the guise of questioning.

A witness should not be invited to comment on the evidence of another witness. Questions from a prosecutor such as 'You have heard the evidence of the officer. Are you saying he is lying?' or 'Can you think of any reason why the officer should lie about this?' are not permissible.

Setting the scene

It is an important technique to be able to require a witness in cross-examination to describe a location. If the advocate knows the scene being described and consequently has an accurate mental picture of it, his task in guiding the witness through his description is that much easier. However, an experienced advocate with no knowledge of the scene under description should be able to apply this technique equally effectively.

This technique is of great importance in summary trials where the preparation by the prosecution is likely to be less thorough than in a Crown Court jury trial. For example there may well not be plans or photographs.

It may be necessary for the defence advocate to require a witness to give in cross-examination a description of the geography of the scene in which the offence occurred before the rest of his cross-examination can have its full impact. (The experienced advocate carries out this exercise in the Gorringe case in chapter 13 – see pp 81–83.) Without this sort of description the magistrates may fail to grasp the points being made in the balance of the cross-examination.

The exact layout of the scene of the offences may be crucial to the defence case. For example, it may be the prosecution case that police officers were on observation and saw an offence being committed while it is the defence case that the prosecution witnesses could not have seen what they claimed to have seen. The defence advocate may wish to obtain from the prosecution witnesses a conclusive description of their version of the layout of the scene in unequivocal terms that can later be shot down. The defence advocate may not wish to put forward a plan for fear of forewarning the prosecution witnesses as to the points they face later in the cross-examination and may thus need to ask the witnesses to describe the scene in answers to questions. If the witness is not aware of the extent of the defence knowledge, it may be that he will attempt to re-arrange the geography of the scene in order to avoid the consequences of the more telling points in cross-examination, thereby sowing the seeds of the witness's own destruction. For example, a store detective from shop A claimed to find a label from an allegedly stolen jacket outside shop C. In his evidence it became clear that the store detective had not gone further than shop B when he followed the defendant from shop A before stopping him and taking him back to shop A. In cross-examination the store detective claimed that shop C was between shops A and B. He was then handed a photograph showing shop C on the far side of B from A. End of case. Any attempt to agree the layout of the street would have alerted the store detective to the point. The innocent and apparently ignorant request from the defence advocate that the store detective describe the street gave the witness confidence to re-arrange the shops. It is consequently important for an advocate to be able to obtain good descriptions of the geography of the scene of an alleged offence by cross-examination.

A technique for obtaining this form of description is to start from a mental picture of the scene. If this is an accurate one from observation of the scene itself it will clearly be easier. It is not essential that it is accurate. The mental picture gives the advocate a starting-point. The advocate then questions the witness, replacing in his mental picture the features that turn out to be wrong. For example, the advocate sets up in his or her mind a street scene with shops down each side of a broad straight main street.

QUESTION: Whereabouts did this incident happen?

ANSWER: In the main market place. (Advocate replaces mental picture of street by a broad market about 400 metres square full of market booths)

QUESTION: What size of market place?

ANSWER: Oh, it is quite small.

QUESTION: What shape is the market place?

ANSWER: It's not really a market place. It's just a street called the Market Place. (Advocate returns to original mental picture)

QUESTION: Why is it called the Market Place?

ANSWER: It has market booths down each side as well as the shops. (Further adjustment to mental picture)

QUESTION: How wide is the street?

ANSWER: Quite narrow. With the booths there's only room for one car.

QUESTION: How long is the road?

ANSWER: With the booths in? I would say about 200 yards.

QUESTION: Is it straight?

ANSWER: No, it's on a bend . . . quite a steep bend which curves up the hill to the church.

QUESTION: At 4 pm were there many people?

ANSWER: Oh yes, it was very crowded. The pavements were full and there were people milling down the middle of the street.

QUESTION: And the weather?
ANSWER: It was raining quite hard. It was getting dark. . . .

The advocate and the rest of the court now have a mental picture of the scene into which they can insert the actions. Of course without having checked the scene the advocate cannot tell whether the account is truthful.

The relationship between the witness and the advocate

A strong adverse relationship develops between the witness under severe cross-examination and the advocate. This is particularly so with experienced witnesses such as police officers in cases where the credibility of the officers is important. Such witnesses will scrutinise carefully what the advocate says in his question and the advocate's demeanour to calculate what answer the advocate is looking for. The witness is then likely to use this information to avoid giving that answer. This effect is illustrated in sections 13, 16 and 19 of the fictionalised account in Part II.

A police witness will give his evidence-in-chief from his notebook. So far as he is able, he will stick to the account given in his notes throughout his evidence. However, the cross-examination has to be only moderately enterprising to take the officer outside the scope of his notes. The officer then has to assess how he should answer the questions in order not to make himself and his fellow officers who have already given evidence or are yet to give evidence appear foolish or untruthful. The witness will look at the topics on which the defence advocate is questioning him in order to find out what features have assumed importance in the case. He will also examine the content of the questions being asked to see what answers the advocate seems to be looking for. This exercise is often surprisingly easy. An advocate needs to have a rigorously disciplined technique in order to devise a form of cross-examination that does not give the witness this sort of information. Inevitably the advocate questions on subjects that have proved of importance in the evidence of previous witnesses. This tells the witness which topics are important. So far as the individual question is concerned, it is only too easy to frame a question in such a way as to reveal the answer the advocate is hoping for. Many advocates are not aware of how transparent their questioning is. This is especially so if the questioning takes the form of leading questions.

The advocate needs to use a technique that counters both these failings, that does not cause any particular feature of the case to stand out and frames the questions so that the witness is not able to see the answer he is being asked for.

The narrative sweep

An answer to the first problem is to apply a technique that might be described as a 'narrative sweep'. That is to start at a point in the witness's evidence before the occurrence of the critical incidents and require the witness to give a full, detailed description of what occurred step-by-step, taking the witness on until he is past the last feature of importance. In this way each feature of the account is treated in much the same way and the witness is given no indication that any particular feature is or has become of greater significance than any other. The witness has no opportunity to be on guard in relation to critical points because nothing will show him that any feature is more critical than any other. This technique has another significant advantage. Because the advocate deals with every feature and not just features that have become significant, he may well identify other features in the witness's evidence that give scope for effective cross-examination and that had not been apparent before.

It is important in applying this technique to control the witness carefully. If the witness attempts to skate over an area without giving a suitable amount of detail, he must be taken back and required to cover that area until he has dealt with it to the satisfaction of the advocate. Indeed, when a witness skates over an area, the advocate should take particular care in his cross-examination of that area, as it is possible that the witness has some compelling reason for his evasion and is particularly shy of describing that area in detail.

The 'sterile' question

The second technique is to use questions that do not have any leading component in them. It is entirely permissible to use leading questions in cross-examination, but a leading question will usually indicate the answer the advocate seeks. The witness is given the information he needs to avoid assisting the advocate's case. Further, a leading question is easy to answer. The wording of the question provides the format of the answer. The witness does not have to devise an answer in his own words, whether he is agreeing or disagreeing with the question. By posing non-leading questions the advocate makes the witness do the work. A series of questions asking

'And what happened next?' forces the witness to give a description entirely in his own words. There are no words in the question that the witness can adopt. If the witness is uncertain how to deal with a particular point, his uncertainty will show in his answer.

It is almost inevitable that a witness giving evidence in answer to cross-examination put in this way will give details that contradict other evidence in the case, even if the witness is fundamentally truthful.

In posing a leading question the advocate makes assumptions as to what the answer should be. These assumptions and the consequent narrow phrasing of the question limit the witness in the answer he gives in relation to the topic. The advocate will almost certainly stop the witness from mentioning features of benefit to the defence case which might have emerged had the questioning been 'open'. This is illustrated in the cross-examination of the experienced advocate in the Gorringe case in chapter 13.

The discipline of the narrative sweep

There is a diagrammatic manner in which this form of evidence can be envisaged. Two police officers might have written their notes together so as to produce a consistent account in their evidence. These witnesses in evidence-in-chief might produce a narrative based perhaps on ten factual assertions or 'points'. The witnesses link these points by making assumptions or perhaps ignoring completely the intervening gaps. In cross-examination the advocate requires each witness to provide every possible factual point that the advocate can squeeze out of him. The cross-examining advocate might perhaps squeeze an additional 20 to 30 factual details out of each witness. If the witnesses have attempted to co-ordinate their evidence but have only dealt with the ten points that they gave in their evidence-in-chief, a large number of these additional details may well be contradictory as between the two witnesses. The result may well be that while the narrative route based on the ten points that the two witnesses have in common is consistent with the common narrative description they each gave in evidence-in-chief, once each witness is forced to provide the additional 30 factual points, the narratives of the witnesses are seen to be wholly different and contradictory.

The defence advocate requires each of these witness to provide the additional factual points by taking him through his account in every possible detail in a 'narrative sweep', without permitting the witness to make assumptions, and requiring the witness to fill in the gaps that he had left unexplained in his evidence in chief. If the advocate's manner of questioning is 'sterile' and non-leading, the witness will have no idea how he should put the details so as not to contradict his fellow witness.

During the course of this cross-examination the witness should not be permitted to jump further than the next detail. If he does so the advocate should firmly take the witness back and require him to deal with the missing features. The witness is particularly likely to try and evade areas with which he feels uncomfortable, either because he has no real answer or because he knows them to be damaging to the prosecution case. It is consequently essential for the advocate to deal ruthlessly with any evasion of this sort.

Where the advocate is covering important ground in his cross-examination, he needs to control carefully his own reaction to the answers he is receiving. The alert witness may notice that the advocate is excited by a particular answer so that the witness is able to act to negative the effect of the answer by qualifying it in some way. The advocate may give himself away by repeating the answer with unexpected emphasis or by going over the question again or simply by pausing. On the other hand, the advocate may decide that it is necessary to repeat an answer given by the witness to ensure that the magistrates have heard and noted it or perhaps to shake the witness. It is important that the advocate devises each step deliberately and to an end and not inadvertently.

The form of the 'sterile' question

The most effective form of question in furtherance of the narrative sweep is the non-leading, simple, single-sentence question. With this form of question the witness is left to do all the work in devising his answer. In addition the advocate uses a minimum of resources. His energy is then available for assimilating and assessing the answers he is being given and deciding the future route for the cross-examination.

The advocate needs to observe closely not just the words of the answer, but the witness's demeanour and the tone of his voice. The advocate must listen carefully for the throwaway remark that might easily be missed but that may be of significance. A change of tone may signal that the witness feels he is in difficulty or is unsure of what he is saying. The witness must absorb the cross-examining advocate's full attention. If the question is simple ('What happened next?' or 'And then what was said?') the advocate is immediately ready to watch the witness closely.

There is always a need for the advocate to remember the question he has just asked. The advocate needs to ensure that the witness answers the question asked. If the witness does not do so, the advocate needs to repeat the question until the witness does answer it. The more reluctant the witness appears to be to answer the question, the more the advocate should persist in seeking an answer. The witness may well be evading the question because it reveals some hidden material for the advocate's case. Even if there is some less significant reason for the evasion, it is not good for the advocate to seem to be easily fobbed off without an answer.

The witness or someone else may require the question to be repeated. If the question is long, the advocate may not remember it. It gives a poor impression of the advocate's control of his questioning if he has to admit that he has forgotten the text of the question. If the question is short, it is easily remembered and in any case is less likely to need to be repeated.

It is a standard technique for an obstructive witness asked a complicated question to ask for the question to be repeated. The advocate loses ground if he is unable to do so. If the witness fails to direct his answer to the question asked, it is an effective technique to repeat the question in exactly the same form until the witness does answer it. This is only possible if the question is short and easily remembered.

Where the questions are long and involved there is also a danger that the advocate will spend more energy and concentration on the devising of the questions than on listening to the answers and observing the demeanour of the witness. This process is illustrated in the Gorringe case in chapter 13 by the inexperienced advocate (see p 72).

The advocate may not be able to write down answers as he is standing up but he should be able to make a mental note of important answers and then commit them to writing at the end of the cross-examination.

There is a further advantage to questioning by way of short, single sentence, non-leading questions. In addition to gleaning information from the content of the questions, the witness tries to achieve a sense of reassurance by judging how successful the advocate feels in his cross-examination. If the witness can satisfy himself that he is scoring off the cross-examiner, his own morale and ability to cope with the cross-examination strengthens. In a long complicated question the advocate not only gives information as to the answer he seeks, he also gives information as to how he considers he is progressing. Uncertainty is everything in fully exploiting a witness in cross-examination. To achieve this sense of uncertainty the witness must be told nothing on how well the cross-examination is going beyond what the advocate chooses to tell him explicitly.

In order to obtain more information, a witness may try to force the advocate to adopt a leading question. For example:

ADVOCATE: How far away were you?
WITNESS: I have no idea.
ADVOCATE: You must be able to give some estimate.
WITNESS: I have no idea.
ADVOCATE: Well, were you 20, 30 or perhaps 40 metres away?

The advocate has been forced into leading the witness. The witness now knows the range of distances that he is being asked to consider. He may well still say 'I have no idea' but his state of uncertainty is reduced by the knowledge given to him. In addition the witness has the satisfaction of having forced the advocate to assist him. To that extent the advocate's dominance of the witness is weakened.

It is not easy to say what the correct solution to this sort of situation is. The advocate may need a figure for some other calculation in his case. On the other hand, if it is clear that the witness is not going to be of any help even if led, the advocate has achieved nothing by his leading question and should therefore not have used it.

The advocate who cross-examines effectively develops a hold over the witness. An important characteristic of this hold is that the advocate builds up a feeling of uncertainty in the witness. This sense of uncertainty is cumulative and is an important cause of the witness giving evidence that damages himself or his side's case. The build up of uncertainty can be reversed or completely destroyed. If, for example, the magistrates intervene in the cross-examination and the advocate is unable to see off the intervention decisively, the advocate's hold over the witness may be reduced. A sequence of simple non-leading questions may build up uncertainty in the witness who does not know whether he is dealing with the answers satisfactorily. If the witness is then able to force the advocate into putting leading questions of the sort set out in the paragraph above, the advocate's dominance in the cross-examination will be broken or at least interrupted and the witness allowed to recover his equilibrium. This may well show in a reduced level of usefulness in the witness's answers to the advocate's cross-examination.

A prosecutor seeing his witness in trouble may be tempted to intervene to relieve the pressure on the witness. It is therefore essential that the advocate is ready and able to see off such interventions swiftly and decisively, thereby increasing the sense of siege in the witness.

Cross-examination by reference to a document

The advocate must know in full the rules that govern the use of documents in cross-examination. They are set out in any good work on evidence and procedure. Of these rules the most insidious is that once a document has been used in cross-examination it is open to the opposing advocate to re-examine on the basis of other parts of the document not referred to in the cross-examination, even if the document could not have been introduced in evidence-in-chief.

The advocate needs to work out fully the necessary sequence of questioning to establish the basis for using a document. It is also important if points are to be made on a document that the witness is seen to be treated fairly. For example, in relation to a previous written statement made by the witness under cross-examination:

QUESTION: Would you look at this document please? (Witness is handed a copy of his statement.) Have you seen this statement before?

ANSWER: Yes. It looks like my statement.

QUESTION: Have you had the opportunity to read it through recently?

ANSWER: No.

QUESTION: Well would you please look at the signature at the bottom of that page and the signature at the bottom of the next page.

ANSWER: Yes.

QUESTION: Whose signatures are they?

ANSWER: Mine.

QUESTION: Is that the statement you made to the police about this matter on 22nd October 1990?

ANSWER: Yes.

QUESTION: I'm going to ask you some questions about that statement. I don't want you to be at a disadvantage, so would you please read the statement over thoroughly to yourself taking your time. . . .

The advocate can then make his points in cross-examination on the document without there being any feeling that the witness is at a disadvantage.

If a document is to be used to undermine a witness's evidence, it is more telling to make the witness read out the passages the advocate intends to rely upon than for the advocate to read them out. The court takes greater notice of documents read by the witness. In most cases the document will be one the witness has written or at least signed. If the witness is required to read it, this point is emphasised to the magistrates. If the document creates difficulties for the witness, it is likely the witness will sound shifty. Sometimes the witness will attempt to remedy the position as he reads it, and usually he will make his position worse. An example: a police officer had corrected the mis-spelt name of an arrested person in his notebook by crossing it out and writing the correct version over the top. Every officer who gave evidence had written the name of the defendant in his notebook with the same wrong spelling and then crossed it out and put the correct version. This officer, on being requested to read out the original entry, read out the new corrected entry. On the request being repeated, he did it again and then again. Finally he felt forced to read out the true original entry. The point on the witness's honesty was made more by his conduct in the cross-examination than by the original offending change in his notes.

The principle throughout cross-examination must be 'More of the witness, less of the advocate'.

3. Police notebooks

A high proportion of public order offences are tried summarily. Many of the trials of these offences involve extensive police evidence. Police officers rely heavily on evidence given from notebooks. The manner in which notebooks are prepared by police officers probably creates more problems for the police witness than the use of the notebook solves.

The legal convention is that the officer commits his evidence to a note at a time soon after the incident when it is still fresh in his memory to assist his memory when he later gives evidence. The legal convention is that the note is no more than an *aide-memoire*.

The reality is very different. The reality is that officers in a case will together write in their notebooks an agreed version of what occurred in the contested incident and then at court read out the agreed version from their notebooks as their evidence. In training the police officer is warned to stick to the account given in his notebook and not to stray outside it. Under methodical cross-examination it is quite impossible for the officer to do this and retain credibility. Under this principle the only way to deal with features that are clearly outside the note is to deny remembering them. If lack of memory is claimed too often, the court begins to doubt the witness's sanity or truthfulness.

When a notebook is written up, the account can only include certain features of an incident however detailed it may be. It is therefore inevitable that the cross-examination will take the witness outside the note. Where a number of officers have devised a carefully co-ordinated note, at least in some respects some of those officers have to abandon their own genuine recollection in favour of the agreed note. It is inevitable that one officer or one group of officers imposes an account on the others. The non-predominating officers are put in an impossible position once the cross-examination forces them to describe features outside the note as their own real recollection may not be consistent with the agreed note. On occasions the agreed note will have the officer giving evidence of features of which he is unaware. It is almost inevitable that the evidence the officer gives in cross-examination will sound unconvincing and is likely to contradict the evidence of other officers. If the technique of the 'narrative sweep' is applied rigorously, each officer will be forced to deal with features that do not appear in his agreed note. Answering a rigorous narrative sweep is difficult enough even if the witness is relying upon a genuine recollection. In this instance the witness is forced to devise his answers by second-guessing what his colleagues are going to say or have said in evidence. Even if generally the prosecution case is a correct one the police officer's task is extremely difficult. It will be a feeble defence advocate who is not able to trawl a basketful of inconsistencies from this form of evidence.

There is almost always a sharp contrast between the manner in which the police witness gives evidence when reading from his note and when dealing with matters not set out in the note. It is the difference between the self-confidence generated by reading an agreed account whose consistency can be guaranteed and the floundering about required when dealing with matters outside the note. This contrast does the witness no favours and is virtually unavoidable.

Although the police practice of writing up notes with other officers has been approved by higher courts, it is not difficult to show justices that in principle the practice is insidious and produces misleading evidence even before attacking the evidence itself in cross-examination.

A form of questioning along the following lines can show how notes written with other officers produce absurd results.

QUESTION: Officer, why did you write your notes with the other officers?
ANSWER: It's standard practice.
QUESTION: I understand that. But why is it necessary to do it?
ANSWER: . . . er . . . So that we can make sure that we have all the information recorded.
QUESTION: Do you mean so that you all give the same evidence?
ANSWER: No.
QUESTION: Well, what do you mean?
           (silence)
QUESTION: Is it meant to be a pooled recollection?
ANSWER: Something like that, yes.
QUESTION: Does that mean that you recorded in your notes some things that the other officers remembered but that you hadn't?
ANSWER: Er no, I have only recorded in my notes what I remembered.
QUESTION: Then did the other officers record in their notes things that you remembered but that they hadn't?
ANSWER: I don't think so.
QUESTION: Well if you all had identical recall of all the events that occurred, why was it necessary to make up your notes together?
ANSWER: Well to make sure we did remember it all.
QUESTION: So that if there had been something in the pooled note that you had not remembered it would have gone in your notes anyway?
ANSWER: No, certainly not.
QUESTION: Then I fail to see why you needed to make your notes up together.

Other clues

There are other clues that suggest that police officers' notebooks may not contain a truly independent contemporaneous record. An officer may have included information about the defendant that he could not have had without being told it by one of the other officers. There may be consistently wrong spellings that suggest that one note has simply been copied from another note. On occasions an officer will describe the defendant as '. . . whom I now know to be' when at the time he claims to have written the note the identity of the defendant was not known. The note may contain in its narrative a description of the charging or bailing of the defendant when the officer claims to have written the note some time before the times of charging and bailing.

Police officers are extremely vulnerable on the content and the making of their notes. A feature that does not assist police officers is that often the easiest way for the witness to deal with a difficult question in cross-examination is to claim amnesia. To lay the ground for such a claim the witness may be tempted not to read through his note fully before giving evidence. This prevents the officer from preparing himself for the exacting task of giving evidence under rigorous cross-examination.

On some occasions, particularly in the Metropolitan Police, more than one officer will rely on the same notebook. If anyone notices and challenges this practice, the officer will assert that he read through the note of the other officer and signed it as correct. The handover of the note is either done surreptitiously as the officers pass in the court or by the first officer leaving the notebook in the witness stand. In the second instance the defence advocate should remove the notebook and pass it to the prosecutor, leaving the officer to justify his use of the other officer's notebook to the court. In either case the second officer will have considerable difficulty explaining his adoption of a note that will undoubtedly use the first person singular when it does not refer to him.

One of the principal sources of dishonesty in relation to police notes concerns the time and circumstances of compiling the note. The content of the note itself may not be capable of effective challenge. However, if the officer can be shown to be unreliable on the making of the note, his whole evidence may be thrown into doubt. The cross-examination of any such police officer should begin with establishing time, place and circumstances in which, and the officers with whom, the notes were made. As each officer gives evidence the information given on these features by earlier officer can be compared with the present officer's evidence.

4. What to do with the information gleaned in cross-examination

The defence advocate may choose to confront the witness with points made in cross-examination and use the revelation of the inadequacy to try and discomfort and discredit the witness further. It is hard to resist the pleasure of showing a witness how stupid and dishonest he has been and how clever the advocate is in catching him out. The main danger with this technique is that the witness may be able to reduce the impact of the point once its damaging quality is revealed to him by qualifying his answers in some way. This problem does not arise if another technique is used.

The second technique is to note the damaging answer without comment during the witness's evidence and use the point in the advocate's closing speech. It may, however, be necessary to underline the fact that the answer has been given at the time so that the magistrates remember the answer. This might be done by asking the question twice or by repeating the witness's answer back to him and to the court. It may be sufficient if the advocate is satisfied that the clerk of the court has noted the answer. It frequently happens that all-important answers are given in cross-examination without anyone other than the cross-examining advocate appreciating the significance of the answer. This can increase the impact of the point when it is revealed in the closing speech. The danger is that everyone else in the court may deny that the witness gave the answer that the defence advocate is relying upon. Hence the importance of ensuring that some note of the answer is taken by someone other than the defence advocate at the time of the answer.

CHAPTER 7

The advocate and the court

1. Concentration and noting during the trial

During the trial the advocate must be alert to all that is going on in the court. The advocate should note each stage as fully as possible. It is impossible to predict what detail may not turn out to be of use. For instance, it is always a good practice to take a full note of the prosecutor's opening. The prosecutor may make some ill-advised comment that is incompatible with the burden of proof he has to discharge or the prosecution witnesses may give evidence on some feature that contradicts what the prosecutor said in opening.

When the prosecution witnesses are giving evidence, it is important to observe not just what they say but how they say it. An experienced advocate will be able to detect, for example, that a police officer reading from his notes during his evidence-in-chief has added a word or a section that is not written in the notes. A subtle change in the form of the witness's delivery will often give him or her away. A witness may hesitate before answering a question and look to someone in court for assistance. The defence advocate may be able to cross-examine the witness on the point that provoked this reflex action if he has noticed it.

2. Interventions

There are a number of situations in which the defence advocate may have to consider intervening in the conduct of another person in the court. This may be the prosecutor but may also be a co-defending advocate or the clerk or one of the justices. It is extraordinarily difficult to handle interventions with complete tact and accuracy. By their nature interventions are unlikely to be welcomed by the person interrupted. Interventions against the prosecutor may be resented by the magistrates who may be unable to see the impropriety the prosecutor is committing in the eyes of the defence advocate.

It is essential therefore that the defence advocate is able to intervene in a correct and suitably measured manner. A correct intervention states the fact of the intervention ('I hesitate to interrupt Mr Groggins . . . ') and then states the nature of the objection ('but that question is objectionable as a leading question and I object to it') and the steps that the advocate urges the court to take ('I would ask the court to rule the question to be unlawful').

It would probably be rare for an objection to be stated in such full terms. Usually the words 'object' and 'leading' would be sufficient to trigger consideration by the justices of the objection, either sympathetically or otherwise. When he makes an objection, the advocate must have in mind all the arguments that it may be necessary to deploy in support of the objection in case it is not immediately resolved but leads to extended argument.

The same applies in reverse. The defence advocate must have at the back of his mind the arguments necessary to justify every action he takes during the course of a summary trial so that he is able to cope convincingly and decisively with an unjustified intervention by the prosecution.

The defence advocate should listen carefully to ensure that the prosecutor does not lead his witnesses on important features of the evidence.

The defence advocate should be alert to intervene where the prosecutor becomes unfair or overbearing towards defence witnesses. One example of abuse is for the prosecutor to ask a defence witness to comment on the evidence of another witness: 'Are you telling this court that the police officers in this case are all lying?' The defence advocate should immediately intervene before the defence witness is made to answer such an insidious and unlawful question. A prosecutor may be keen on the form of comment or cross-examination that challenges a defence witness because a feature of his evidence was not 'put' to the prosecution witness concerned by the defence advocate. Apart from the question of the general duty to put the defence case to prosecution witnesses, in a summary trial there is no such specific duty (see p 32 above).

In many instances an objection can be used as an opportunity to advance the advocate's case. For example, a prosecutor when challenged over questions put to the defendant in cross-examination may seize the opportunity given to him by the objection to make what is in effect a closing speech to the justices. Equally the defence may do the same thing. The defence always labours under the difficulty that the purpose of a cross-examination may not be apparent to the court because the defence has had no opportunity to explain its case to the justices at that stage. If an objection is made to a line of cross-examination and the defence advocate is challenged to justify it, this may be an ideal opportunity for the defence advocate to 'open' his case to the justices at length and in detail. (Rachel uses such an opportunity in Part II at p 196.)

CHAPTER 8

The defence advocate's closing speech

1. The content of the speech

There are three main subjects that the defence advocate needs to cover in his closing speech:

1 The burden of proof.
2 The law applicable to the charges in the case.
3 The features of the evidence that support the defence case.

The closing speech in a summary trial rushes upon the advocate often with no real opportunity for preparation. It is usually a feat of extemporisation. For the experienced advocate the techniques are all in place in the mind, honed (or not) through experience. The facts and the law may be different but the techniques of presenting a speech are broadly the same for every case, and the advocate simply adapts the old arguments to the particular circumstances of the present case. For the beginner advocate, on the other hand, the closing speech in a summary trial is a moment of frightening effort.

The closing speech for the defence in a summary trial is of great importance. The prosecution has no closing address and there is no equivalent of the summing up from the judge in a jury trial. Consequently it is often the defence advocate who gives the justices their final guidance on how to deal with the case. If the justices trust the integrity and judgement of the advocate they will listen closely to what is said in the closing speech and if it appears to be well reasoned and correct there is a strong possibility that they will adopt the arguments presented in it.

There will be little opportunity to prepare the closing speech unless the case runs to more than a day. Few summary trials are that long. While a degree of advanced planning for the closing speech may be possible on the basis of the assumed route that the case will 50 take, it is essential that the advocate remains sufficiently flexible to take into account the progress made in cross-examining the prosecution witnesses and other features of the case. If no such progress has been made, it is unlikely that the defence has any really prospect of success anyway.

Probably the parts of the speech that are most susceptible to advanced planning are the start and the finish. A competent speech requires a sure launch, but even more it requires a confident finish. These can be arranged in such a way that the unexpected changes in the case do not affect these features.

It is most important that while delivering the main body of the speech the defence advocate remains sufficiently flexible to deal with the changes that may have occurred in the nature of the case during the trial. In particular, the advocate needs to be sensitive to expressions of view from the justices and to take them into account in his speech. These views may be expressed during the closing speech itself, making necessary a sudden and radical alteration in the content of the rest of the speech.

It is important not to assume that the justices have any knowledge of the law. The speech should contain a full explanation of the law appropriate to the case. Magistrates may, for example, have a knowledge of the constituent elements of theft sufficient for a court involved in sentencing and bail applications. This knowledge may not be sufficient to analyse properly a contested theft case in which the concepts of 'dishonesty' or 'intention permanently to deprive' are the keys to conviction or acquittal. One of the advantages of having to explain the law to the justices is that the advocate is forced to look it up. It is disconcerting how often parts of the law turn out on careful examination to be not quite as the advocate had assumed them to be. Interesting new points can only be discovered by such routine research.

It is comparatively rare, even in busy magistrates' courts, for individual justices to have much experience of trying contested summary trials. Most justices sit for one morning or afternoon session per week. Usually that session will be in a remand court. Only infrequently will justices sit in courts trying fully contested cases. It is therefore of great assistance to the bench if the defence advocate in his closing speech indicates to them the way in which the case should be analysed. While this analysis may lead to a conviction, if the justices find themselves adopting the defence advocate's approach they may be that much nearer to adopting his arguments on the merits of the case as well.

The defence speech will often hinge on the manner in which the justices should apply the burden of proof. There is a difficulty in that justices are inclined to feel that the burden of proof is so much a part of the system that it applies itself without effort on their part. They may consider it an impertinence on the part of the defence advocate to hint that they might not apply it correctly. Nevertheless it is essential in the closing speech to remind the justices how they should use the burden of proof. One of the easiest ways is to remind them that it is not a question of which account, that of the prosecution witnesses or that of the defence witnesses, they prefer, but rather that they must have no reasonable doubt of the correctness of the prosecution case, bearing in mind all the evidence, before they convict the defendant.

Each advocate will develop his own formula for presenting the burden of proof point to the court. It is important, however, that an advocate should vary his delivery between trials. If an advocate has personal clichés which he delivers without variation to the local court too often, they will eventually be treated with levity and not given full attention.

The reality of the summary trial is that all too often, even in the most enlightened magistrates' courts, the burden of proof unconsciously shifts onto the defence and that the defence has to disprove the prosecution case. This may be only on a balance of probabilities in the courts that strive to apply the true burden of proof, nevertheless the burden is often without a doubt firmly on the defence. By placing great emphasis on the true principle of where the burden of proof lies, the defence advocate can do something to redress the balance.

It may on occasions be irresistible for the defence advocate to declare the prosecution witnesses to be liars (as Rachel Red does in section 30 of Part II). Even then the advocate, having had his fling, should draw the justices back to the true application of the burden of proof:

> . . . having said that, your worships, it is of course not a question of whether you feel that the prosecution witnesses were lying in their evidence. You don't have to find that to acquit the defendant. Your worships need to consider the evidence as a whole and decide whether there is a doubt about the correctness of the prosecution account of the incident . . .

As part of the defence closing speech the advocate must of course refer to the parts of the evidence that support the contentions that he makes. It is important to be highly selective. The speech needs to be as short as it can reasonably be to retain the interest of the justices.

Therefore when the evidence is referred to only those parts that are important and decisive should be used.

2. The style of the speech

When the advocate addresses the magistrates he should speak in short and complete sentences. He will need to make a conscious effort to achieve this. Each sentence should contain a minimum of conditional clauses. Preferably there should be none.

The long rambling sentence containing numbers of clauses is in danger of not finishing unless it is very lucky and the points contained in the sentence become lost and probably again if not very lucky may well contradict themselves within the one sentence if they don't tail off and become lost... The style that contains long sentences is difficult to listen to. If it is difficult to listen to and it has been a long case, the magistrates may just not listen at all.

The differing use of the personal pronoun is important. The advocate can express a view in the first person singular. When the advocate wishes to invoke higher authority he moves to the third person. 'I would urge your worships that . . .' becomes 'The law on this point is clear and is that . . .'

When details are being given of the evidence that supports the defence case, it is important that the points are concise and fit readily into the argument.

If the justices are to be referred to legal texts, particular pitfalls arise. There is an unconscious tendency when reading for the reader's voice to lose its accentuation and volume, for the delivery to speed up and for the voice to rise in pitch. All these features are signals to the listener that what is being read is of little interest and should not be listened to. If the advocate needs to read from a written text such as a law report, statute or a witness statement, the advocate must take deliberate steps to counter these tendencies in order not to lose the attention of the justices. The advocate should speak slower and louder, with a deeper tone and should exaggerate the accentuation of the text. The advocate should look at the justices in turn at intervals to show that he is concerned that they should be listening and to check that they are listening. The justices are then more likely to listen and take in the text. If the text really is of little interest, the advocate should avoid reading it.

CHAPTER 9

The court's decision

The professional advocate takes the court's decision without argument or emotion and with unabated vigour moves on to the next stage of the case. That does not mean that if the court makes a decision with which the advocate does not agree, the advocate cannot take an opportunity to indicate that he disapproves of that decision. This step must be taken in a calculated manner and to a particular advantage. Sometimes a questionable decision on the verdict can be used to persuade the magistrates into a lenient decision on sentence. There are magistrates who find themselves unable to give a finding of not guilty in a summary trial when they feel that this has the implication of branding police witnesses as untruthful, even if it is clear that this is what they are. With some magistrates, the more conclusively the police officers have been shown to be untruthful, the more determined they become to convict. Often the corollary of such a decision is for the magistrates, motivated by their disquiet, to be lenient in sentencing the defendant they have wrongly convicted.

The advocate's reputation

The advocate should at all times conduct himself with courage and rectitude. He should never give way to the substantial temptations to be underhand when he thinks he cannot be caught out. The advocate's greatest strength comes from his own high opinion of himself. If he is deceitful, there is always someone who knows and that is the advocate.

The advocate should never sacrifice his good name or integrity for advantage in one case. The advocate's greatest asset to his client is in being an advocate that his local courts trust and admire, and that the magistrates in those courts have confidence in the advice that he gives them when addressing them on the law.

The advocate's reputation is his greatest asset. It is to be cherished and improved and never to be squandered.

CHAPTER 10

Bail applications

It is essential for the advocate to put himself in a position to deal with questions of bail whenever they arise. In some cases difficulty over bail can come out of the blue. If, for example, the prosecution have decided that the defendant is interfering with witnesses, a hearing that the advocate expected to be a routine remand or committal may become the critical contest of the case. For a defendant in custody, how his lawyer handles the application for bail can be the most important feature in deciding whether the defendant retains his services or not.

1. When to apply for bail

The simple answer is as soon as possible and as often as possible. There may be genuine tactical reasons for delaying a bail application, for example to await full details of sureties or to see the full prosecution papers, but few defendants accept any delay in applying for bail as justified. They are probably correct. If there is a feature of the bail application that will be improved by a delay, a resourceful advocate will probably be able to convince the court that another application can be made after the improvement as well as straight away.

There are two pressing reasons for a relentless pursuit of bail for a defendant.

1 Many defendants consider the question of bail or custody to be the most important consideration in their case. It is often more important to them than the verdict. If the defendant considers that his lawyer is not trying sufficiently hard on this aspect, he is likely to change lawyers.

2 Until the question of the pursuit of bail is exhausted, the

defendant in custody may find it difficult to concentrate on the preparation of the case itself.

2. The requirements for bail applications

1 A good working knowledge, constantly refreshed, of the statutes covering bail applications. Probably more than in any other area of advocacy, the advocate needs to be able to quote to the magistrates verbatim the relevant statutory provisions. For instance, bail or custody in a case may turn on the advocate's ability to point out that the test for a remand in custody is whether there are 'substantial' grounds for believing that the defendant will commit further offences, whereas the prosecutor has stated that he 'fears' or 'suspects' that the defendant will behave in such a way.
2 A full note of the defendant's background containing the sort of information needed for the antecedents section of the proof of evidence (see p 134 below).
3 As much information about the case the defendant is facing as can reasonably be obtained. If the bail application is to the Crown Court at an advanced stage of the case, this information will be virtually complete. If the bail application is on the defendant's first appearance soon after his arrest, it will be a matter of scratching around obtaining scraps of information from the Crown Prosecutor, the police officers and any other source available. It is necessary to find out the basis on which the prosecution is objecting to bail.

3. Assessment of tactics

The advocate has to make an assessment as to how to make his contested bail application. There are probably two general methods of approach that may be used.

1 To attack the prosecution objections head on.
2 To concentrate on the defendant's financial and domestic circumstances.

It will be rare not to include 2) in an application. Very often both features will be present. If there are flaws in the prosecution reasoning that bail should be withheld, the advocate may decide to make his main application dependent on an attack on the prosecution objections. For example, the prosecutor may make some claim that he cannot sustain. Or there might be some essential ingredient missing from his case. If however the prosecution arguments are strong, the advocate may decide to make his bail application solely on some feature of the defendant's background or domestic circumstances.

The bail application is probably the area of advocacy in which the greatest creativity is required in the advocate. In a summary trial much of the content of what the advocate says is dictated by the facts of the case. In a bail application the content is entirely the choice of the advocate.

4. Incontrovertible matters

Where there are matters put before the court by the prosecution that are damaging and difficult to explain, it is often better to ignore them in the bail application than attempt to explain or excuse them. The test to apply is that if the matter cannot be quickly and completely explained it is better ignored altogether. If the defence advocate takes up an apparently damaging point against the defendant it will be emphasised to the justices that the defence advocate agrees with the prosecutor that the point is a telling one. Also, the more time the defence advocate spends on the point, the more fixed it becomes in the justices' minds. If the result of a lengthy address on the point is that it has not been satisfactorily disposed of, the justices are left with the point in sharp focus. This is particularly true since the defence advocate's bail application will be the last address the justices hear before making their decision (other than in those rare and eccentric courts where the prosecutor is allowed the last word). If the damaging point is ignored by the defence advocate and the application for bail is made on a different basis altogether, it is unlikely that the court will attach as much weight to the point as it would if the defence advocate attempted unsuccessfully to deal with it.

5. Facts in a bail application

The basis of a bail application should almost always be to give as much information about the defendant as possible to the justices. The more magistrates know about an individual, the less easy they find it to remand that person in custody. Curiously this applies even if much of the information is not particularly favourable. This is because it is easier to make an unpleasant order on an unknown being. The more familiar that being becomes, the more difficult it is to do something unpleasant to him. It is a conundrum that probably there is no fact in a defendant's background that a resourceful advocate cannot turn to good use in a bail application. If the defendant has a string of previous convictions, the advocate urges the justices that they might be worse or that the very fact of the previous convictions in some way makes the defendant a good bail risk. The various ingenious arguments that can be put forward cannot be itemised. The resourceful advocate always finds something in favour of bail for the defendant, even if it's only that it's Christmas.

6. The prosecutor in a bail application

The prosecutor in a bail application has a difficult and unrewarding role. Usually the objections to bail have to be read from a file and have been written by someone else. Reading is a notoriously unconvincing form of advocacy. It builds into the advocate's voice all the signals to the listener inviting him to switch off. There is consequently an immediate contrast between the prosecutor's objections and the defence advocate's stirring application (provided that is what it is). The prosecutor cannot really choose his ground. He is bound to stick to the few areas opened to him by the Bail Act, principally that the defendant will not turn up for his trial, commit further offences, obstruct the course of justice or be a danger to himself. The test for most of these grounds is that there must be *substantial* grounds for believing this to be so. It is essential that the defence advocate has an immediate and comprehensive knowledge of the important parts of the Bail Act. Indeed the defence advocate will need to quote the text of the Bail Act as part of his application.

7. The prosecutor's objections

The defence advocate should take a full note of the prosecutor's objections to bail and should listen carefully to the wording the prosecutor uses. The prosecutor may use language that falls below the test of 'substantial grounds'. For example, the prosecutor may say that he considers there are 'grounds for considering that the defendant may abscond'. If he uses these words, a powerful bail application can be built around the fact that even the prosecutor does not believe that the statutory test has been discharged. In many cases the objections to bail are written by the police officer in the case and not the prosecuting lawyer. On many occasions the officer will not have had at the forefront of his mind the specific and demanding requirements of the Bail Act and puts the objections to bail in a way that gives good material for a bail application. As in a contested summary trial where there has been a substantial mistake in the prosecution case, it is an effective tactic to turn the hearing into a consideration of that mistake rather than one on the true merits. For example, the defendant in a bail application may have been charged with an offence of causing grievous bodily harm but there is no information available to the prosecutor at the bail application as to what the injuries were. This leaves it open to the defence advocate to urge the justices that they should consider the case as if it was a charge of assault occasioning actual bodily harm or even common assault.

8. Magistrates and the decision-making process in a bail application

It is important that the advocate in making the application understands the thought processes and dilemma of the justices who are deciding the bail application. Most justices on most occasions will if possible grant bail. There is therefore a leaning towards the defendant. However, a remand in custody is an easier decision to put together and to agree upon than to grant bail with conditions. This is particularly so as there are usually several magistrates making the decision and they have to come to an agreement on the conditions. It is therefore essential that the advocate making the application does as much of the work as possible for the justices. The advocate does this by assessing what conditions should realistically be imposed if the defendant is to be granted bail and by working those conditions out in as much detail as he can. For example, an advocate in a particular case might urge the justices to grant the defendant bail with conditions:

1 that he lives and stays every night at X address,
2 that he reports daily between the hours of 6 pm and 9 pm to Y police station,

3 that there be two sureties for his attendance at trial, namely A and
  B, each in the sum of Z pounds, and
4 that the defendant surrenders his passport.

If these are appropriate conditions, the advocate has left the justices
with the straightforward decision, bail on these terms or custody.
The advocate can introduce these conditions to the justices in such a
way as to cause them to write them down for later consideration.
This is done by saying, 'I would invite your worships to consider bail
on these conditions . . . ' Most magistrates will then reach for their
pens. If the justices think the advocate's suggestions on the conditions are sensible, they may well be more likely to accept the
advocate's other submissions on the merits of granting bail in
principle.

9. The form of the application

Broadly, an application for bail could contain the following sections,
although not necessarily all of them and not necessarily in this order:

1 Comment on the objections to bail made by the prosecutor.
2 A description of the defendant's background.
3 Comment on the defendant's involvement in the case.
4 Reasons for granting the defendant bail.
5 The law relating to the grant of bail.
6 Suggested conditions of bail.

10. Sureties

If bail is granted with sureties, the surety may go straight into the
witness box to be taken, depending on the court's practice. It is
important that the advocate ensures that the surety has the necessary
attributes and is correctly briefed. In many areas the prosecution will
object as a matter of course to a surety with criminal convictions,
but the magistrates may still accept that surety. The advocate needs
to sort out with the surety the sum for which the surety is prepared
and able to stand bail. The surety will have to satisfy the justices on
oath that he has that sum in his own name, either in money or in
convertible belongings. Some courts as a matter of policy will not
accept sureties based on the value of their residence. This is particularly so if the residence is in the name of a spouse as well. The

advocate should go through with the proposed surety the questions he will be asked in the witness box when his surety is taken. These questions will usually be:

1 How long have you known the defendant?
2 Are you prepared to stand bail for his attendance at court in the sum of £XXX?
3 Are you aware of the charges that the defendant faces in these proceedings?
4 Are you worth £XXX when all your debts are paid?
5 Do you appreciate that if the defendant fails to attend court for any hearing while you are his surety, you stand to lose £XXX?
6 And that if you were unable to pay that sum you might be sent to prison?

The advocate needs to know that the answers to all these questions are going to be satisfactory, or at least to be prepared for the answer that may cause difficulties. For example, in answer to question 1: 'I have never met him. His mum asked me to stand surety for him.'

The other matter that needs to be clear is whether the surety is continuing to trial, to committal or just until the next appearance. Further attendance for the surety at court will be arranged in accordance with this order.

CHAPTER 11

Pleas in mitigation

In many ways pleas in mitigation involve similar techniques to bail applications. The advocate needs to assess the punishment he intends to persuade the justices to impose upon the defendant. The advocate moulds his submissions to that end in much the same way that in a bail application the advocate seeks to persuade the justices to adopt a particular bail package. Usually the direction the plea should take is indicated by the probation report, often accompanied by a pre-sentence report. The probation report will usually do much of the work of mitigation for the advocate, unless the report recommends a form of disposal that the defendant does not wish for.

As with a bail application, the basis for a plea in mitigation needs to be information about the defendant. This is the sort of information contained in the antecedents section of the proof of evidence. As with questions of bail, the more the justices know of the defendant, the more difficult it becomes for them to sentence harshly.

It is not appropriate to set out any rigid rules for the content of a plea in mitigation. The content must be a matter of what seems correct to the advocate at the time and in the light of the offences and the other information available. A format which will often be a useful one is to set out features of the defendant's circumstances so as to explain how the offences came to be committed and then contrast this with features of the defendant's circumstances which, the advocate urges the justices, show why he will not commit such offences again.

1. Expressions and ploys

One of the most useful ploys in a plea in mitigation is to turn it into a plea not for the defendant but for society or for the defendant's

63

family. The advocate ceases to say 'It need not be necessary to send this defendant to prison . . . ' and says instead, 'The interests of this man's family and society at large are overwhelmingly that the defendant be left in a position to continue with his job and support his family rather than putting his family in a position of being financially dependent on the state . . . ' This is not a dishonest ploy in any way, for the consequences of a defendant's sentence fall directly on his family. 'Society' has an immediate financial interest in the sentencing of a citizen and in keeping him out of prison. It is really an oratorical feature to change the appearance of the submissions being made from the solely selfish perspective of the defendant. The advocate reminds the justices that the sentencing exercise involves the interests of many more people than the one defendant standing before them and that the public interest is intimately bound up in sentencing policy.

2. The nature of the offences

It is impossible to generalise as to what an advocate should say about the offences for which the defendant has been convicted. Every case will raise different considerations. In the case set out in the Part II (see p 256), Rachel Red makes no comment on the offences for which her client has been convicted. He had pleaded not guilty and Rachel Red considered that he had been wrongly convicted. She did not feel inclined to make the concession that he had committed the offences in her mitigation. Probably an apology or explanation would have sounded somewhat hollow in view of the vigorous defence she had mounted. However, in most cases the advocate should consider an apology and an explanation of the offences so as to reduce their apparent seriousness in the eyes of the bench, although an apology should only be given if the defendant specifically authorises it. The advocate may, however, decide that any reminder of the offences will only exacerbate the defendant's position.

3. The content of the plea in mitigation

It is even less valid than with a bail application to try and lay down subjects that the advocate should include in the plea in mitigation. All that can be said is that the following categories of information or comment might be considered in some order or other:

1 The defendant's past in some detail.
2 The defendant's current circumstances: job, family life, medical conditions and finances.
3 Any explanation or apology for the offences committed
4 The sentence that the justices are urged to consider
5 The defendant's future prospects.

4. References

References from employers, friends or relatives, either in writing or by way of oral evidence before the justices, may well help a defendant. The advocate should check that either form of reference is suitable and going to be of assistance in the case. Provided the reference passes that test, it is bound to assist to some extent. Justices are impressed, as is any court, that there is someone who thinks sufficiently highly of a defendant to come to court and say a few words about him.

CHAPTER 12

The novice advocate

There is no one 'correct technique' for a beginner to learn. There is just the tortured path of experience. But the path can perhaps be smoothed a little.

1. Use of the voice

It is rare for an advocate to make a conscious effort to school the voice. Usually the use of the voice develops with experience. If the volume adopted by the novice advocate is not sufficient for a court to hear, he has to increase the volume in response to the protests of the court. He should therefore make a conscious effort to speak clearly and loudly. The advocate with training in public speaking will have less difficulty than those without. The voice needs to be of sufficient volume to be heard throughout the courtroom, not just by the bench. Advocacy is a declaration of self. It has the useful by-product of self-advertisement. The loud, clear voice is a declaration of confidence in the advocate's own powers and in the strength and correctness of the case the advocate is putting forward. The voice should dominate and carry clearly to everyone in the court room. The occupants of the public gallery must be made to wish that they were represented by this powerful and self-confident advocate and the tribunal to think that whatever it is that this advocate is saying must be listened to with respect.

2. Advocacy and public speaking

There are fundamental differences between public speaking and advocacy. Advocacy requires of the advocate a high degree of awareness of the behaviour and reactions of all the parties to the trial, and at the same time the ability to work out what to say next and the form of its delivery. Experience enables the advocate to carry out many of these functions automatically. The beginner has to do it all deliberately, an extraordinarily demanding and difficult exercise. The novice advocate should not therefore be surprised that he is unable to perform as glibly and tellingly as the more experienced.

3. Nervousness and how to overcome it

Nervousness is an inevitable component in advocacy, even in the experienced. Without some degree of nervousness, the advocate is complacent and likely to be ill prepared. In the beginner, however, nervousness can be excessive and is liable to be debilitating. It is exacerbated by the unknown nature of the ordeal the beginner is facing.

There are various steps the beginner can take to reduce the impact of nervousness. Uncertainty is the main aggravator of nervousness. On his first case the advocate may even be discomposed by worries about how to get to the court and how long it will take. It may be a good idea to reconnoitre the route the day before. The advocate may suffer from uncertainty as to the role played by the personnel in the court or where to sit. The advocate must acknowledge these problems and take deliberate steps to reduce their impact. A reconnaissance of the court, and getting to the court in good time so that the advocate can sit in and watch what goes on, will be invaluable. The procedure and the order in which advocates speak may be uncertain in the mind of the beginner. Again arrival in good time and just watching other cases should make it clear.

Thorough preparation of an advocate's case is another good means of reducing the impact of nerves. If the advocate has researched and ransacked every corner of the case, he gives himself a confidence that should make an outbreak of nerves easy to quell. Once the case starts and the advocate is able to see the good grasp he has of the case, his nervousness should dissipate to an even greater extent. Preparation stimulates the thought process. If the advocate is thinking about the case, he has less energy to worry about it.

4. The list of common terms

The novice advocate would do well to prepare a list of common terms used in the court, for example the expression 'advance disclosure.' At the moment of truth as the beginner advocate rises to request an adjournment for 'advance disclosure' to be given by the Crown Prosecution Service, the expression flees from the advocate's mind. If it is in a list in the advocate's note on the desk before him the problem accompanied by apparently life threatening embarrassment is resolved.

5. The use of facts, not opinions

With experience the advocate's mind develops the facility to take a half-formed idea and clothe it in suitable argument. Probably the experienced advocate deploys each argument in his stock many times each year with only slight variations due to differing facts. The arguments are fundamentally the same. The beginner does not have this armoury of argument, nor a mind well trained in taking the half-formed idea and kitting it out in suitable expression. The consequence is often that the idea in the beginner's mind, sound though it may seem when conceived in the brain, emerges from the advocate's mouth in stilted and inappropriate words.

It is consequently a good idea for the beginner to avoid deploying opinions until thoroughly at home in court and to base his advocacy on facts alone. Most advocacy is based principally on statements of fact. Argument and opinion is then used to develop the submissions. In many instances argument can be kept to a minimum and pure facts relied upon. This is particularly so in the criminal courts. A bail application is primarily a deployment of fact. So is a plea in mitigation. Once the novice advocate is confident of putting forward fluent arguments, the diet of fact can be garnished.

6. The urge not to look foolish

The beginner suffers particularly from the urge not to look foolish. This urge dies in older advocates. Although they generally retain the ability to make themselves look foolish, they cease to be concerned at the prospect or even in many instances to notice when they do. For the novice advocate it is a potent force. The beginner will suspect that something needs to be done but will hang back because of this understandable worry. The beginner should as soon as possible dispense with this hobble and take the plunge. If something appears to be necessary, it should be tackled. If it turns out to be entirely wrong, no matter, the advocate is likely to get it right the next time. The advocate needs to adopt the battle cry of the infant show jumper: 'Throw your heart over the jump and then follow it.'

7. The beginner and cross-examination

It is appropriate that this section should follow the section on the urge not to look foolish. It is in cross-examination that the beginner is particularly vulnerable. Suddenly the novice advocate is confronted with a witness of whom he has to ask cunning and devastating questions. The principal quality of such a question seems to be length. The importance of keeping such questions short and simple has already been emphasised (see p 39). The novice is particularly prone to expend more energy on the devising of the question than on listening to the answer and studying the demeanour of the witness.

8. Lists and reconnaissance

The novice advocate should be scrupulous in providing himself with every aid that releases energy and thoughts for the very taxing procedure of advocacy. He should make sure he has notes of all the essential names, dates, places, car numbers, addresses that may be of importance in the case. He should have easy access to the exact wording of relevant passages of law. With all these to hand, the advocate can concentrate on the surroundings, the demeanour of the justices, the witness and his opponent. He can then make comprehensive and compelling notes and can absorb readily the points on which to base his speech.

9. The beginner and formulation of questions

In all forms of criminal advocacy the advocate has to assume that the court he is addressing and the witnesses he is questioning are less well educated and intelligent than himself. This may not always be so, but it is important for his technique to make this assumption. The beginner needs to apply deliberately the technique of speaking in simple sentences with as few conditional clauses as possible. He will need to make a conscious effort to keep sentences short. In this way the beginner will be adopting a manner of speaking that makes it seem that he knows what he is saying.

10. The beginner and self-criticism

It is a consequence of inexperience that triumphs and successes loom too large. With experience comes the acceptance that the result of a case may be due to the advocate's efforts but is more likely to be due to the nature of the case or the outlook of the court. With experience the advocate will be able to make an assessment of his efforts and learn from his mistakes without being unduly cast down or elated by his conclusions. The beginner needs to bear this fact in mind. It will not prevent the beginner from being unduly elated or depressed, but it may assist him to remember it nonetheless.

CHAPTER 13

An illustration of effective and ineffective cross-examination

The author conducted a series of courses on summary advocacy that involved the participants in cross-examining witnesses in fictional summary trials. The author recorded the cross-examinations of a novice participant and an experienced participant. The record is instructive.

1. The case

R v Fred Gorringe

2. The charge

The defendant is charged with assaulting Police Constable Taffrail, a constable of the Metropolitan Police, in the execution of his duty on 14 July 1988 in Titan Street, London W1, contrary to section 51 of the Police Act 1964.

3. The police officer's witness statement

The witness statement of PC 286 M Snotty:

On 14th July 1988 at about 4pm I was on duty outside the Titan Embassy in Titan Street, W1 with other police officers facing an unruly demonstration. I saw a man I now know to be Fred Gorringe throw a bottle at another police officer PC 222X Taffrail. The bottle struck PC Taffrail on the head. I took hold of Gorringe, told him I was arresting him and cautioned him. Gorringe said 'Fuck you coppers.' I then took Gorringe to the charging centre where I wrote up my notes after Gorringe had been charged.

4. The defendant's proof of evidence

The defendant's rather inadequate proof of evidence reads:

> My name is Fred Gorringe. I have been charged with assaulting PC
> Taffrail in the execution of his duty. I have pleaded not guilty. On the
> day in question I was in a demonstration outside the Titan Embassy. I
> was jammed right up against the crush barrier by the rest of the crowd
> and could hardly move. Bottles were being thrown from the back of the
> crowd. Suddenly one of the policemen on the other side of the crush
> barrier started swearing. He grabbed me and hauled me over the barrier.
> He was helped by another policeman who had no helmet on and had a
> cut on his head. The first policeman said 'You're nicked, sonny.' He
> started taking me away. I said, 'Why, what have I done?' He said 'You'll
> find out'. I was taken by the policeman to a van and then driven to a
> police station. At the police station the policeman told the sergeant,
> 'This lad was throwing bottles. They were all throwing bottles. I saw one
> of them hit another officer.' I did not throw any bottles or anything else.
> I was just standing there shouting slogans. I work in an architect's
> office as a clerk. I have no convictions. In fact I have never been
> arrested before.

5. The inexperienced advocate's cross-examination of the officer

Q: First of all I would like to ask you . . . you say that it was an unruly
demonstration . . . in what way was it unruly?[1]

A: It was very much the sort of crowd one gets outside embassies where
they're being besieged by demonstrations like this . . . there was a
great deal of pushing and shoving going on . . . a large amount of
shouting.[2]

Q: What was the demonstration about?

A: Ah it would be some . . . I don't know too much about these sort
of things . . . I believe that everyone knows about the Titan oranges
one's supposed not to buy like the South African ones . . . but I
don't follow politics myself . . . I believe it was something to do with
that . . .

Q: About how many people were involved in the demonstration?

A: Several thousand I would put it as . . .

---

1 The advocate has not thought out how to start the cross-examination and this
shows in the question. The witness will immediately receive this message and his
confidence will be boosted.

2 This is a long, confident answer. The witness appears to feel he has little to fear
from the cross-examination.

Q: A lot of noise?[3]
A: Yes, a considerable amount.
Q: What were all these people doing basically?
A: I believe it was my impression and other police officers' impressions that they were trying to storm the embassy at that stage . . . certainly that was what we were trying to prevent them doing at that stage.
Q: What exactly were they doing? What were their actions broadly speaking?[4]
A: Well, all of . . . er . . . shouting, pushing, trying to knock down the crush barriers . . .
Q: Anything else?
A: In what way, sir?
Q: Any other actions that you may have observed amongst the crowd?
A: Well, as I say, a lot of shouting, things being thrown, shoving, surging . . .
Q: (This question asked while the previous answer is being given[5]) What sort of things being thrown? What sort of things being thrown?
A: Bottles, pieces of stick, a number of things . . .
Q: Are we talking about many bottles, many sticks?
A: A considerable number, yes sir.
Q: Were you able to see from what section of the crowd this was coming?[6]
A: They were coming from all parts of the crowd.
Q: And what were you doing all this time?[7]
A: I was standing next to the crush barriers with other uniformed police officers attempting to stop the crowd from going through the crush barrier and . . . er . . . obviously invading the embassy . . .
Q: And what were you . . . what did you have to do exactly to stop them?[8]

3 A leading question that does not progress the cross-examination. The advocate is treading water while waiting for inspiration.
4 The correct sort of question, but it need not have been repeated. However, it is still all too clear that the cross-examiner has not found a sense of direction.
5 This is a clear sign that the advocate is more concerned with the devising of the question than the answers the witness is giving.
6 This is a badly formulated question. The witness could legitimately have answered 'yes' or 'no'. The question should have been 'Where in the crowd were they coming from?' Even when correctly formed, however, it is still a useless question.
7 The right sort of question but little sense of direction. The witness will still not be feeling under any pressure.
8 The two sections of the question are not connected. The advocate began speaking before deciding what the question was to be. He should have remained silent until he had decided what to ask. It is clear that the advocate is unable to plan more than half a question in advance.

A: At that stage, nothing.

Q: How did you propose to stop them then?

A: Well, should they move the crush barrier . . . obviously many police-men had their feet on the base of the crush barrier to keep them firm . . . had they surmounted the crush barrier, then obviously they would have been arrested . . . as many were, indeed . . .[9]

Q: Did some of them come over the crush barrier then?

A: Yes . . . I believe they did.

Q: Large numbers?

A: No, not very many.

Q: What was PC Taffrail doing?

A: Much the same sort of thing...it was a line of police officers, sir . . .

Q: (This question asked while the previous answer is being given[10]) Crowd control? Crowd control basically?[11]

A: Exactly sir, yes.

Q: Were either of you in uniform?[12]

A: Er . . . we were all in uniform, sir . . . yes . . .

Q: Now you saw this bottle strike PC Taffrail on the head . . . can you say how far approximately he was away from you at that point?[13]

A: PC Taffrail, sir?

Q: Yes.

A: Um . . . approximately thirty yards, sir . . .

Q: Were you able to see from what direction the bottle came?[14]

A: Oh yes, sir . . . yes.

Q: And where was that in relation to you?

A: Well, the gentleman, the defendant was almost immediately in front of me . . . slightly to my right on the other side of the crush barrier

---

9 The language the witness uses and the form of his answer shows his self-confidence. The cross-examination is not causing him any difficulty.

10 This is a clear sign that the advocate is more concerned with the devising of the question than the answers the witness is giving.

11 This question allows the witness to give an impression that the witness and cross-examiner are in agreement. The question is pointless and at best does not advance the cross-examination at all. The wholehearted and patronising nature of the answer shows how little the witness feels under pressure.

12 A pointless question.

13 The two sections of the question are not connected. The advocate began speaking before deciding what the question was to be. He should have remained silent until he had decided what to ask.

14 In the context of the witness' specific evidence that Gorringe threw the bottle this is a leading question that will have the sole effect of enabling the witness strongly to affirm his evidence. The question enables the witness to appear resolute and consistent. It is consequently pointless and damaging to the defence case.

. . . and . . . er . . . approximately a yard away. . . so I was easily able to see him . . . a long-haired fellow . . .[15]

Q: And how far would he have been from PC Taffrail?

A: About the same as me, sir . . . thirty yards . . .

Q: And there were other bottles being thrown at the same time, were there?

A: There were a number of objects being thrown throughout the afternoon, sir, yes.

Q: And at that particular time?[16]

A: Er . . . probably, sir. My attention was drawn to the gentleman in question as he was so close to me, so to speak . . .

Q: Now you say you took hold of the defendant . . . did you say anything to him at all just prior to doing that?[17]

A: Well, I told him I was arresting him and cautioned him . . . that was after he had thrown the bottle, sir . . .

Q: Yes . . . yes indeed . . . Did you say anything else apart from that?

A: That was what I said, sir . . . and he replied as I mentioned in my evidence, sir.[18]

Q: You took him back subsequently, didn't you, to the charging centre? Erm . . . did you say anything to anybody when you got back there? Any conversation with anybody there?[19]

15 This answer shows the self-confidence of the witness and how little he feels under pressure.

16 The advocate quite rightly notes that the witness has failed to answer the preceding question and presses the point. The advocate, having obtained the answer he is seeking, then fails to follow up what might have been a promising line of cross-examination, that there were many missiles being thrown on this occasion and it must have been difficult to attribute any particular missile to any particular person. This would have been a cross-examination point to establish the witness's unreliability and does not directly advance the defence case.

17 The two sections of the question are not connected. It is clear once again that the advocate began speaking before deciding what the question was to be. He should have remained silent until he had decided what to ask. If the advocate had had some sort of strategy, he would not have had to agonise over each question.

18 The witness evades the apparent purpose of the question which is to require him to say specifically what he said in direct speech. The advocate allows him to do so and then moves on to another topic. It is thereby clear to the witness and the court that the advocate has no real aim in asking that line of questions and little idea what to do with the answers. If the witness is evasive, it may be because he is worried about answering the question asked. It is precisely in these circumstances that the advocate has an opportunity to cross-examine to effect and he must follow up properly.

19 The two sections of the question are not connected. If this was really the topic the advocate intended to question on, the question should have been: 'What was said at the charging centre?'

A: I told the custody sergeant that I had seen . . . that I had seen him throw the bottle.

Q: Did you tell the custody sergeant you had seen him do anything else?[20]

A: Er . . . I don't think so, sir . . . I said I had seen him throwing bottles and one of the bottles had hit PC Taffrail on the head . . . I think that's about it, sir.

Q: Did you not describe what had been going on generally at the scene?[21]

A: Er . . . no, sir. It was common knowledge. There were large numbers of police there, it was common knowledge what was going on there, generally speaking . . .

Q: You didn't mention then that other people had been throwing bottles?

A: I think that er . . . I am sure that the custody sergeant would have known that.[22]

Q: These . . . this bottle that hit PC Taffrail, did you, did you observe any injury to PC Taffrail?[23]

A: Well, I saw his helmet being knocked off and it appeared to me to be a cut on his head . . . and I . . . er . . . he sort of wobbled. . .[24]

Q: And at what point did you observe this injury?

A: Well, immediately after the . . . er . . . bottle had hit his head . . .

Q: It must have been quite a nasty business, this demonstration?[25]

A: That's a fair comment, sir, yes.

Q: Could have turned out very nasty, couldn't it?

A: Yes . . . I was aware of what was going on, sir.

Q: Anxious no doubt to do your best to keep control?

A: Yes, sir.

Q: Anxious no doubt to see to it that nobody got hurt?

A: That's one of one's duties, sir, yes.

Q: Including yourself?

---

20 If the cross-examination had sufficient form to give the impression that the advocate knew what he was doing, the witness would have been alerted by the form of this quesion that this was a topic of importance and put on his guard.

21 This is a leading question of no value and too general to be answered.

22 Another evasive answer.

23 The second section of this question does not require the first section as an introduction and the two sections are not logically linked. It will be clear to the witness that the advocate has no particular direction in his cross-examination and probably had no real idea what the question should be about until he began speaking the first section.

24 The witness, in spite of the poor quality of the questioning, is not answering well. With properly devised and delivered questions he would be in trouble.

25 This is a ludicrous comment in the form of a question. The only result may be to engage the court's sympathies for the witness.

A: Well yes, sir . . .

Q: Colleagues, other people in the crowd?

A: That's right, sir, yes.

Q: In fact you must have been concentrating I would think fairly hard on the task in hand?

A: Well, I don't think one had time to sleep on the job, sir . . . not on a job like that, sir.

Q: No . . . there was quite a lot going on all around you, wasn't there? People milling around, things flying through the air?

A: Yes.

Q: In fact I should think it must have been pretty difficult to fasten your attention on all the little incidents going on all around you?

A: Er . . . yes, sir, yes.

Q: So in that case there would be some scope, wouldn't there, for . . . er . . . for error in terms of what you may or may not have seen?[26]

A: Well, if you mean, sir, I didn't see the gentleman in question, the defendant throwing the bottle, he was right in front of me . . .

Q: If you could just answer my question . . . there must have been some scope, must there not, for error? Quite a lot going on, wasn't there?[27]

A: Well not in this case, sir.

Q: How do you mean 'not in this case'?

A: Well, the gentleman was right in front of me.

Q: Yes, but there's a whole crowd of people in front of you.

A: Yeah, but he raised his hand with a bottle in it.

Q: Yes, but you've said yourself, haven't you, that it wasn't possible for you to fasten your attention on everything that was going on.

A: No . . . but my attention was drawn to the bottle and the gentleman in front of me at that particular point.

Q: But it would be easy to miss other things wouldn't it?[28]

A: Well yes, because you can't watch everything, sir.

26 For the first time the advocate has produced a line of questions that shows he is thinking more than one question ahead. It is a promising sequence, dealing with whether the witness could have identified the defendant as the thrower of the bottle. Unfortunately the sequence culminates in a leading question that the witness is able to contradict decisively and convincingly.

27 It is unrealistic to expect the witness to say in general terms that his evidence is wrong.

28 In this sequence the cross-examination has degenerated into an argument between the advocate and the witness. The advocate must avoid this. The sympathies of the court will be with the witness and there will be a swift intervention from the court to bring the argument to an end. The advocate will have lost ground.

Q: It would be easy to get things wrong, wouldn't it? It would be easy to misobserve things.[29]

A: I don't accept that, sir.

Q: You see, you've said that there were quite a number of people throwing objects through the air . . . were you really able to say that this defendant threw a bottle at all?[30]

A: I saw the bottle in the defendant's hand and I watched him throw it and I followed its trajectory.

Q: Yes. You see, his instructions to me are that he did not throw a bottle or anything of that sort. . . . I put it to you that you might be mistaken about that . . .[31]

A: I'm not mistaken about that.

Q: Are you sure that he threw it at this particular point?[32]

A: Oh yes, sir.

Q: Might you perhaps have seen him throw a bottle earlier on or later?[33]

A: No . . . I would have arrested him earlier if I had seen him throw it earlier.

Q: Can you really say that it was his bottle that hit the officer?

A: Well, I followed the trajectory of the bottle.

Q: Yes. And there may or there may not have been other bottles flying through the air at the same time . . . isn't that right?[34]

A: There may or there may not have been.

Q: They also would have had a trajectory wouldn't they?

A: Undoubtedly, sir, yes.

29 It is unrealistic to expect the witness to agree with this question. This is really a comment for the closing speech and there is consequently no point in putting it in cross-examination. The witness is able to deny the point decisively. Every time the witness is allowed to contradict a defence point decisively his evidence appears more reliable to the court. The essence of cross-examination is to cause the witness's evidence to appear shaky and unreliable not the reverse.

30 It is unrealistic to expect the witness to agree with this question.

31 Again it is unrealistic to expect the witness to agree with the question.

32 The *only* consequence of this sort of question is that the witness is given the opportunity to confirm his account.

33 It is unrealistic to expect the witness to agree with this question. It is also a question of despair. The advocate has put two directly opposite questions into one. The advocate cannot have expected any useful answer from this question. It is in effect an invitation to the witness to say anything he likes. It is the most pointless type of leading question.

34 This question shows that the advocate has in mind this very important point but is unable to formulate the correct questions to illustrate the point in cross-examination. The witness has little difficulty dealing with the point in this form. The court will not be critical of the witness's evidence so that this form of parrying answer is quite adequate for the witness's needs.

Q: Isn't it conceivable that it was one of those bottles that struck him?[35]

A: Er, not to my knowledge, sir . . . not to my recollection . . .

Q: You say not to your knowledge or recollection?

A: Well I'm certain that it was that bottle that went through the air that I followed that hit PC Taffrail.

Q: Well that's not what with respect you said a moment ago . . . you said not to your knowledge or recollection . . . isn't it?[36]

A: I'm certain that that was the bottle.

Q: You see, I'm not suggesting that you're not telling the truth but I do want to put to you a slightly different scenario . . . that boils down to you may be mistaken in this case . . . is that not right?[37]

A: No . . .

Q: Would you not concede that there's a possibility?[38]

A: Not in this case . . .

Q: There's some thirty yards between you and the other officer . . . isn't there?

A: That's right, sir . . .

Q: A similar distance between the accused and the . . . that officer as well?

A: Yup.

Q: There's an awful lot going on?

A: Oh yeah.

35 Again this is the right point put in the wrong way. It is unrealistic to expect this witness to agree with a proposition the implication of which is that the witness is wrong in the key point of his evidence.

36 The advocate is taking issue with the witness over his use of 'knowledge or recollection'. It is hard to see what other basis the witness could give evidence from. The court's sympathies will be with the witness.

37 In this sequence of questions the advocate has the germ of a good idea, that is that it seems strange that the witness should happen to follow the route of this one bottle which turns out to be the one that hits the second officer. In order to exploit this idea in effective cross-examination the advocate has to conduct a narrative sweep with the witness to establish exactly what he did at each point. Instead the advocate puts to the witness a series of propositions in leading questions that the witness has no trouble in contradicting. A witness is only really put in difficulties when dealing with facts. A witness knows that he can contradict a general proposition without any danger of being proved wrong by other evidence. Nor is it a good idea to reassure a witness that it is not being suggested that he is not telling the truth. Uncertainty is a substantial weapon in cross-examination. This assertion will have reassured the witness to some extent. In any case it is a matter for the court, not the advocate.

38 It is unrealistic to expect the witness to agree with this question.

Q: And it's right, isn't it, that when you got the accused to the charging centre you spoke to your colleague there? That's right, isn't it?[39]

A: To the custody sergeant, sir, yes.

Q: And one of the things you said was along the lines of that this lad was throwing bottles, they were all throwing bottles . . . I saw one of them hit another officer . . . is not that right? those are my instructions. . .[40]

A: No, sir . . . I said I had seen . . . I'd seen the defendant throwing bottles . . . I may have said I had seen them all throwing bottles at one point . . . I certainly said . . . I said to the sergeant I'd seen him . . . the lad . . . throwing bottles and that one of those bottles hit PC Taffrail on the head . . .

Q: No . . . those are not my instructions . . . it rather sounds, you see, as if you'd seen a number of bottles and you weren't quite sure which one it was . . .[41]

A: That's not . . . that wasn't my intent, sir, or indeed what I said.

Q: I've no further questions.

Comment

The advocate has achieved nothing by this cross-examination other than to permit the witness to reaffirm his evidence-in-chief. Conviction of the defendant is certain to follow. There were two sequences of questions that seemed to be following promising lines but the advocate abandoned them before they achieved anything. The third sequence ended in a blind alley through the use of a highly inappropriate leading question which required little effort to deflect. Many questions were begun before the advocate knew what question he was intending to ask, so that the question changed subject during delivery. It was clear that the advocate was not listening to some of the answers he was given. His uncertainty and indecision was obvious to the witness, who was consequently entirely comfortable during the cross-examination and able to put himself over as a

---

39 This question does not follow with any logic from the previous sequence. The advocate is asking questions without any real strategy in mind. He is also simply repeating the witness's evidence-in-chief. This is the classic sign of a cross-examination with no purpose.

40 With the last sentence the advocate makes the error of indicating the source of his information. Without this indication the officer might have been uncertain as to whether he could safely deny the question. The advocate tells the witness that the source of the information is the defendant and the witness's uncertainty is resolved.

41 It is clear from this weak question that the cross-examination is winding down. The advocate's final lack of inspiration is obvious.

confident and truthful witness. Other than the three sequences most of the questions were 'one-offs' with no indication that the advocate was able to think beyond his next question.

6. Cross-examination of the same officer by the more experienced advocate

Q: What station are you from?

A: Bow Street, sir.

Q: How many officers from your station were there that day?

A: There were a good thirty, sir, at that stage. . .

Q: And they were all from that district?

A: What, at the demonstration, sir?

Q: What district are you from?[42]

A: M District, sir.

Q: Were there other officers there that you knew?

A: There were officers that I knew from my station there, sir. . .

Q: Did you know any of the other officers?

A: Er . . . not . . . not apart from the ones from my station, sir.

Q: Did you know all the ones from your station?

A: I knew all the officers from my station sir, yes. . .[43]

Q: Where were they standing?[44]

A: The officers from my station were mainly to my left . . . one or two to my right. . .[45]

Q: Now what sort of area does the embassy stand in?

42 The advocate suddenly remembers the need to emphasise that Taffrail was from a different division. Hence the abrupt and uncomfortable change of direction.

43 The advocate has begun the cross-examination with a good pace of questioning using short single sentences. When a witness repeats a question before answering, it can mean that he is feeling his way and wants to be sure of the question before he answers it. Perhaps the speed and manner of the cross-examination has put him on the defensive.

44 All the questions in this cross-examination so far have been short, single sentences. Each question is asked as part of a sequence obtaining the answers the advocate needs. This sort of sequence can be delivered quickly and a momentum is built up that gives the witness little opportunity to think where he is being taken.

45 The advocate needs to establish which officers the witness knew and where they were standing. He opens his cross-examination with this unexpected topic because he wants the information on the record for the later stage but does not want the witness to have in mind the drift of the questioning when he moves to the second stage. The advocate then moves to the description of the scene that he needs for several features of his cross-examination. The abruptness of the change disconcerts the witness.

A: I'm sorry?

Q: What sort of area does the embassy stand in?[46]

A: It's a rather large square in London and there are three embassies on each side of the square.

Q: One on each side of the square bar one side?[47]

A: Bar one side, that's right, sir.

Q: What sort of size of square is it?

A: It's about the same size as Russell Square. . .[48]

Q: And what does the square contain?

A: It contains large buildings and in the middle of the square there is a sort of wooded area . . . a small park.[49]

Q: And does anything separate the wooded area from the street?[50]

A: Just the pavement, sir.

Q: And where is the street?

A: The street we are talking about?

Q: Yes.

A: There is a sort of rather a large sort of a road between the embassy and the park.

Q: Going all the way around the square?

A: That's right, sir.

Q: And where are the entrances to the square?

A: The entrances to the square are in each corner as I recollect.

Q: And where in that particular side of the square is the Titan Embassy?

A: The Titan Embassy is on the south side of the square.

46 On being asked to repeat the question the advocate is able to do so verbatim because the question is a simple, complete sentence and because he remembers the question he has asked.

47 The advocate has thrown in this leading question to ensure that the magistrates have grasped the scene correctly.

48 The square outside the courtroom.

49 The advocate could put this detail to the witness in leading questions and invite him to agree. It is better to make the witness describe it. The advocate does not know but that somewhere in the information the witness may not create an opportunity for a cross-examination coup. The witness may re-arrange the geography in order to allow for some evasion or untruth. If the witness's later evidence is inconsistent with this description it is easier for the witness to say he was mistaken if he has simply been agreeing with detail put to him in leading questions rather than if he has himself asserted the detail to be so. The advocate is listening carefully to the witness and is likely to latch onto any feature that the witness seems sensitive about relying solely on the manner of the witness's delivery. The more information the witness gives, the more vulnerable he is to cross-examination.

50 The advocate has been to the scene and questions from a position of knowledge, as the witness will have understood. The description is for the justices, not for the advocate, and to put the later answers in context.

Q: Whereabouts on that side?

A: It takes up most of the side in fact. . .

Q: Where were the police positioned?

A: The police were positioned immediately in front of the Titan Embassy. . . the crush barrier was in position immediately in front of the police . . . it was like a police line except there was a slight arc.

Q: And where did the police extend from and to?

A: It covered the extent of the building as a matter of fact . . .

Q: What, and ended at each end?

A: Yes . . . there were a few officers a bit further on. . .

Q: And what was the density of police?

A: We only had about . . . at that stage we only had about a line of two at the very most . . . two deep . . .

Q: And how far away was the officer on your left?

A: Er . . . you mean the officer we were referring to?

Q: No . . . the next officer along.

A: He was right next to me, sir.

Q: Shoulder to shoulder?[51]

A: Shoulder to shoulder, that's right.

Q: And on your right?

A: The very same, yes . . .

Q: So there were police shoulder to shoulder all the way along?[52]

A: Yes mostly. . . two deep, sometimes one deep . . .

Q: Were you in the square before the demonstration arrived?

A: Er, yes, sir.

Q: And where did the demonstration come in from?

A: They came in from the left-hand side . . . from the left.

Q: Is that all of it?

A: Yes, the entire demonstration came in from there, sir.

Q: And how many people were there in the demonstration?

---

51 The advocate should not have lead the witness in this question. If the witness had been on his toes he would have realised that it suited the advocate to say the police officers were standing shoulder to shoulder and said something else. Perhaps the advocate's estimate of the witness was that he would agree and he wanted to hurry the witness to this conclusion to keep up the momentum of the cross-examination. Even so, the advocate should not have lead the witness, he should have allowed the witness to give his own description. A witness more on his toes would have rejected the advocate's form of words not because it was wrong but because an antagonistic witness avoids any form of words put to him by a cross-examiner.

52 The advocate repeats this answer because he wishes to make sure the magistrates have grasped this graphic and fundamental feature. This is deliberate technique and not filling in a gap because the advocate cannot think what to ask next.

A: Very difficult to say sir . . . several thousand . . . they swept into the square . . .

Q: And how much of the square did they fill?

A: Most of the square . . . in fact all of the square I would say . . .

Q: How long did the demonstration go on for?

A: The entire demonstration went on for about three hours I would say . . .

Q: Starting when?

A: Starting approximately three o'clock.

Q: And what was the behaviour of the demonstration?

A: Well they were very unruly . . . some speeches were made at some point . . . from a makeshift platform. . . and that was approximately half an hour before this incident took place . . . and shortly after the speeches they became more unruly and . . . er . . . then they tried to assault the embassy . . .

Q: And what time did the assault on the embassy start?

A: Shortly before this incident, about ten minutes before . . .

Q: Whereabouts was the platform that the speeches were made from?

A: That was to my right and to the east side of the square as I recollect . . .

Q: And what was your responsibility?

A: Crowd control, sir . . . stop them getting through the crush barrier.

Q: How did you do that?

A: Well, by leaning hard on the crush barrier and standing on the base of the thing . . .

Q: Anybody trying to get over it?

A: Several people tried to get over it . . . some were arrested . . . it was difficult to arrest them.

Q: Anybody try and get over your section?[53]

A: One or two, yes . . .

Q: At what sort of time did they do that?

A: I can't recollect exactly . . . sometime before the main incident . . . as I say, the main surge took place about ten minutes before the incident . . .

Q: And whereabouts on the police barrier did the surge take place?[54]

A: Er, different points . . .

Q: How many different points?

A: Difficult to say, sir . . . one could only see so far . . .

Q: Was the crowd surging against the police barrier all the way along?

---

53 This is a sequence of leading questions with no apparent point in view. Perhaps the advocate was just testing the witness to see what opened up.

54 The witness in his previous answer uses the word 'surge' for the first time. The advocate takes up the word in his sequence of questioning.

A: Pretty well, yes . . .

Q: And you were concerned to stop people coming over your section of the barrier?[55]

A: That's right.

Q: How many people did you see throwing bottles?

A: Again very difficult to say, sir . . . too numerous to say . . . I mean there were numerous missiles flying around . . .

Q: Can you make any sort of estimate?

A: Er . . . many, sir . . . as I say, there were missiles flying around all the time . . .

Q: And what were the main targets for the missiles? Any idea?

A: Either police officers or the embassy . . .

Q: Now you say you saw the defendant with a bottle?

A: That's right, sir . . . yes . . .

Q: Was this the first time you had seen him that afternoon?

A: Yes . . . the first time I noticed him was when he had the bottle in his hand . . .

Q: How far away from you was he?

A: Just over a yard . . .

Q: And that's the other side of the barrier, is it?[56]

A: That's right, yeah.

Q: So at this stage the crowd were surging up against the barrier?

A: Yes . . . that's right . . . yes.

Q: Did you see anyone else with him with a bottle?

A: Er, not at that point, no.

Q: What did you say he did?

A: Well I saw him raise his hand with a bottle in it. And then I watched

55 This sequence of questions is designed to establish the point that the witness would have been unlikely to stop watching his section of barrier in order to follow the path of one bottle which then landed some distance to this right. The point is not put in cross examination but reserved to the closing speech. If the advocate had put the point to the witness, the witness would have been given the opportunity to avoid or demolish the point.

56 The advocate should not have lead the witness on this point. The advocate should have made the witness put this answer in his own words. The advocate is following a point which requires this answer. By posing a leading question the advocate permits the witness to agree or disagree without effort and destroys the opportunity for making the witness devise his own answer and possibly create more material for cross-examination. It is essential to make the witness do the thinking and the talking.

him throw the bottle. Then I followed the movement of the bottle
until it hit PC Taffrail.[57]

Q: Can I ask you this?[58] How did you actually arrest him?

A: Well, I told him I was arresting him.

Q: How did you physically arrest him?[59]

A: Well, I had to pull him over the barrier.

Q: No, before that. What did you do?

A: Well, I told him I was arresting him.

Q: Before that, what did you do? You were standing on the police side of
the barrier . . . what did you do?[60]

A: Well, I saw that the bottle had hit PC Taffrail. And then I looked back
to him. I told him I was going to arrest him, cautioned him and then
he said 'Stuff you, coppers'. And then I pulled him over the barrier.

Q: You're standing on the police side of the barrier. The defendant is on
the other side of the barrier. What did you do?[61]

A: Well, I had to move forward and across the barrier.

Q: What do you mean by that?[62]

A: Well, I had to virtually clamber over the barrier.

Q: Did you actually clamber over the barrier?

57 There is an inherent implausibility in this answer that the advocate was hoping
the witness would give. The advocate will use it in his speech. The implausibility
is that a police officer in this situation is most unlikely to decide to watch the
path of one bottle out of many and see it land some way to his right. The
advocate could put the implausibility to the witness as part of this sequence. He
chooses not to.
   This is the answer the advocate was heading towards with his sequence of
leading questions. It may be that there would have been promising material to be
had if the advocate had not lead the witness in this way. The advocate has
blundered over a number of blooming flower beds in order to plant his geranium
in the end bed.

58 This is a superfluous sentence but it cushions slightly the abrupt change of
subject.

59 The advocate knows this is an area that police officers are often reluctant to deal
with in full. He is therefore ready to repeat questions and persist until he has the
full detail he requires. The witness is likely to evade the questions because he
knows that the arrest stage can be a minefield of awkward technicalities that the
defence can exploit.

60 As part of his evasion technique the witness tries to move past the awkward part
without giving any detail. With the inexperienced advocate this technique
worked and the advocate carried on from this further point. This advocate
just takes the witness back to the start of the section he has evaded and makes
the witness go over it again until he has given a satisfactory answer.

61 The advocate persists in requiring the witness to describe in full each stage of the
arrest.

62 The advocate does not permit the witness to skate over parts that are awkward
to describe.

A: Yeah well that's the only way you can do it, sir.

Q: What do you mean by that?

A: Well, the barrier is quite wide.

Q: Did you climb over the barrier or not?

A: Er, partially, sir. I partially climbed over the barrier and I partially pulled him over my side of the barrier.

Q: He made no effort to escape?

A: Well no . . . no . . . he couldn't have.

Q: Did you have any trouble getting him over the barrier?

A: Well yes a bit.

Q: How did you do it?

A: Well . . . by brute force.

Q: And then what happened?

A: Well . . . then he went quietly to the van.

Q: Yes but before that . . . you were pulling him over the barrier and then what happened?

A: Well, as I say he said 'Stuff you, coppers' after I cautioned him and then we went to the van.

Q: But whereabouts were you when you arrested him?

A: I was facing him.

Q: And where were you in respect of the barrier?

A: Well, the other side of the barrier from where he was.

Q: What sort of hold did you have on him when you arrested him?

A: Well, as I recall I gripped him by the shoulders.

Q: In what way?

A: Well, can I demonstrate sir?

Q: Yes, please do.

A: it was a question of taking him by the shoulders like that and pulling him over.

Q: Did anyone help you?

A: Er, no, I was on my own at that stage.

Q: What sort of build would you say the defendant is?

A: Sort of medium build.

Q: And you just lifted him over by his shoulders?

A: It's not that easy, sir, no.

Q: But you say you did it?

A: Yes I did . . . with some difficulty.

Q: Wasn't there another policeman who helped you?[63]

---

63 It is not easy to see why the advocate handles the matter of the second officer assisting in the arrest in quite this way. It is the defendant's case that the second officer was the injured one, ie, Taffrail. Perhaps the advocate merely wants confirmation of the defendant's account. The only point that comes out of this sequence is the failure of this witness to mention the other officer in his notes as assisting in the arrest, probably only a minor point.

A: Well, another policeman came to my assistance immediately afterwards. I actually arrested him and . . . er . . . pulled him over. I did that on my own.

Q: Who was the policeman who came to your assistance?

A: I can't recall . . . he disappeared soon afterwards.

Q: What station was he from?

A: I can't recall.

Q: Do you make any mention of him in your notes?

A: I don't believe I do . . . no, sir.

Q: Why not?

A: I didn't think it necessary, sir.[64]

Q: What did you say to the defendant?

A: Well, I told him I was arresting him.

Q: What did you say to the defendant?

A: I said I am arresting you for threatening behaviour.[65]

Q: Yes . . . then?

A: And . . . er . . . then I cautioned him.

Q: And?

A: He then replied 'Stuff you, coppers'.

Q: What do you mean when you say you cautioned him?[66]

A: Well, I told him he wasn't obliged to say anything but anything he said would be written down and given in evidence.[67]

---

64 The advocate will use this material in his speech to support the defendant's contention that there was another officer who helped arrest him. The advocate chooses not to confront the witness in cross-examination with this point. This would seem to be a valid approach.

65 This sequence has produced the general point for the defence closing speech that there is an inherent lack of plausibility in the witness's description in what took place during the arrest. But this answer gives a much more powerful point. That is that this could not be the appropriate offence to arrest the defendant for if the witness had really seen his fellow officer hit by a bottle and possibly severely injured. The witness's problem, as the advocate knows well, is that the witness cannot claim to have arrested the defendant for any other offence because the fact of arrest for threatening behaviour is too extensively documented. The witness's only option was to try and avoid saying what his grounds for arrest were. Hence the extensive evasion. The advocate was quite happy to put the witness through a lengthy and agonising sequence of questions to extract the answer. The magistrates will have seen how reluctant the witness was to give the full answer. This strengthens the point to be made in the defence closing speech immeasurably.

66 The advocate persists in making the witness describe everything that was said.

67 This is probably a point this advocate makes in all public order cases. It is unlikely that the magistrates think much of the point although without a doubt the witness did not give a caution and is lying when he claimed that he did. No one could blame an officer for delaying the giving of a caution until calmer circumstances. Nevertheless police officers will claim to have administered cautions when they clearly could not.

Q: You said that to him in the middle of a riot?

A: Well yes.

Q: And what did he say?

A: He said 'Stuff you, coppers'.

Q: What were you arresting him for?

A: Er, threatening behaviour.

Q: What was the actual act you were arresting him for?

A: Well, for threatening behaviour.

Q: What was the act you were arresting him for?[68]

A: Well, I had seen him throwing the bottle.

Q: And that was the complete act you were arresting him for?

A: Yeah . . . I thought the appropriate thing to arrest him for was threatening behaviour at the time.[69]

Q: Who's PC Taffrail?

A: He is a police officer from another division.

Q: Which division is he from?

A: Er, may I check my notes sir?[70] . . . X Division.

Q: You say he was injured?

A: Er, yes, he was.

Q: Did you have the opportunity to inspect his injuries?[71]

A: No, but I saw the injuries when I saw the bottle strike his head.[72]

Q: Didn't you have the opportunity to examine his injuries later on?

A: Er, no, I didn't, no.

Q: When did you see him again after the arrest?

68 The witness has evaded the true question so the advocate repeats the question as near verbatim as possible.

69 Again this is a point the advocate chooses to use in his speech to the justices and not to confront the witness. The point is that if the witness had really seen the defendant throw a bottle that hit a police officer on the head he would not have arrested him for threatening behaviour but some more serious offence of assault. It is interesting that the witness harps back to the 'reason for the arrest' point when his answer is primarily addressed to a completely different question. It indicates how vulnerable the witness feels on the 'reason for the arrest'.

70 The witness knows he may refer to his notes at any time. He is giving himself time to cope with an area of the cross-examination he knows is going to give him difficulty. The asking of this sort of superfluous question shows a witness to be under pressure from the cross-examination.

71 This is a sequence of questions leading to the damning point that this witness cannot explain the presence of PC Taffrail's name in his notes if his description of when he wrote his notes is accurate. The advocate attempts to conceal the real purpose of the questioning by basing it on the witness's opportunity to examine Taffrail's injuries.

72 This sort of self-contradictory answer shows that the cross-examination is now striking the witness at a vulnerable area. The account in the witness's notebook does not allow the witness any room to explain these points adequately.

A: Er, the next day in court.

Q: Did you have the opportunity to examine his injuries then?

A: Yeah I saw he had the mark on his head.[73]

Q: Was he an officer you knew?

A: No . . . I didn't know him at the time. He's from another division, sir.

Q: You had the opportunity to speak to him at court?

A: Yes, that's right, sir.

Q: You didn't see him before that at the charging centre?

A: No, I didn't, no.

Q: You sure?

A: Yeah, I'm sure about that, yeah.

Q: Did anyone tell you who he was?

A: No I found out the next day in court.

Q: What do your notes say about him?[74]

A: Er, what do you mean sir?

Q: Well, do you mention him in your notes?

A: Well yes, sir . . . I say that a bottle was thrown at a police officer, PC 222X Taffrail.

Q: When did you write that?

A: Well, I wrote those notes in the charging centre quarter of an hour after the incident took place.[75]

Q: When did you find out who he was?

A: Er, well I next saw him at court the next day.

Q: Well, how did you put his name in your notes?

A: Well there must be a mistake or perhaps I did see him at the station, I can't recall, or perhaps he gave his name at the station.[76]

Q: Or perhaps you wrote your notes the next day?

A: No, I wrote them a quarter of an hour after the incident took place.

Q: And perhaps you haven't told the court the truth about this?

A: No, that's right, sir.

---

73 There is a good point revealed by this answer. A 'mark' is hardly consistent with being struck by a bottle thrown from 30 yards. The advocate is concentrating on a particular line of questioning so that he sweeps past this answer. It may be that the answer has registered sufficiently for the advocate to use it in his closing speech. The advocate ought to be analysing everything the witness says in his answer and not just the parts of the answer that are relevant to the sequence of questions the advocate is currently following.

74 It is very much better technique to make the witness read out the section rather than to put it to the witness in a leading question. The witness almost inevitably will sound shifty as he reads out the excerpt.

75 The advocate knew that this would be his answer because the witness had given the time that he wrote up his notes in his evidence-in-chief.

76 This sequence of questions should win the case for the defence. The inescapable conclusion is that the witness is lying.

Q: You haven't told the court the truth?[77]
A: No, I have told the truth about everything.
Q: Whereabouts was PC Taffrail standing?
A: Er, he was approximately thirty yards to my right.
Q: How do you know?[78]
A: Well, that was where I saw him.
Q: Police officers standing shoulder to shoulder?
A: More or less, yes.
Q: How many police officers standing between you and PC Taffrail?
A: Something like twenty-five I suppose.
Q: From different stations?
A: Yeah that's right . . . yes, from my station.
Q: No . . . the officers between you and him were from different stations.
A: Some were, yes.
Q: Most of them were, weren't they?
A: Well some of them were. I knew some of the officers were from my station.[79]
Q: Well, you said that most of the officers from your station were standing on your left?
A: That's right yeah . . . some were standing to my right.
Q: So if there were three or four standing to your right . . . there are twenty officers standing between you and PC Taffrail that you don't know?
A: There were officers I didn't know yes.
Q: All of them wearing helmets?
A: Yes that's right.
Q: And PC Taffrail you didn't know either?
A: No, I recognised his face when I saw him, you know, hit.
Q: You say the barrier was in a crescent shape?
A: Yes that's right.
Q: With a surging crowd up against it all the way along?
A: Yes, that's right.[80]
Q: And you say you saw the bottle hit PC Taffrail?
A: Yes, that's right.

77 This is a deliberate misunderstanding of the witness's answer to enable the advocate to make the comment on the witness's truthfulness. A legitimate ploy.
78 The advocate has moved straight into the linked point. How could the witness see what happened to Taffrail from where he was?
79 The witness has forgotten that the advocate tied him down on this point at the beginning of the cross-examination.
80 The advocate has set this point up for comment in his speech, the point being that the witness could not possibly have seen the bottle strike Taffrail in these circumstances. Again he chooses not to make any comment in cross-examination.

Q: And what happened when it hit him?[81]

A: Well, it struck his helmet which kind of got knocked off sideways and I could see the blood on the side of his head.

Q: What happened to him?

A: Well he kind of slumped and . . . er . . . a couple of his fellow police officers sort of pulled him up, stopped him hitting the ground you know.

Q: Did he hit the ground?[82]

A: Er no, he didn't, no. As I say, a couple of police officers who were nearby sort of held onto him and I could see that they sort of pulled him back a bit and . . . er . . . obviously his place was taken by someone else while he was recovering.

Q: You must have been watching for fifteen or twenty seconds?[83]

A: Er, well I . . . er . . . saw what was happening, yes.

Q: So what was happening to your section of the barrier while you were watching him?

A: Er, it was quite a short time, nothing particular was happening.

Q: You weren't watching PC Taffrail at all were you?

A: Well I saw him get struck, sir, and I saw him get help.

Q: Do you ever play cricket?[84]

A: I did when I was a lad, sir, yes.

Q: What's the distance you reckon you could throw a cricket ball?

A: Well it depends how strong you are, sir.

Q: Yes exactly. You couldn't throw a bottle thirty yards, could you?[85]

A: Well I would have said so, yes.

Q: It's a long throw for an item like that, isn't it?

A: I wouldn't have thought so, sir.[86]

81 With this sequence the advocate is exploring for how long the witness was watching Taffrail. The longer this period the longer the witness had the bottle thrower out of his view. Set this against the brief view the witness had of the bottle thrower before the alleged throwing and the advocate is able to establish considerable difficulties for the prosecution on identification.

82 The advocate asks the question using the witness's own words. The witness is given no unnecessary assistance in formulating his answer.

83 With the impetus the cross-examination has built up it is probably legitimate to put this leading question.

84 For some reason the advocate embarks on this absurd diversion. It makes no point and brings the cross-examination to a halt. Fortunately the main points have already been made.

85 The advocate is trying to make the point that this must have been a very long throw for a bottle. He does not do it in a convincing way. A 30-yard throw for a cricket ball is a usual throw.

86 This sequence of questioning goes badly wrong for the advocate. The police officer to some extent gains the initiative and recovers his poise.

Q: What did you say to the custody officer when you got to the police station?[87]

A: Well, I told him that that lad had been throwing bottles and one of the bottles had hit a police officer.

Q: So you told the custody officer that you had seen him throw more than one bottle?

A: Well I meant that I had seen him throw the bottle that had hit PC Taffrail.

Q: But you didn't know who PC Taffrail was then did you?

A: Well no, I said a police officer at the time.

Q: Officer, you didn't see the defendant throw a bottle at all did you?

A: Oh indeed I did, sir.

Q: I have no further questions.

Comment

This is on the whole an effective cross-examination. The advocate has established several points for his speech. In relation to one point the only conclusion the magistrates could come to is that the witness is lying. That is the point dealing with how Taffrail's name came to be in the witness's notebook. The points made in the cross-examination should be sufficient if presented in an effective closing speech to persuade a reasonable bench of magistrates to conclude that there is a doubt as to Gorringe's guilt and acquit him. The points were each established by well thought out and properly disciplined sequences of questions. Each sequence appeared to have a particular and a realistic goal. Each sequence was executed by way of simple, single-sentence questions that extracted the necessary evidence from the witness. The only real failing in the cross-examination was the impulsive diversion into the 'throwing a cricket ball' sequence.

87 The advocate needs to escape quickly from the cricket ball fiasco and has this last topic up his sleeve. Unfortunately, he moves on from there back to the 'naming Taffrail' topic, a seam he has already mined to exhaustion, so that the cross-examination ends on a less effective note.

Part II

A Summary Trial: A Case Study

CHAPTER 14

The preparation

1. Billie and Terry are charged with public order offences

'I'm going to get myself a really good brief for this one,' growled
Terry Turquoise as he and Billie Blue emerged from Heeling police
station. They stopped and stood on the pavement. 'Who are you
going to get, Billie?'

'Rachel Red. Like I always do,' said Billie.

Billie and Terry had just spent the night in the cells of Heeling
police station, and each been charged with theft and assaulting a
police officer in the execution of his duty.

'I'm going to try that posh firm up the West End my uncle uses
when he gets caught blagging,' said Terry.

'You're not a blagger, Terry. Ruby Red is a good enough firm of
solicitors for us. Rachel always does us proud.'

Terry snorted derisively. 'Well, I'm moving up in the world. I'll
have a really brilliant barrister while you're scrubbing around with
your local solicitor. You'll see.' Terry turned and made his way up
the road. A night in the cells always made him tetchy.

Later that morning Billie went to Ruby Red's offices. He arrived
as Rachel Red was opening the door.

'Rachel, I got nicked last night,' said Billie.

'Sorry to hear that Billie.'

'Yeah. I'm going to court Thursday.'

'Want us to act?'

'Yes please, Rachel. There's no one else I want.'

'Come on in and we'll fill in the legal aid application form.'

Rachel Ruby collected the form and took Billie into her office.

'Got your charge sheet, Billie?'

'No. I left it at home.'

'Bring it to court. I need to see all the documents. What were you
charged with?'

'Theft and assault on police.'

'Doesn't sound like you, assault on police, Billie.'

'I didn't do it, Rachel. It was a stitch-up.'

'OK. We'll sort it out. Tell me what happened.'

'The coppers who nicked us say they saw us two weeks ago stealing from cars. They say they recognised us. They just grabbed us. Then they charged us with theft and assaulting them in the execution of their duty.'

'Have you got any witnesses?'

'Yeah. There's Terry who was charged with me and a whole lot of people standing around.'

'Any idea who these people were?'

'I don't know. I think I've seen some of them before. I'll look around for them.'

'OK. Get the names and addresses to me as quick as you can so I can get statements from them. Perhaps I should ask was it you stealing from cars two weeks ago?'

'Course it wasn't. Why would I nick from cars?'[1]

Rachel finished the legal aid form. 'OK. I've filled in all your details. I think I know most of them by heart. Just sign here. . . That's it. See you in court on Thursday. The Crown Prosecution Service will have the advance disclosure at court if we are lucky and we can decide where to have the case tried. It's got to be Crown Court really.'

'I don't want to go to Crown, Rachel. Me and my girl are going abroad travelling in a month and we want it out of the way.'

'We'll talk about it at court.'

In the afternoon Terry contacted his solicitors. Terry had not used these solicitors before. He had heard that all the big blaggers used them so he thought they must be good. It was expensive going up town just on spec, so he telephoned them first.

'Rose Madder, solicitors. How may I help you?'

'Er. I've been charged with a criminal case. I'm going to court Thursday. At Heeling Magistrates' Court and I want you to represent me.'

'Do you have legal aid?'

'Not yet.'

'Well obtain a form from your local court. Fill it in and submit it

1 The classic evasion.

to the court and once you have legal aid we can give you an appointment.'

'Oh right. I'm pleading not guilty.'

'Yes.'

'And I've got witnesses.'

'Yes. Just fill in the form and that will enable your case to be prepared.'

'Who will I see?'

'That will depend on who is available. Just go to the court and fill in the form. The sooner you do that the better.'

'Oh right. I'll go straight down the court and do it now.' Of course he didn't.

On the morning of their first court appearance, Billie and Terry arrived at court together at 10.15 am. Rachel Red met them in the hall.

'I'll see you later,' Billie said to Terry.

'Yeah.' Terry wandered off to the legal aid office.

'The prosecutor has arrived late, Billie,' said Rachel. 'He is in a bit of a lather. I don't think I'll be able to speak to him before we get on.'

'Terry is going to want an adjournment to get his brief to court.'

'Yes, but if you elect trial at the Crown Court on the theft, the case will go over anyway and Terry gets his adjournment.'

'Yeah. But as I told you I don't want to go to Crown. I want to get it over with as quick as possible.'

'Look, Billie. With your record if you're convicted you could go inside. Anyway before we go in I want some details from you.'

'What? Now? Why don't I give them to you when I come into the office?'

'No. There are some details I always get before I go into any court, so just sit down and give me them.'

'You're a real drag, you know that Rachel?' said Billie.

'Yes I know. Full name?'

'Billie Blue.'

'Address and telephone number? . . . age and date of birth? . . . are you married? . . . have you got any children? . . . the last school you attended? . . . How old were you when you left and what exams did you have? . . . What jobs have you had since you left school? . . . I need to know the dates for each job and why you left . . . What are you doing now? . . . Where is the job? . . . What hours do you work? . . . What is your income? . . . What are your weekly outgoings? . . . What sort of accommodation are you living in? . . . How long have you lived there? . . . Have you got any particular plans for the future?

. . . Have you got a girlfriend? . . . Give me a list of your convictions with the approximate date, the court, the offence and the penalty. . . Have you had any major illnesses either physical or psychiatric? . . . Were you ever in care? . . .'[2]

'Blimey, Rachel, you'll want to know how many babies my small brother's hamster had last Christmas next.'

'Not quite, Billie.'

Billie gave Rachel the information she was after. Rachel went into the courtroom. It had recently been 'done up' by the local authority. Several brass fans suspended from the roof revolved languidly in the overpowering centrally heated atmosphere. Rachel took her seat in the advocate's row.

The case the magistrates were considering when Rachel entered the court finished. The usher stepped forward.

'The next case, your worships, is Terry Turquoise and Billie Blue'. The usher opened the gate and ushered them into the dock.

The clerk shuffled through his papers. 'Are you Terry Turquoise?'

Terry nodded.

'Date of birth?'

'Twenty-fifth of the third, sixty-eight.'

'Are you Billie Blue?'

'Yeah.'

'Date of birth?'

'Fourteenth of February nineteen seventy.'

Before the Crown Prosecutor could speak, Rachel Red stood up. 'I appear for the defendant Billie Blue, your worships.' Heeling was Rachel's local court so her mannerisms were well known. Rachel felt strongly that a defendant was reassured if his advocate made her presence known unambiguously and early on. This was particularly so if the defendant was in custody and came out of the cells to be confronted by a courtroom filled with unknown persons. To hear a familiar voice speaking forcefully on his behalf and saying his name was exactly what he needed in his first few disoriented moments after his journey from the cells.

'Thank you, Miss Red,' said the clerk.

The Crown Prosecutor stood up, peering at his file.

'Do you have advance disclosure, Miss Red?' asked the clerk.

---

2 Rachel ensures she has this basic information for every person she represents before going into court, so that she is in a position to cope with any bail emergency that may blow up unexpectedly.

'Not yet,' said Rachel.

'I am putting a new charge today of vehicle interference,' said the Crown Prosecutor.

' . . . and the theft charge?' asked the clerk.

'I am discontinuing that charge.'

'Can I put this new charge, Miss Red?' asked the clerk.

Terry looked agitated. 'My solicitor said I was to get an adjournment for legal aid.'

'Well, Mr Turquoise, the charge of vehicle interference can only be tried in this court' said the clerk. 'You now have no right to elect trial at the Crown Court.'

'My solicitors told me to get an adjournment so that I can see them before I do anything.'

'I am sure you know whether you are pleading guilty or not guilty without seeing your solicitor?' said the clerk.

'Yeah, I suppose so' said Terry glumly.

The clerk looked round at the chairman briefly. 'I propose to take a plea, sir, so that we can set a date for trial if it is needed.'

'Certainly,' said the chairman.

'Terry Turquoise and Billie Blue, you are charged that on 22 April 1996 at Arbuthnot Street, Heeling you did interfere with a motor vehicle intending to commit an arrestable offence, namely theft. Do you plead guilty or not guilty? . . . Terry Turquoise?'

'Not guilty.'

'Billie Blue?'

'Not guilty.'

'And then there are two charges of assault on police. Mr Turquoise, you are charged that on 6 May 1996 you assaulted Cuthbert Crimson, a constable of the Metropolitan Police. Do you plead guilty or not guilty?'

'Not guilty.'

'And Mr Blue, you are charged that on 6 May 1996 you assaulted Orlando Orange, a constable of the Metropolitan Police. Do you plead guilty or not guilty?'

'Not guilty.'

The clerk turned to the prosecutor. 'How many prosecution witnesses?'

The prosecutor shuffled through the papers. 'There seem to be three.'

'How long do you think the trial will take?'

The prosecutor looked blank. Rachel Red stood up.

'There may be several defence witnesses. I would ask that a day be set aside.'

'Fifteenth July, all day in court four?' asked the clerk.

'Fine,' said Rachel Red. The prosecutor nodded. Terry looked unhappy.

'Unconditional bail?' said the clerk.

'I have objections to unconditional bail,' said the prosecutor.

'Thanks for warning me,' Rachel muttered at him.

At the sound of the word 'objections' the magistrates reached for their pens and looked alert. 'Yes, Mr Scarlet?' said the chairman.

'Your worships . . .' The prosecutor was peering closely at the file. 'I am sorry, your worships. This file is not typed and I have considerable difficulty reading this officer's handwriting . . . It seems that this offence . . . was committed some weeks ago . . . The officers . . . '

'Which offence was that, Mr Scarlet. There are two on different dates.'

'It must be the vehicle interference, sir,' said the clerk.

'Yes, of course. How silly of me. That was on the 22nd April?' said the Chairman.

'Yes sir . . . the theft . . . ' continued the prosecutor.

'You've discontinued the theft,' said the clerk.

'Yes. I mean the vehicle interference . . . this offence was committed some time ago . . . the officers caught these two defendants committing the offence and tried to arrest them. The defendants evaded capture and escaped . . . it is the Crown's feeling that they may not appear for their trial.'

'What are you asking for, Mr Scarlet?' enquired the chairman.

'I'm just trying to see,' said the prosecutor peering closely at the file. 'Ah yes. I am asking for . . . I am asking for a remand in custody, your worships. These defendants have a number of convictions. May I hand in their records?'

'I would like to see Mr Blue's first,' said Rachel.

'I am so sorry,' said the prosecutor, handing her a copy. He turned to the usher. 'Perhaps Mr Turquoise could be shown a copy of his?'

The clerk turned to the chairman. 'Sir. Mr Turquoise is not represented. In view of the fact that the prosecutor is asking for a remand in custody it may be better that the case is put back so that he can speak to the duty solicitor.'

Rachel Red stood up. 'Sir. I couldn't help overhearing what your clerk said. May I suggest that I address you on behalf of each of these defendants? I know a substantial amount about the circumstances of them and their case. I find it hard to see why the prosecution should be applying for a remand in custody. You may feel the reason this application is being made is that it is the police officers in the case who wish the defendants to be remanded in custody and that this application is not being made as a result of a considered assessment by the Crown Prosecutor. Mr Scarlet clearly has not had the opportunity to read the file properly before the case was called on.

'Your worships,' Rachel continued. 'As you are aware there are very stringent requirements laid down by the Bail Act before a defendant can be remanded in custody. The only ground for refusing bail Mr Scarlet has referred to is failure to attend court. The wording of the Bail Act is that a defendant can only be remanded in custody if there are 'substantial grounds' for believing that he might not attend his trial. Mr Scarlet's words were that the Crown . . . perhaps that ought to be the police, fear that the defendants may not attend court. Your worships, even the police do not use language that establishes the required test, laid down by the Bail Act. The only matters the prosecutor puts forward in support of his contention are that the defendants are alleged to have run away on 22 April and that they have criminal convictions. Your worships, these two defendants have pleaded not guilty to the offence on 22 April. I can tell you that the basis for that plea is that they each deny they were in Arbuthnot Street on 22 April. The defence is that this is a case of mistaken identity.

'Your worships, neither of these defendants has a substantial criminal record. Neither has served a custodial sentence. Each is in work. Mr Billie Blue works as a panel-beater with XYZ Panel Beaters in Heeling. He has worked there for eighteen months. Mr Turquoise works at the same place. Mr Blue lives with his girlfriend and their two year old baby at 33 Claribel Mansions, the Glen, Heeling. That is a flat of which his girlfriend is the tenant but he has lived there for some months. Mr Blue's mother lives in the next door block. He has lived all his life in the area. Mr Blue has nothing on his record showing an inclination to fail to appear.

'Your worships, perhaps the most compelling argument for granting them bail is that they have turned up on time today for their first appearance. The custody sergeant who charged them clearly considered them a good bail risk. Your worships, as you can see, the custody sergeant was right . . .'[3]

---

3 It is an effective ploy to import an argument from a third party, particularly if the third party is a police officer.

'Yes, thank you, Ms Red.' The chairman turned to the two other magistrates. 'I don't think we need . . .' The other magistrates nodded in agreement. 'We don't need to trouble you further. Yes, we will grant unconditional bail to 15 July. You can stand down.'

Mr Scarlet shrugged and turned to the next indecipherable file.

Outside the courtroom Rachel spoke to Billie.

'Right. I am sure they will grant you legal aid. As soon as you get the notification, I want you to make an appointment to come and see me. I am going to represent you at the summary trial so I want to make sure I prepare the case and I am going to do it thoroughly. OK?'

'OK.'

'That means you make an appointment and you keep it. If you mess me around, I won't do the trial.'[4]

'I understand, Rachel.'

'In the meantime I want you to find out the identities of as many of these witnesses as you can.'

'Yes.'

'And make sure Terry gives his solicitors all the information they need.'

'Rachel, you're as bossy as the Old Bill.'

'Well, I want to get this one right.'

Back in her office, Rachel wrote to the police station.

Dear Sir,

We are representing Billie Blue who was in custody at your police station on the night of 6th/7th May 1996. Please would you send us a copy of Billie Blue's custody record.

In reply to which Rachel duly received the custody record.

2. Taking instructions from Billie

Billie made his appointment and turned up for it only half an hour late. Rachel eyed him from behind her desk.

'I hope you have got a good long time.'

'Yes. As long as you like. Half an hour?'

'More like two hours.'

'I don't think I can sit still for two hours. Can I smoke?'

---

4 While Rachel has an east relationship with her clients, there are some points on which she disciplines them ruthlessly.

'No. But when you find it too much we'll have a break and you can go outside for a smoke.'

'Well, actually I've written out what happened.' Billie produced a page of scrawled handwriting.

'Sorry, Billie. That isn't good enough.'[5]

'Doesn't earn you any money?'[6]

'No it doesn't. And it won't win you the case either. It's most unlikely you have written down the things I need to know. I'm afraid I'm going to go through this case with you and you are going to sit there and give me the answers.'

'And if I don't?'[7]

'You can get another solicitor.' Rachel was becoming irritable.

'OK, OK. Keep your hair on!'

'Right . . . your full name.'

'Billie Blue.'

'Address?'

'33 Claribel Mansions, the Glen, Heeling . . .'

'Telephone number?'

'855 5656.'

'Your age and date of birth?'

'26 . . . 14 February 1970.'

'What was the last school you went to?'

'Heeling Comp.'

'And you left aged?'

'Yes, very . . . '

'Thank you, Billie.'

'16.'

'Any exams taken?'

'Why are you asking me all these questions, Rachel? Why should it matter to you what exams I've taken? Are you nosey or what?'

'I need to know as much as I can about the people I do cases for.'

'Why?'

---

5 It is bad practice to rely upon a statement prepared by the witness himself. It is most unlikely that the witness will have addressed his mind to the correct points or expressed them in the right way. Also the procedure of taking a statement from a witness is an essential part in finding out what the case is about for the solicitor and a rehearsal for the witness in giving evidence at a trial.

6 Many people consider this an amusing jibe. For the dedicated lawyer it is tasteless and unpleasant.

7 The problems of preparing a case can be as much about dealing with awkward or defective personalities as about the facts of the case.

'Because I can represent them much more effectively if I understand them. Also there are important stages in the proceedings when this information is needed. You saw it yourself when the prosecutor opposed bail.'[8]

'OK. GCSE art and technical drawing.'

'And then what did you do?'

'I went straight into me grandad's panel beating business. . . . I've worked for him ever since.'

'Doing?'

'Beating panels . . .'

'Wages?'

'A ton a week.'

'What do you pay in rent?'

'Thirty.'

'Any other outgoings?'

'Usual bills.'

'Yes. Any fines outstanding?'

'Yeah. One to this court.'

'How much outstanding?'

'About fifty.'

'How much are you paying a week?'

'Ten.'

'Are the payments up-to-date?'

'Yeah. Me mum's paying them.'

'OK. Any other outgoings?'

'Not that I can think of.'

'And who else lives at that address?'

'Me girl and the baby. . . Cologna.'

'Yours?'

'Course . . . I think.'

'Aged?'

'Six months.'

'How long have you lived with her?'

'Five months.'

'Whose flat is it?'

---

8 Another reason is that it breaks the ice between the lawyer and the client. Everyone likes to talk about themselves and tends to be more friendly towards the person who asks them questions about their personal circumstances. Yet a third reason is that there may well be features in the background that have a direct bearing on the facts of the case.

'Hers.'

'How old is she?'

'Eighteen.'

'Does she have any income?'

'Yeah. She's on the dole. I just pay her the thirty.'

'Where did you live before you moved in with her?'

'With me mum and sister.'

'What happened to your dad?'

'He moved out when I was twelve.'

'Do you see him?'

'No. He's in Liverpool.'

'Ever been in care?'

'Yeah, for a year when I was thirteen.'

'Ever been inside?'

'Yeah. Six months YC when I was eighteen. I only did two months.'

'For?'

'For assaulting a copper. I didn't do it. It was like this one, a stitch-up.'

'How many convictions have you got?'

'Three . . . no four.'

'Are these them?' Rachel handed him the list the prosecutor had given her at court.

'Yeah, that's them.'

'All for nicking radios or taking cars except the one for assaulting police?'

'Yeah.'

'So you're in breach of a conditional discharge if you're convicted of this one?'

'Yeah.'

'OK, so let's look at the charges. First, interfering with a motor vehicle with intent to steal from it on 22 April . . . did you do it?'

'No way.'

'OK, number two, on 6 May assaulting Police Constable Orlando Orange in the execution of his duty. Did you do that?'

'Well, there was a fight but I didn't start it and I didn't hit him at all.'

'So far as you know, is there any link between these two charges?'

'Yeah, one of the coppers claims he saw us interfering with cars two weeks before and then saw us in the High Street last Tuesday. . . tried to arrest us and says we assaulted him.'

'Right. Tell me about 22 April and Arbuthnot Street.'

'Well it's difficult. Me and Terry weren't in this Arbuthnot Street on 22 April. I spent the evening with my cousin in her flat.'

'What time did you get there?'

'I think it must have been about seven-thirty.'

'Who else was there?'

'Just me cousin.'

'What did you do?'

'Just watched telly.'

'Until when?'

'About ten.'

'And then?'

'I went home.'

'Where does your cousin live?'

'In Heeling . . . 15 Clarence Close. Are you writing all this down?'

'Of course. I need a full statement about all this. How often do you go to your cousin's?'

'Quite often. Once, twice a week.'

'OK. I'll leave that for the moment. I'll come back to it later. And I'll need to see your cousin.'

'What do you need to see her for?'

'If you were with her at the time they say you were nicking from cars, we'll need to call her to show it wasn't you.'

'That's going to cause problems.'

'How so?'

'Well, me girl thought I was down the pub. She doesn't like me cousin.'

'I see. What's your cousin's name?'

'Purple . . . Paula Purple.'

'Let's leave that and go on to the night your were nicked.'

'Yeah well, me and Terry were in the High Street . . . '

'Hold on, let me ask you the questions.'

'Right.'

'Did you go to work that day?'

'Yeah, a'course.'

'What time did you leave work?'

'About five . . . five-thirty . . . six . . . perhaps six-thirty.'

'Well which?'

'Does it matter?'

'Just tell me.'

'Well to tell the truth I can't remember exactly. We'd been busy at work. When we're busy, I'm lucky to get away before six.'

'Where did you go from work?'

'Home.'

'How do you get home?'

'Drive me motor.'

'How long does the journey take?'

'Five . . . ten minutes.'

'What did you do then?'

'I had a bath and me tea.'

'How long did that take?'

'An hour, maybe forty-five minutes.'

'And then?'

'I always play snooker Tuesdays with Terry. I met him in the Dog and Bone.'

'Where's the Dog and Bone?'

'Heeling High Street.'

'How did you get there?'

'I drove.'

'What time did you get there?'

'About seven . . . seven-thirty.'

'Did you go straight to the Dog and Bone?'

'Yeah.'

'And who was there?'

'Terry . . . and some of me mates.'

'What did you do?'

'Played snooker for a bit.'

'And then?'

'Me and Terry decided to go for some chips.'

'And did you?'

'Yeah. We went along to the chippy on the corner.'

'What time was this?'

'About eight . . . eight-thirty . . . nine.'

'Can you be more precise about the time?'

'No. I don't think I can.'

'What happened?'

'We were going to the chippy . . . '

'Sorry. Can you describe your journey in more detail?'

'How do you mean?'

'The pub is on the other side of the road from the chippy?'

'Yeah.'

'How far are they apart?'

'Two hundred metres . . . two-fifty . . . three hundred . . . something like that.'

'So when you came out of the pub did you cross the road or what?'

'Oh I get you . . . no, we came out of the pub and walked along the road on the same side. We were going to cross the road opposite the chippy.'

'And?'

'This Bill car suddenly pulls up and this copper jumps out and nicks us and takes us to the Bill shop . . . '

'Hang on, hang on. Where did this Bill car come from?'

'Behind us.'

'What made you aware of it?'

'Terry sees it and shouts "Old Bill".'

'So what did you do?'

'Legged it, of course.'

'Why did you do that?'

'I don't know really. You just do when the Bill arrive.'

'But why?'

'I don't know. I just do.'

'Had you been looking for a car to nick from?'

'No, of course not.'

'Well, why did you leg it?'

'Do you really want to know?'

'I don't know.'

'Terry had bought a bit of draw in the pub and he had it in his pocket.'

'Oh, brilliant.'

'I'm only kidding.'

'Look, Billie, don't muck me about. We've got problems here. Why did you leg it if you weren't doing anything wrong?'

'I don't know really. We could see the Bill car was stopping for us. Terry shouted, "Let's go", and we did. It was a joke in a way. These Bill are all so out of condition they can't catch you.'

'And these ones?'

'We got it wrong, didn't we? The two in this car were young and play rugby or something for the cops. They run really fast. They caught us round the corner.'

'What happened then?'

'They caught me first . . . '

'Where?'

'About twenty metres up this side road.'

'How did he catch you?'

'He grabbed me by the neck . . . '

'What did he say?'

'What did he say? . . . What do they usually say?'

'I don't know . . . what did he say this time?'

'He said something like, "Got you, you bastard . . . you're fucking nicked".'

'What happened then?'

'He took me down the nick.'

'No . . . after he had said, "You're fucking nicked".

'He just held me while his mate chased Terry. Christ that bloke had a turn of speed. He just steamed up the pavement. Terry is quite fast and he used to be fit . . . but not any more. I heard a scream and then the other copper brought Terry back. I heard him say to Terry, "I saw you in that car, you dirty little thief".'

'Yes?'

'Terry said, "I weren't in no car. We've just come out of the pub. We were just going for some chips".'

'Yes?'

'The copper said, "Well, why did you run then?"'

'Yes?'

'Terry said, "Just for a laugh." And the copper who had hold of me said, sort of sarcastic, "So you just run for a laugh?" And I said, as best I could because he had hold of my collar really tight and I couldn't speak easily, "Yeah, honest, it was just for a laugh. We haven't touched no car." Then the second copper said, "Well, you're both fucking nicked anyway." And I said, "Well which car are we meant to have been in?" And the first copper said, "Just you shut up. We'll sort that out down the nick." And I said, "No. If you say we were in a car, you show us which car we were in and see if it's open." And they said, "Just shut up and get in the panda". And Terry and me said, "No. If you say we were in a car, you show us which one." Then the first copper said to the other one, "We'll have to get the van." So they radioed for the van. We stood there waiting for the van and quite a crowd gathered. So me and Terry started shouting at the crowd, "These coppers say we were in a car over there." And we told them to try the car doors and see if any of them were open. And several of them started trying car doors and none of them were open.'

'You could have locked the doors when you got out,' said Rachel.

'Yeah but the coppers didn't think of that, I don't think. I think they got worried because of the crowd trying the car doors. I think they changed their minds about saying we had been in a car.'

'What happened then?'

'The van arrived and a sergeant came out of it and we started on at the sergeant.'

'What were you saying to him?'

'We said, "These officers say we were in a car in the High Street but we weren't," and "We want you to try the car door handles and see if they are open," and Terry said "Yeah. We want you to fingerprint all the cars in the High Street an' all and see if our fingerprints are on any of them, which they couldn't be." This was a bit silly but I think that Terry was getting a bit carried away.'

'What did the sergeant say?'

'He didn't say anything, he just looked a bit surprised and then said "Put them in the van." And the two officers put us in the van and we were taken down to the station.'

'What did the two officers do?'

'How do you mean?'

'How did they get back to the station?'

'Oh yeah. They must have gone in the panda car.'

'Didn't either of them travel with you in the van?'[9]

'Now you mention it, I think one of them may have come in the van with us.'

'Which one?'

'I think it must have been the one who nicked Terry.'

'Was anything said in the van on the way to the nick?'

'No. We just kept saying to him that he couldn't have seen us in a car because we hadn't been in one. We told him that there was a group of our mates who came out of the pub after us and had seen that we couldn't have gone into a car. This wasn't true but it worried him. Then he said, "Well you run and I know why you run, it's because you were the ones my mate caught breaking into cars last week".'

'Yes?'

'Then we got taken to the nick.'

'Yes, but didn't you say anything to him when he said that to you?'

'What do you mean?'

'He said he and his mate had seen you breaking into cars the week before?'

'Yes.'

'Didn't this surprise you?'

'Oh, yeah.'

---

9 Rachel knows from experience that Metropolitan Police officers are required to stay with their prisoners at all times until they are handed over to the custody officer if at all possible.

'So what did you say to him?'

'We said we hadn't been breaking into cars and if he had seen us why hadn't he arrested us.'

'And what did he say?'

'He said it was because we had run away like we had tonight.'

'What was said then?'

'I don't think much else was said because we had arrived at the nick. It's not far to the nick.'

'Did he tell you where he and his mate had seen you in the cars and when?'

'No. He didn't say any more about it.'

'Did he say what happened when they had chased you?'

'No. We just got to the nick and the coppers bundled us out and into the charge room.'

'What happened in the charge room?'

'The sergeant behind the desk took our particulars. When he took mine he asked the first officer why I had been arrested and the officer said, "Breaking into cars, sarge".'

'Let's see what they have recorded on the custody record. The reason for arrest says, "Interference with motor vehicles", and then in the main narrative section it says, "Relevant time begins 12.04. DT arrested interfering with motor vehicle chased and arrested." It's curiously worded. It seems to be suggesting that you were interfering with motor vehicles on the night of your arrest. We'll have to see.'

'OK.'

'What did the custody sergeant say to you?'

'He didn't say anything, he just said, "Put them in the cells".'

'Did he offer you a lawyer?'

'No.'

'Did he ask if you wanted anyone telephoned?'

'No.'

'Did he get you to sign anything?'

'No.'

'Have a look at this custody record . . . Is that your signature?'

'Yeah . . . it seems to be.'

'Do you remember signing it?'

'Not really . . . I suppose I must have signed it.'

'It says you said you didn't want a lawyer.'

'Yeah, well I thought I would be out of there quick.'

'What happened next?'

'They put us in the cells.'

'Who did?'

'The copper who had been in the van with us.'

'Did you say anything to him?'

'Yeah. I asked him what we were being charged with.'

'What did he say?'

'He said he'd think of something.'

'Where did he say that?'

'In the cell corridor.'

'What happened then?'

'I went into the cell.'

'How long were you there?'

'About three hours.'

'And then?'

'They got us out and charged us.'

'Who got you out?'

'The custody sergeant.'

'The same one as the first one?'

'No, a different one.'

'What did he say when he got you out?'

'He just said "This way please, Mr Blue."'

'And then?'

'He just charged me and Terry.'

'Did you say anything?'

'No.'

'Why not?'

'I didn't know I could say anything. Anyway what was there to say? I'd been saying all along it was a stitch-up and they took no notice. Why say anything more? Anyway he read the charge out so fast there wasn't really the opportunity to say anything. I'd been asleep when he got me out. I wasn't really awake. I didn't really take in what he said. It was all dates and such. I wasn't sure which day he was referring to.'

'There are two dates. 22 April, when you and Terry are meant to have interfered with motor vehicles. Then 6 May, when you and Terry assaulted a police officer each when they were trying to arrest you.'

'Yes. I know now.'

'Did you do either of these?'

'No.'

'Were you in Arbuthnot Street on 22 April?'

'No, Rachel. They've made this up. Terry and I weren't in Arbuthnot Street together nicking from motors, then or any other time. I've never seen these two coppers before . . . and I don't think they've ever seen me before.'

'Right.'

'You do believe me, don't you, Rachel?'

'Look Billie. It's my job to represent you. I put your case forward as well as I can and I will do just that. It makes no difference whether I believe you or not. Does it?'[10]

'I suppose not. But I'd be happier if you did.'

'In fact I don't even think about it. OK. I've got all that down. A few last questions. Have you ever come across either of these two officers before?'

'No.'

'Did they seem to know who you were on the night they nicked you?'

'Well, I heard the one who'd arrested me when we were waiting in the custody area talking about me to an older officer. The older one said, "That's Blue." The copper who arrested me said, "Yeah, I know." They both laughed.'

'Did you know the older officer?'

'Yeah. He's quite well known locally. He's called Sid.'

'Do you know his full name?'

'No.'

'What does he look like?'

'He's tall with a beard and a bald head. He's a Northerner. He drives one of them Rovers.'

'Did you see any more of him?'

'No. He just left the custody area. I didn't see him again.'

'OK. Now can you give me descriptions or better still names of the people there when you were arrested?'

'No, I'm afraid I can't, Rachel. I'll have to ask around and find out if anyone knows anyone who was there.'

'OK. But do it straightaway. Now what about interviewing your cousin?'

'What do you mean?'

'Well we'll need her to give evidence.'

'What? You mean come to court?'

'Yes.'

---

10 Clients, particularly in criminal cases, frequently seek to obtain this concession from their lawyer. Often it is from a liar seeking reassurance that the lies he has concocted are convincing. In some instances it is a form of emotional blackmail. Advocates are well advised to evade this form of question in much the way Rachel did.

'I don't think I want that.'

'OK. I'll write to her after the case and tell her which prison to visit you in.'

'I'll ask her first and then get her to come and see you.'

'Right. I'll put all this in a statement and send it to you. You check the statement is correct and sign it and send it back.'

'OK.'

'Now there's one final thing and it's important. These two charges relate to different days. We could probably have them tried in different trials in front of different magistrates.'

'What do you think?'

'I think that we are going to be much better off having the two charges tried together. The policemen's motives for saying you interfered with cars on the first occasion must arise out of the incident when they arrested you. It is going to be easier to show they are lying if the charges are heard together in my view.'

'You're the governor, Rachel.'

'Yes I am, aren't I?'

3. Taking instructions from Terry

Terry Turquoise arrived at the offices of Rose Madder at about ten o'clock on Wednesday 15 April. They were smart but cramped offices in Regent Street, London W1. The receptionist looked at him censoriously.

'Can I help you?'

'Yes, I've got an appointment.'

'Who with?'

'I'm not sure.'

'Have you got your letter of appointment?'

'No. I'm afraid I lost it. I didn't think it would be important.'

The receptionist sighed.

'What's your name?'

'Terry Turquoise.'

'What an unusual name,' said the exquisitely groomed person. She studied her large diary.

'There's no entry for you today. What is it to do with?'

'I am appearing at Heeling Magistrates' Court next Thursday.'

'And the charge is . . .?'

'Interfering with motor vehicles and assault on police.'

'Mmm . . . quite the little Ronnie Cray. Just a minute.'

The receptionist picked up her telephone.

'Jemma. I've got a chap here says he's got an appointment for this morning. He's not in my book. The charge is interfering with motor vehicles and assault on police . . . Heeling Magistrates' Court next Thursday . . . right . . . Yes, I'll do that.'

She turned to Terry.

'Your appointment was for yesterday. If you wait over there, someone will be down to see you and sort something out.'

Terry disconsolately sat by a rubber plant and, selecting a glossy magazine from the glass table, picked his way through an article.

'Mr Turquoise?'

'Yes.'

'I'm Belinda Burnt-Umber. Could you come this way please.'

Terry followed Belinda up thickly carpeted stairs to an interview room. Belinda gestured at a Scandinavian canvas-backed stainless steel chair, in which Terry sat gingerly. Belinda Burnt-Umber placed a writing pad on the table in front of her and removed the top of her arrow headed fountain pen with elegant crimson tipped fingers.

'You've missed your appointment and come on the wrong day, so we haven't very much time to prepare your case. However, as it is next Thursday, we'll have to do the best we can.' Belinda looked at her watch. 'I'm afraid I only have a few minutes.'[11]

'Oh right.'

'Now, what are you charged with?'

'Interfering with motor vehicles and assault on police.'

'Have you got your charge sheet?'

'No.'

Belinda sighed.

'Can you tell me the dates of the offences you are charged with?'

---

11 The firm of Rose Madder is in fact a highly efficient firm. All its procedures are laid down and tightly controlled. The staff are well trained. The firm has a heavy workload. Terry's case is minor with little interest in it compared with Belinda's main workload. Terry does not help himself by missing his appointment. He does not know it, but appointment-missing is the bane of a criminal practice. Terry does not have the intelligence or ability to concentrate to enable this firm to prepare his case. Probably he just does not have the mental equipment to play that most demanding of roles, defendant in a contested criminal trial. On the other hand, Rose Madder ought to make more effort to make its clients feel part of a team as Rachel Red does. For Rachel it is 'our' case, and not 'your' case.

'They must be the same day as I was arrested.'

'And what date was that?'

'It's about a month ago.'

'Don't you know the date?'

'Er . . . no . . . I'm not very good on dates.'

'Well, what about the day of the week?'

'I'm pretty sure it was a Wednesday . . . or a Thursday.'

Belinda Burnt-Umber stared at him stonily.

'That's not very helpful.'

'I'm sorry.'

'You come to us expecting us to prepare your case. You come on the wrong day. You don't have your charge sheet and you don't even know the date of the charges you face.'

'Look I'm really sorry. I think it was the Wednesday and it was early March.'

'Are you pleading guilty or not guilty?'

'Not guilty.'

'You didn't do it?'

'No.'

'What do the prosecution say you were doing?'

'I don't really know.'

'You don't know?'

'No. Other than the charge they didn't tell me.'

'But you know you didn't do it? Whatever it was that you didn't do.'

'No. Look I'm sorry but I'm really confused about this case.'

'You're not the only one. Well I suppose I'll just have to do the best I can, but it's not very promising. Most of the people I interview at least know what they are meant to have done.'

'I'm sorry.'

'Yes, so you keep saying.[12] Where were you arrested?'

'In the High Street in Heeling.'

'When? . . . of course you can't remember, I forgot.'

'It was about ten o'clock at night.'

'What happened?'

'These two coppers turned up and nicked us.'

'They just turned up and nicked you?'

---

12 It is extraordinarily easy to bully a client without really meaning to. Belinda has had a hard day, no doubt, and takes it out on Terry because he is not bright and badly organised. Terry just thinks it is the price for having a 'blagger's firm'.

'Yes.'

'What for?'

'I don't know.'

'What did they say you had done when they interviewed you?'

'They didn't interview me.'

'They didn't interview you? Look, I find that a bit hard to believe. Just think will you. Just about everybody gets interviewed.'

'I don't remember being interviewed.'

'Mr Turquoise, were you stoned?'

'No I wasn't.'

Belinda Burnt-Umber held up her pad. 'Mr Turquoise, I've got one paragraph written here. All it says is on a day you can't remember you were arrested for reasons you don't know. That's it. I'm not used to instructing counsel with so little information. Isn't there anything more you can tell me?'

'No. That's all I know. I really am sorry. Look can I have a smoke?'

'I'm afraid we operate a smoke-free office.'

'Right.'

'Have you got any witnesses?'

'No . . . at least not yet.'

'Well we'll just have to do the best we can. I'm going to have to go now. Please fill in this antecedents form before you go.'

'This what form?'

'Antecedents form, Mr Turquoise. Antecedents. It is your life history . . . or some of it . . . so that we know about you. You put down whether you have ever won a Nobel prize . . . or . . .'

'What sort of prize?'

'Never mind . . . Here's the form . . . Have you got a pen?'

'Er, no.'

'Well, Jasmin in reception will lend you a biro. There will be a barrister at court to represent you.'

'What's his name?'

'Why do you assume it will be a man? Our best barristers are women. And I'm afraid it is not possible to know who it will be until the night before the case.'

'Can I phone up and find out the night before?'

'You could but it will be most inconvenient. In any case you won't know the person. If I was you I would just go to court and meet her there. You can be confident the barrister will know her stuff.'[13]

---

13 It is common for the lawyer to feel that the running of the case is none of the client's business.

'Right.'

When Terry emerged into reception Jasmin was on the phone, so he left to fill in the form in the seclusion of his own home.

Once there Terry studied the antecedent form closely with every intention of completing it. Somehow he was stumped by the section dealing with his employment. After ten minutes of frenzied effort his concentration was exhausted.[14] He stuffed the form into the jar where all awkward family documents were kept and it stayed there until the following Christmas when his mum was looking for her Christmas club membership card and threw it away.

4. Taking statements from Billie's witnesses

Billie came into Rachel Red's room followed by a teenaged girl.

'Rachel, this is my cousin Paula Purple.'

'Hullo Paula, thanks for coming along.[15] Sit down.'

'Can I sit down too, Rachel?'

'Sure Billie, there are lots of chairs in the waiting room.'

'Can't I sit in on the interview?'

'I'm afraid not.'

'I want to hear what Paula says.'

'In the waiting room please, Billie.'

'Oh OK. You're a real tyrant, you know that, Rachel?'

'That's what my gerbil says.'

'Hey, I didn't know you was married, Rachel.'

'The waiting room, Billie . . . Now Paula, can I ask you some basic questions? How old are you?'

'Seventeen.'

'You live alone?'

'With my little boy, Neddie.'

'Neddie?'

'His full name is Nebuchadnezar . . . Neddie for short . . . his father's Egyptian.'

---

14 Much opportunistic crime implies a lack of concern for the future on the part of the criminal. That sort of personality is unlikely to consider the preparation of his case of great significance while still wanting to win when actually faced by the trial. It is therefore quite pointless to expect the defendant to assist in the preparation other than under the immediate supervision of the lawyer.

15 This sort of courtesy eases the way with the witness. It is also reassuring for the defendant to hear the lawyer being considerate to his witness.

'Right. Have you any criminal convictions, Paula?'

'Me? No.'

'Have you had any dealings with the police?'

'No. I've never been nicked.'

'Do you know anything about Billie's case?'[16]

'I know he's been nicked for nicking from cars. . . . He couldn't have done it.'

'What do you mean?'

'Well, on the night he's meant to have done it he was with me at my place.'

'How do you know?'

'Well I was there. He was with me.'

'When was this?'

'It was Wednesday two weeks before he got nicked.'

'When did you find out he had been nicked?'

'He phoned me the next day and said he had been nicked.'

'When did he tell you what he had been nicked for?'

'Then . . . when he phoned me and told me he had been nicked.'

'What did he say?'

'He said he had been nicked for nicking from cars.'

'Did he say when?'

'I think he did.'

'And what did you say?'

'I didn't say anything.'

'What, nothing?'

'Well I just talked to him.'

'What about?'

'I don't remember.'

'Did you talk about the allegation of interfering with motor vehicles?'

'The what?'

'Nicking from motors.'

'Yes.'

'What was said?'

'Billie said he couldn't have done it because he was round my place that night and I said, "Oh yeah, so you was".'

---

16 Paula is to be an alibi witness. A bad alibi witness can be particularly damaging. Rachel is determined that she is not going to ruin Billie's case with a put-up witness. As a rule Rachel sees witnesses on their own. As she intends to test Paula's evidence to breaking point this is particularly important.

'Which night was that?'

'The Wednesday two weeks before he was nicked.'

'How often does Billie come round your place?'

'Most nights. For a bit anyway.'

'How long did he come round to your place that night?'

'You'll have to ask him that.'

'Well how long do you say?'

'Well I don't know. . . . perhaps an hour . . . two hours . . . maybe three.'

'When did he arrive?'

'Seven . . . eight . . . maybe seven-thirty . . .'

'Who came with him?'

'Who came with him? I don't know.'

'Did anything special happen?'[17]

'Special? No . . . what do you mean?'

'Does Billie come round every night?'

'No, not every night.'

'Did he come round the Tuesday that week?'

'Tuesday? . . . I don't remember.'

'What about the Thursday?'

'Thursday? He may have . . . he often comes round on Thursday.'

'Paula, I know you're trying to help Billie . . . but you haven't the first idea whether Billie came round that night or not. Have you?'

'Yeah. He came round.'

'What time did he leave?'

'Maybe nine? . . . I don't really remember.'

'OK Paula. I will be putting what you've told me into a statement and I will be asking you to sign it.'

'I won't have to go to court, will I?'

'Well if you are to help Billie you will have to give evidence at his hearing. But I don't think what you have to say will help him at all.'

'I don't want to go to court. I can't answer questions. Billie didn't tell me I would have to go to court. He just said I would have to give you a statement and that would be enough.'

'Look Paula, don't get worked up about this. I don't think you should give evidence. I'll speak to Billie. You just sit in the waiting room while I speak to him.'

Rachel took Billie back to her office.

'Billie. I want to tell you that the best way to get convicted is to

17 These are the sort of questions Paula would face in cross-examination.

call a witness who is obviously not telling the truth. And the best sort of witness to help get you convicted is a bad alibi witness.'

'What do you mean?'[18]

'You're suggesting that we put up Paula as an alibi witness to show you couldn't have been nicking from cars on 22 April?'

'Yes.'

'You don't tell her that is what you are accused of until more than two weeks after the alleged incident.'

'I couldn't 'ave, could I?'

'Yes I know. But that is not the point. The longer it is until she finds out that particular night was important, the less likely she is to remember it and what happened. What you have got to understand is that unless there is something unusual about the evening, it is difficult to show why your alibi witness should remember that particular night. Do you see the point? If you weren't the one nicking from the cars, it is quite understandable if you don't have any idea where you were or what you were doing that night. I can barely remember what I was doing yesterday let alone two weeks ago. The court may well accept that. What the court won't wear is if we put Paula forward as a witness when she clearly has no idea whether it was the Wednesday or the Tuesday or the Thursday you went round there that week . . . or what time you arrived or left or who was with you. I'm not having you wrecking our case by putting forward a witness that is just going to fall apart on us. OK?'[19]

'Didn't you tell her?'

'Didn't I tell her what?'

'Didn't you tell her when I got there and that. . . .'

'Look, I am not going to set your witnesses up for you.[20] And anyway if she makes such a poor showing when I am questioning her in my office face to face, she's going to be a disaster in court. Now do us all a favour and stop mucking around with the case. All right?'

'OK Rachel. Keep your hair on . . . what are we going to do then?'

'You are going to do your best to identify proper witnesses who

---

18 One of the hardest and most important parts of the preparation of such a case is protecting the defendant from his own inadequately manufactured evidence.

19 Rachel Red makes a point of referring to a case as 'our' case rather than 'your' case when talking to the defendant. It is an effective gesture that reassures Billie that Rachel is firmly on his side.

20 Rachel is ruthlessly firm in rejecting any impropriety. Suddenly they are 'your' witnesses.

were present when you were arrested and you are going to leave it to
me to try and deal with the police evidence; unless, that is, you can
genuinely remember where you were that night and can describe
exactly what you were doing.'

'Rachel, I probably was at Paula's . . .'

'Can you say for certain? What was on TV, something like that?'

'No.'

'Well, leave it. It'll cause too many problems otherwise.'

'OK.'

'I want you to show me where you were arrested.'

'What? Now?'

'Yes. It's just down the road.'

'OK.'

Billie and Rachel left the office and walked the quarter of a
mile to the end of the High Street. Billie stopped by a boarded-up
shop.

'We were just walking along here. We were going to cross the
street to the chippy over there. The cop car pulled up behind us
there.'

He pointed back up the road. 'And there's the pub we came out of
. . . the Dog and Bone.'

'Where did the police stop?'

'Just by where that red Metro is now.'

'Were there any parked cars there then?'

'No. They stopped by the curb.'

'What did you do then?'

'Me and Terry legged it round the corner. . . .' Billie walked
round past the shop into the side street. 'I had just got to that
tree there when the cop grabbed me by the shirt.'

'How far did Terry get?'

'I didn't really see. He ran into the dark with the copper behind
him. Then they came back with the copper holding him.'

'What was the lighting like?'

'Well you can see there's that street light on the corner.'

'What's it like at night?'

'It gives some light. The houses give some light but they tend to
shine into their front gardens and not far beyond.'

'Where were the witnesses standing?'

'There was a group over there outside the chippy . . . on that
corner. Then there were some walking up the road towards me.'

'So, some of them may have seen that you didn't assault the
policeman?'

'No reason why not.'

'How are you doing in tracking them down?'

'I've started but I've not made much progress.'

'Well, how about making some progress? You want to win the case, don't you? With your record you'll be in trouble otherwise.'

'Yeah. OK. Terry and me can go to the pub this Friday and ask around.'

'Good. You do that. Now you can shove off. I am going to make a sketch plan.'

Once she had finished the plan, Rachel drove to Arbuthnot Street. Billie had said he had no idea where it was in Arbuthnot Street the police officers said they had seen him interfering with the motor vehicle, so there was little point in taking him along. Rachel found that Arbuthnot Street was a residential road of about two hundred and fifty metres in length. It linked two mainish routes through Heeling. The road was a continuing bend the whole of its length. There were four street lights in the road. The road was lined by mature trees down one side. Again Rachel made a sketch plan. She went back to her office, where she took the opportunity to work a little later than normal. Once it was completely dark she went back to the chip shop in the High Street with a photocopy of her sketch plan and studied the area, making additional notes on the plan. From there Rachel went to Arbuthnot Street and examined that road in darkness.

The next morning Rachel wrote a letter to the local authority.

Dear Sirs,

We are representing a defendant charged with a criminal offence that is alleged to have been committed in Arbuthnot Street, Heeling. The offence is alleged to have occurred during the hours of darkness. We have observed that of the four street lights in this road, two are not working. We would be most grateful if you could inform us when these various lights came to the notice of your authority as being out of operation and which of the lights in this road were working on 22 April 1996.

Yours faithfully,

Ruby Red.

At the end of the following week, Rachel received a letter from Heeling Borough Council Highways Department.

Dear Sirs,

Thank you for your letter concerning the street lighting in Arbuthnot Street, Heeling. The two lights currently out of commission were brought to the notice of the authority on 18 April 1996. It is unfortunate

that it is taking so long to repair these lights. This is due to financial restrai. ⁺ placed on this department by the council treasury.
Yours faithfully,
E. Lightbulb.

Some days later Billie came into Rachel's office.

'Rachel, I've found one of the guys who saw us being nicked. He's called Nipper White.' He indicated a man standing behind him. 'Nipper, this is my solicitor Rachel Red.'

'How do you do, Rachel.'

'Hullo Nipper. How did you find him, Billie?'[21]

'He was in the pub last Friday when me and Terry went there.'

'OK. You leave Nipper with me and I'll take a statement from him.'

'Right you are Rachel. Now Nipper remember what I told you and the fifty notes will be behind the bar for you at the Dog and Bone . . . Just joking, Rachel, just joking.'[22]

'Billie will drive me to drink one day,' Rachel said once Billie had gone. 'Now, Nipper, I take it that is a nickname?'

'No, that's me real name.'

'It can't be.'

'No. It isn't really. Me real name is William White. That's why I'm called Nipper.'

'Ah . . . I see. . . . And what's your address?'

'47 Bluebell House, Heeling.'

'And your telephone number?'

'993 4592.'[23]

'How old are you, Nipper?'

'Twenty-eight.'

'What's your work?'

'I work on the railways as a ticket collector.'

'How long have you done that?'

'Six years.'

'Have you any convictions, Nipper?'

'Not for eight years.'

---

21 This is not a casual enquiry. Rachel Red is only going to use a witness that can be shown in evidence to have come to light in an honest manner and is not just one of Billie's cronies.

22 Rachel and Billie have the right sort of relationship. Out of it will come a case prepared to its full.

23 Rachel Red makes notes of telephone numbers whenever she can. Whenever a crisis strikes and a telephone number is needed, it can never be found.

'And what did you have then?'

'I've got some for theft and fighting.'

'Ever been to prison?'

'No.'

'OK. Now how did Billie get hold of you?'

'I went into the Dog and Bone last Friday and the landlord, Sid, said there was a guy trying to find if anyone had seen him being arrested the other day opposite the chippy. I had, and Sid pointed out Billie to me and I spoke to him. He asked me to come and see you and here I am.'[24]

'What did Billie say to you about the incident?'

'He just asked me whether I thought he had been fighting with the copper and I said I didn't think he had. I remember thinking at the time that the coppers were out of order.'

'Did you discuss the incident with Billie?'

'No not really. Just enough to see we were talking about the same night. Billie didn't tell me what he thought had happened. I just told him what I saw.'

'What do you think of the police?'

'I don't think about them at all really. When I come across them they seem all right. It was just that night. I think they were young ones and got a bit carried away.'

'Where were you when the incident started?'

'I was outside the chippy.'

'Where was the incident involving Billie?'

'Across the road.'

'Which road?'

'The chippy is in the High Street. The incident was across the High Street.'

'OK. What happened?'

I heard some shouting so I looked across the road. I saw these two coppers getting out of their car. There was these two geezers legging it down the High Street and round the corner. Billie was one of them.'

'Did you recognise him.'

'No. But I know now that Billie was one of them.'

'OK. But can I ask you to stick to things you know from what you

24 A competent prosecutor is going to explore how Nipper came to the notice of the defence and his relationship with the defendant in detail in his cross-examination.

saw and not what you've learned since? Call them the first guy and the second guy or something like that.'[25]

'Oh right.'

'Carry on.'

'Yes. Well the coppers went off after them really fast. One caught the first guy just into the road round the corner and grabbed him by the collar. The other one went past Billie . . . the first guy and after the other geezer.'

'Yes.'

'Well the copper was holding Billie . . . the first guy and talking to him, holding him by the collar and the arm. They weren't struggling or anything. Then the other copper comes back with the second guy.'

'What happened then?'

'I watched for a bit. They seemed to be just talking. Then a police van arrived. I went into the chippy to get me supper.'

'Was there any fighting between the two guys and the coppers?'

'Well the coppers seemed a bit rough with them, but I didn't see that either of them was resisting at all.'

'What was the lighting like?'

'There's a street light on that corner. I only live just down that road and on the right so I know the area well. Billie and the copper were standing about fifteen yards from the light. I could see them clearly.'

'Where were Billie . . . the first guy and the other bloke when you first saw them?'

'They were running down the High Street.'

'And where were the police officers?'

'They was just getting out of their car. One of them shouted at them and that was what made me turn round. They slammed their car doors just after I looked at them.'

'Were there any cars parked by the curb in front of the police car?'

'I don't think there can have been because I remember catching sight of the first guy's feet and he was wearing white coloured trainers. I could see them sort of flashing when he run.'

'Did you see anything more?'

---

25 It is important that the witness statement does not attribute to the witness knowledge he does not have.

'No. I went into the chippy and the windows were all steamed up. When I came out everybody had gone.'

'Can you remember which day all this happened?'

'No, not really. It must have about two months ago, something like that. I think it was a Friday.'

'Did you recognise Billie when you saw him last Friday?'

'No. I can't say I did.'

'What about his friend?'

'No. I hardly saw him at all.'

'What was the name of the road they ran down?'

'It's called Doggett Street.'

'Right. Would you be prepared to come to court and say all this in evidence?'

'I don't mind. Can you give me a letter for me guv'nor?'

'Certainly. The hearing is on 15 July. Can I just explain that I will be there representing Billie. As you're a witness you won't be able to come into court before giving evidence. You'll have to wait in the entrance hall. The usher will call you in and you go into the witness box. You will see me there and I will be the first lawyer to question you. After I have taken you through your evidence, you will be questioned first by the lawyer representing the other guy, Terry Turquoise, and then by the prosecutor. You need to be on your guard with the prosecutor because he will try and catch you out.'

'Try and make out I'm a plonker?'

'Something like that. Now there are a number of things I want you to remember about giving evidence. The first is that you must listen to the question, and listen carefully whoever asks the question. OK?'

'OK.'

'And then answer the question you have been asked. OK?'

'Right.'

'You must make sure your answer is directed to the question.'

'What do you mean?'

'Well, in the courts precise wording is of great importance in a way that in ordinary life it usually isn't. Very often witnesses listen to the general wording of a question and form an impression of the subject that the question is about and then ramble on about that subject. They fail to catch the precise meaning of the question.'

'Oh.'

'This can make the witness seem evasive. Or worse still a witness may make an assumption about the question that no one else does and so appears to contradict himself. For example the witness might be asked, "When you met your neighbour at the bus stop, did you talk to him?", and the witness answers, "No. We just talked about the weather." The witness has assumed perhaps that the question was, "Did you talk about anything important?" It is an unwarranted assumption and causes the witness to contradict himself within one answer. The witness makes himself look a pillock and lays himself open to damaging cross-examination by a quirk of speech that would not raise an eyebrow in ordinary conversation.'

'Right.'

'Think before you give your answer so that you have sorted out in your mind what you are going to say before you say it. If you don't do that, again you will be liable to contradict yourself. It frequently happens that the human mind throws up an answer in immediate response to a question before it has had time to think it through, and then within seconds throws up a second contradictory answer. If the question is one that needs a little thought, don't answer immediately, think about it and then answer. Nothing is worse than answering immediately, having second thoughts and then giving a second answer that contradicts the first answer.'

'Sounds sense.'

'Then keep your answer as short as is sensible and reasonable to enable you to say what you intend. This has a number of advantages. In a short answer you are less likely to contradict yourself within the answer. You will find it easier to remember what you have said, so you are less likely to contradict yourself in a later answer. It is conventional wisdom in the Anglo-Saxon culture that a person who gives short answers to the point is more reliable than the one who doesn't.'

'OK.'

'Good answer . . . once you have finished your answer just stop talking. Don't ramble on.'

'Sounds like sense.'

'Make sure you read your statement carefully before you go into court. I will be working from a copy of the statement. You aren't bound by the statement, but reading it will probably bring the facts we have been going through back to your mind and it will make it more likely that we are each thinking in the same sequence.'

'Right. Can I refer to my statement when I am in the witness box?'

'No, I'm afraid you can't. If your mind goes blank when you go into the witness box, don't worry. I'll be starting off with dead easy questions like "What's your name?" and "Where do you live?" If you can't answer them, then you have got problems! Then I'll take you into the important part.'[26]

'I think I'll manage.'

'Of course it always happens that witnesses add things they have never mentioned before or even change the account completely. I will be happier if you don't do that, but I am well aware that giving evidence in a court has a curious effect on people, and I'm used to that happening . . . unfortunately. Some witnesses you think are going to be brilliant turn out to be useless and vice versa.'

'I'll try to be brilliant.'

'Don't try and be anything except truthful and careful. Anyway, thanks for coming, Nipper. I'll get what you told me to you in the form of a statement. I would be grateful if you would sign a copy and send it back to me. I'll see you in court on 15 July. I'll also write to you saying I need you to come to court and you can show the letter to your boss. If you need anything more, please let me know.'

'Fine.'

'I really appreciate your help. Thank you very much indeed.'[27]

'No problem, Rachel. Good-bye then.'

5. Terry's witness

Terry phoned Rose Madder.

'My name's Terry Turquoise. I'm in court on 15 July. I'm phoning to say I've got a witness.'

'Who is doing your case Mr Turquoise?'

'A barrister.'

'No. Who at this office is doing your case?'

'I don't know.'

The was a sigh at the end of the telephone.

'Have you been in to see anyone about your case here?'

'Yes, a bird.' A frosty pause.

---

26 It is important that a witness is briefed on how to give evidence to full effect. An explanation of the procedure and how to handle questioning is as reassuring for an inexperienced witness as a knowledge of procedure is for the inexperienced advocate.

27 Simple techniques of bonding the witness into the case and making him happier to help.

'What was the woman's name?'

'I don't remember. It was a bit posh.'

'Hold on a moment please. . . .'

'Hullo Mr Turquoise?' A different voice.

'Yeah.'

'I'm not the person doing your case, but as you don't seem to know who is, perhaps I can help you.'

'Yeah. I'm in court on 15 July for my trial and I've got this witness.'

'Great. Can you get the witness to come in to our office and give us a statement?'

'No. You see he's working. He says someone will have to come and see him at home in the evening.'

'I'm afraid that won't be possible. Can't you persuade him to take a day off and come into our office?'[28]

'No. He's only just started this job. He says he can take the day off for the trial but he can't take two days off or he'll lose the job. He might just be able to manage six o'clock one evening.'

'I'm afraid this office closes at five thirty.'

'Well, what am I going to do?'

'Hold on a minute . . . I've asked one of the solicitors and he says to bring your witness to court on the day and the barrister can take a statement from him there.'[29]

'Will that be good enough?'

'Well, it's not perfect, but it will have to do.'

'Shall I get him to write out what he saw?'[30]

'Yeah, why not. Do that and send it in to us.'

'OK. Thanks.'

28 This is bad practice. The obligation, once the witness is identified, is on the solicitors to see him by hook or by crook and to take a statement from him.

29 There are several reasons why this is not acceptable practice. The advocate has enough to do on the day without having to take a statement from a witness. The witness may raise points that need further investigation.

30 This is the worst of practice. A statement written by the witness is unlikely to cover the points of concern in the case and in particular is unlikely to cover material that sorts out his vulnerability to cross-examination in addition to the direct facts of the case.

6. Correspondence

Rachel Red wrote to the Crown Prosecution Service.

Dear Sirs,
Blue and Turquoise, Heeling Magistrates' Court 15 July
We represent Billie Blue in this contested summary trial. A full day has been set aside for the hearing. We are writing to ask that you disclose the prosecution witness statements to us. This will enable us to take instructions on those statements prior to the trial and thereby avoid the necessity of taking instructions during the hearing and taking up court time unnecessarily.

A further reason for requesting the statements is that we do not understand from the charges the nature of the allegations that Mr Blue faces. As the charges relate to different dates we will on the face of it need to seek separate trials. A study of the statements may enable us to agree to a single hearing.
Yours faithfully,
Ruby Red.

Rachel wrote to Billie:

Dear Billie,
I enclose 2 copies of the statement I took from you. Please read the statement through carefully and if you agree that it is correct, sign and date one copy and return it to me in the enclosed stamped addressed envelope. Please keep the other copy and read it every now and then between now and the trial. If anything further occurs to you write a note on your copy and tell me about it when we meet.

We have one witness, William (Nipper) White. I think he should be quite good. I have written to him giving him all the details of the case and where and when to be at court. I have also sent him a copy of his statement.

However, please do not assume that we have finished preparing the case. I would be grateful if you could have another go at finding any more witnesses there might be.
Yours sincerely,
Rachel.

She also wrote to William White:

Dear Nipper,
Thank you very much for coming to see me the other day. I enclose two copies of the statement I took from you. I would be grateful if you would read the statement through and if you are happy that it is correct, please sign and date one copy and send it back to me in the enclosed stamped addressed envelope.

Please keep the other copy and read it through every now and then before the trial. If anything occurs to you then please make notes on your copy.

I should be most grateful if you could be at court on 15 July 1996 at 9.30 am so that we can have a quick word before the trial starts.

Please remember that you are not allowed into the courtroom until you are called to give evidence.

Can I say how grateful I am for your help in this case.

Yours sincerely,

Rachel Red

7. The statements

Billie's proof of evidence read:

Billie Blue of 33 Claribel Mansions, the Glen, Heeling, telephone number 081-855 5656 will say in evidence:

1   I am 26 years old, date of birth: 14 February 1970.
2   I attended Heeling Comprehensive School, leaving at the age of 16 with GCSEs in art and technical drawing.
3   I then joined my grandfather's panel-beating business as a trainee panel-beater. I am still employed there as a panel-beater. The business is called XYZ Panel Beaters of 13 Wingnut Crescent, Heeling. I earn around £100 per week in hand.
4   I have outgoings of: £35 per week rent, £5 per week getting to work, then the usual electric and gas bills, details of which I will get, and £5 per week on an outstanding fine of which £200 remains outstanding.
5   I live at the above address with my girlfriend, Noreen and our baby Cologna who is aged six months. The address is a flat of which Noreen is the tenant. I have lived with her for five months. Before that I lived with my mother and family at 35 Dresden Drive, Heeling.
6   My family consists of my mother and my sister Esmeralda. My father left home when I was 12 years old. He now lives in Liverpool. We never see him.
7   I was in care for a year when I was 13. I think that this was because I was not going to school and my mother could not cope with me.
8   I have been shown a list of convictions in my name. They are correct. I have been convicted seven times of which five were by Heeling Juvenile Court. In 1989 I was given a sentence of six months' youth custody for theft from motor vehicles. My remaining convictions are all for theft or interfering with motor vehicles or taking a motor vehicle without consent. I was on probation for one year from 1990. My probation officer was Sid Silver of Heeling Probation Service. I had a good relationship with him.

9 I am in breach of a conditional discharge for taking a motor vehicle without the owner's consent which was imposed on me on 25 August 1992. The facts of that offence were that I had been to play football at a club in Bedford. When I phoned home I was told that my mother had been taken to hospital. I panicked and took a car to get to the hospital. I left some money for the petrol in the car which was why I was not given a custodial sentence, I think.

10 I have never suffered from any major illness or operation. I have no history of psychiatric disorder.

11 I am charged in this case with two charges:
   1. Interfering with a motor vehicle with intent to steal from it on 22 April 1996 in Arbuthnot Street, Heeling.
   2. On 6 May 1996 assaulting Orlando Orange, a constable of the Metropolitan Police in the execution of his duty.

12 I have pleaded not guilty to each charge.

13 In this case I have a co-defendant, Terry Turquoise. He is charged with 1. as above and a charge of assaulting another officer on 6 May 1996. Terry has also pleaded not guilty.

14 All I can say about the first charge is that I was not in Arbuthnot Street on that day and I have no knowledge of the incident. I believe that the officers have made up this allegation because they did not feel able to charge us with motor vehicle interference on 6 May.

15 On 6 May 1996 I was in the High Street, Heeling. I left work that day between 5 pm and 6.30 pm.

16 From work I drove home, which took about five to ten minutes. I then had a bath and my tea. This took about an hour.

17 I then went to the Dog and Bone pub, High Street, Heeling to meet my close friend Terry Turquoise to play snooker with him. Terry works for my grandfather as well. I have known him for about ten years. All my last five convictions except the one where I got the conditional discharge were committed with Terry. He got six months' YC when I did.

18 I met Terry at between 7 pm and 7.30 pm. I drove to the pub in my car. I then played snooker with Terry and other people who I know but not by name until about 9.30 pm or 10 pm.

19 Terry and I then left the pub to go to the chip shop which is about 200 to 300 metres from the pub on the other side of the road opposite Doggett Road.

20 During the evening I had about five pints. Terry probably had the same. Neither of us was drunk. We are used to drinking that amount. When I get drunk I drink about eight or nine pints. I never drink less than four pints when I go to the pub. I go to the pub probably three times per week.

21 The two of us came out of the pub and walked toward the chip shop

walking on the same side of the road as the pub. We would have crossed the road opposite the chip shop.

22 As we were near to where we were going to cross the road, Terry suddenly shouted, 'Old Bill.'

23 I looked round and saw a police car which was driving up the road from behind us. It suddenly stopped and I and Terry ran away from it up the High Street.

24 I think we did this from high spirits. We had not been doing anything wrong and were not worried about being stopped by the police. We could see that the police car was stopping for us and Terry shouted, 'Let's go', so I just ran. I think we did it as a joke.

25 The police officers got out of the police car and chased us. They were very fit and fast.

26 We ran about 30 metres up the High Street and then turned left into a road I think is called Doggett Road.

27 One of the officers caught me when I had run about 20 metres up Doggett Road. He caught me by grabbing me by the collar from behind and swung me round. I was still running when he caught me.

28 As he caught me he said something like, 'Got you, you bastard, you're fucking nicked.'

29 He then stood holding me while the other officer chased Terry. The second officer had a considerable turn of speed. He and Terry went out of sight in the dark up Doggett Road. I heard a scream and then about half a minute later the second officer brought Terry back. I heard him say to Terry, 'I saw you in that car, you dirty little thief.'

30 Terry said, 'I weren't in no car. We've just come out of the pub. We were just going for some chips.'

31 The second officer said, 'Well, why did you run then?'

32 Terry said, 'Just for a laugh.'

33 The officer who had hold of me said sarcastically, 'So you just run for a laugh?'

34 I said, as best I could because he had hold of my collar really tight and I couldn't speak easily, 'Yeah, honest, it was just for a laugh. We haven't touched no car.'

35 The second officer said, 'Well, you're both fucking nicked anyway.'

36 I said, 'Well, which car are we meant to have been in?'

37 The first officer said, 'Just you shut up. We'll sort that out down the nick.'

38 I said, 'No. If you say we were in a car, you show us which car we were in and see if it's open.'

39 One of them said, 'Just shut up and get in the panda'.

40 Terry and I both said, 'No. If you say we were in a car, you show us which one.' We both said this several times.

41 Then the first officer said, 'We'll have to get the van.' So they radioed for the van.

42 We stood there waiting for the van and quite a crowd had gathered. So me and Terry started shouting at the crowd, 'These officers say we were in a car over there.' And we told them to try the car doors and see if any of them were open. Several of them started trying car doors and none of them were open.

43 I think the officers got worried because of the crowd trying the car doors. I think they changed their minds about saying we had been in a car.

44 The van arrived and a sergeant came out of it and we started on at the sergeant. We said, 'These officers say we were in a car in the High Street but we weren't.' We want you to try the car door handles and see if they are open.'

45 Terry said to the sergeant, 'Yeah, we want you to fingerprint all the cars in the High Street and see if our fingerprints are on any of them, which they couldn't be.'

46 The sergeant didn't say anything. He just looked a bit surprised and then said, 'Put them in the van.' The two officers who had arrested us put us in the van and we were driven to the station.

47 The officer who arrested Terry came in the back of the van with us. The one who arrested me must have gone back in the police car.

48 The trip to the station took about five minutes. During the journey in the van, we kept saying to the officer that he couldn't have seen us in a car because we hadn't been in one. We told him that there was a group of our mates who came out of the pub after us and had seen that we couldn't have gone into a car.

49 Although this wasn't true, it seemed to worry him. Then he said, 'Well you run and I know why you run, it's because you were the ones my mate caught breaking into cars last week.'

50 I was surprised at this. We both said we hadn't been breaking into cars and if he had seen us, why hadn't he arrested us?

51 And he said it was because we had run away like we had tonight.

52 I don't think much else was said during the journey to the police station. The officer did not say anything more about us breaking into cars on the earlier occasion. He did not say where it was or when.

53 At the police station we were taken into the charge room where the custody sergeant took my particulars.

54 When he took mine he asked the first officer why I had been arrested and the officer said, 'Breaking into cars, sarge'.

55 The custody sergeant asked me if I wanted a lawyer and I said I didn't. I said this because I thought I would be out soon.

56 The custody sergeant also asked me if I wanted anyone informed that I was at the police station and I said that I didn't. I then had to sign the custody record. The custody sergeant then said, 'Put them in the cells.'

57 I was then put in a cell by the officer who had been in the van with us.

On the way I asked him what we were being charged with. The officer
said he'd think of something. This was in the cell corridor.

58 I was in the cell for about three hours. An officer then opened my cell
door and said, 'This way please, Mr Blue'.

59 This officer took me to the custody sergeant who charged me. It was
a different sergeant that I had not seen before.

60 The charges were of attempted theft in Arbuthnot Street on 22 April
and assault on a police officer on 6 May.

61 I did not say anything in answer to the charges. I didn't know I could
say anything. I'd been saying all along it was a stitch up and they
took no notice.

62 The sergeant read the charge out so fast there wasn't really the
opportunity to say anything. I'd been asleep when I was got out. I
wasn't really awake. I didn't really take in what the sergeant said. It
was all dates and such. I wasn't sure which day he was referring to.

63 I had never seen the two officers who arrested Terry and me before.
When we were in the custody suite I heard another officer, who is
called Sid, say to the officer who arrested me, 'That's Blue'. The officer
who arrested me said, 'Oh is it?' They both then laughed. Sid is tall
and bald with a beard. He drives the area car. He has a Northern
accent.

64 At no stage while I was in custody was I taken from my cell and
interviewed.

William White's statement read:

William White of 47 Bluebell House, Heeling, telephone 081-993 4592
will say in evidence:

1 I am 28 years old, date of birth: 2 February 1968. I am single and
work for British Rail as a ticket collector. I have been so employed for
six years.

2 I have no convictions in the last eight years and have never been to
prison. All my convictions are spent.

3 I have come to be a witness for Billie Blue in this way: I went into the
Dog and Bone on Friday, 10 June 1996 and the landlord Sid said there
was a guy trying to find out if anyone had seen him being arrested the
other day opposite the chip shop. I had seen this incident and Sid
pointed out the man to me and I spoke to him. He asked me to come
and see his solicitor which I agreed to do.

4 I know the man I spoke to in the pub as Billie. This is because he told
me his name. I do not know his surname and I had never spoken to
him before 10 June 1996. I did not discuss what I had seen of the
incident with Billie other than very briefly so that we could see that
we were talking about the same incident. Billie did not tell me what
he thought had happened.

5 Billie asked me whether I thought he had been fighting with the
police officer and I said I didn't think he had. I remember thinking

at the time that the police officers were out of order in the way they behaved.

6   I have been asked what I think of police officers. My answer is that I don't think about them at all really. When I come across them they seem all right. It was just that night. I think they were young ones and got a bit carried away.

7   When the incident started I was outside the chip shop. The incident was across the road from me.

8   I heard some shouting so I looked across the road. I saw two police officers getting out of their car in the High Street. I also saw these two men running down the road and round the corner. The police officers went off after them really fast. One officer caught one of the men just into a side road into which they had run, called Doggett Road, and grabbed him by the collar. The other officer ran past them and after the other man.

9   The officer was holding the first man and talking to him, holding him by the collar and the arm. They weren't struggling or anything. Then the other officer came back down Doggett Road with the second guy.

10   I watched for a bit. They seemed to be just talking. Then a police van arrived. At this point I went into the chip shop to get my supper.

11   I did not see any fighting between the two police officers and the two men at all.

12   I have been asked about the lighting. There is a street light on that corner. I only live just down that road and on the right so I know the area well. The first officer and the first man were standing about 15 yards from the light. I could see them clearly.

13   When I first saw the two men they were running down the High Street.

14   When I first saw the police officers they were getting out of their car. One of them shouted at the two men and that was what made me turn round. The officers slammed their car doors just after I looked at them and started running after the two men.

15   I have been asked if there were any cars parked in front of the police car. I don't think there can have been because I remember catching sight of the feet of one of the men. He was wearing white trainers. I could see them flashing when he ran.

16   When the police van arrived, I went into the chip shop. The windows of the chip shop were all steamed up and I could not see out. When I came out the police and the two men had gone.

17   I think this incident occurred in April or May this year. I would not recognise the men.

18   I am prepared to come to court and give evidence. I will need a letter to my boss saying that I am required.

8. Final preparation

In due course Rachel received a letter from the Crown Prosecution Service.

> Dear Sirs . . .We do not intend to serve the prosecution's witness statements in this case. It is not our practice in summary proceedings and as you know we are not obliged to serve statements in such circumstances . . .

On 13 July at Rose Madders, as no one else wanted to do it, Belinda Burnt-Umber was given the job of preparing the brief for Terry's case. Belinda had decided to instruct an old school friend who had just finished her first six months of pupillage as a barrister.

'Hullo, is that Beryl Black's clerk?'

'Yes it certainly is. What can I do for you?'

'Oh hullo. I would like Beryl Black to do a case for us at Heeling Magistrates' Court the day after tomorrow.'

'Certainly.'

'Is she free?'

'I'll just double check for you . . . Yes she's free. What's the name of the case?'

'It's a summary trial due to last all day and it's called Turquoise.'

'Lovely. And the charges?'

'Interfering with motor vehicles and assault on police.'

'And it's . . .?'

'Belinda Burnt-Umber from Rose Madder.'

'Lovely. . . and the papers?'

'They will be down in the morning.'

'Right, thanks, Miss Burnt-Umber.'

Belinda put the statement from Terry Turquoise with his custody record and a page of instructions. In the instructions she gave what little information she had. . . . 'There is a defence witness who declined to come into instructing solicitor's offices to give a statement. He should be at court to give evidence. His identity is not known to Instructing Solicitors.'

CHAPTER 15

The trial

9. First things at court

On the day before the summary trial the Crown Prosecution Service instructed a barrister to conduct the prosecution, Vernon Violet. The file was sent down to the barrister's chambers, arriving at five o'clock. At the same time, warning messages arrived at Heeling Police Station that Police Constables Orange, Crimson and another officer who had been driving the police car in the Heeling High Street incident, were required to attend court to give evidence the next day.

All converged on Heeling Magistrates' Court for ten o'clock on 15 July.

The magistrates gathered in their meeting room at the back of the court from 9 am onwards. The chief clerk had placed a notice on the board giving the provisional allocation of magistrates to the various courts. In Court 4, where the case against Billie and Terry was to be heard, Mrs Yellow was to be in the chair. With her were two other magistrates, Mrs Beige, a retired local head teacher, and Mr Magenta, a retired army warrant officer, finishing his career in a clerical grade of the civil service. All were astute in their ways. Mr Magenta was hard of hearing but too sensitive to admit it; Mrs Yellow had a soft spot for young policemen in uniform; the experience of Mrs Beige was that the pupils from her school who had ended up in the police force were not the ones she would have chosen as amongst the most reliable and truthful. Mr Magenta liked the idea of discipline and was therefore well disposed towards the police. However, all three magistrates usually did their best to reach the correct verdict and did not automatically accept what police officers or anybody else said in evidence.

The clerk for Court 4 was to be Deirdre Dunn. Deirdre was an 141

unassuming but conscientious person. When she pronounced on the
law she was usually correct. If pushed, she could be forceful.

The usher for Court 4 was Horace Tiddler. Horace had been an
usher at the court for some ten years after retiring from the police
force.

Vernon Violet, briefed by the Crown Prosecution Service, was not
pleased at the prospect of conducting a prosecution in the magistrates' court that morning. The file was largely handwritten and
difficult to read and Violet considered the magistrates' court a
demeaning place to appear. He usually appeared in the Crown
Court, which was easier, more dignified and marginally better
paid. At best he accepted this role with resignation. His clerk had
told him that the case would only occupy the morning. This seemed
to him to be unlikely. On his arrival at Heeling Magistrates' Court
he sought out the three police constables who were waiting in the
police room.

'You are not by chance the officers in the case of Blue and
Turquoise?'

'Yes sir.'

'Ah, excellent. I am the prosecutor. My name is Violet, Vernon
Violet of Counsel.'

'Right Sir.'

'Do you have your notebooks?'

'Yes sir.'

'How many do you have?'

'We have two each sir. One for the motor vehicle interference and
one for the assault on police.'

'Except me, sir. I have only the one,' said PC Pink.

'Excellent. Well I am going to have a strengthening and restora-
tive coffee and I'll see you in the courtroom. I gather that we are the
only case and should consequently be straight on at ten o'clock.
You'll be there ready to go?'

'Yes sir.'

'Excellent. We may then be able to escape from this reprehensible
place by luncheon. Do you know if the defendants are here?'

'Yes sir. I saw them arriving a moment ago.'

'Excellent, excellent.'

Rachel went past the door as this exchange was taking place. She
hurried on to find Billie. She found him in a corner of the hall staring
out of the window. She took him to one of the interview rooms.

'Are you ready to go, Billie?'

'Yeah.'

'Now I want to tell you a few things about what to do during the trial.'

'Oh right.'

'Have you ever been through a contested trial before?'

'What do you mean? I've been to court loads of times.'

'Yes I know that, but so far as I can remember you've always pleaded guilty.'

'Yeah. That's right.'

'Have you ever sat through the whole of a not guilty hearing?'

'I must have . . . no, not the whole of one.'

'Right. This is what happens. There will be the magistrates sitting at the end of the court on the raised bit, as you know. There will probably be three of them. One of them will do most of the talking, but they all count when the decision whether you are guilty or not is made . . .'

'Yes.'

'In front of them is the clerk. I don't know who it will be, but the clerk is important in that it is he or she who advises the magistrates on the law.'

'Right.'

'The first thing that will happen is that you will be asked whether you are guilty or not guilty. You plead not guilty. Say it loud enough for everyone to hear . . .'

'Don't you remember, Rachel, they did that last time . . .'

'Well they may ask you again . . . Then the prosecutor will open the case . . .'

'Open the case? What is it? In a tin?'

'. . . tell the magistrates what the case is about. He will then call the first police officer to give his evidence. The prosecutor will question him about what he says happened. After that I or Terry's advocate will cross-examine the officer . . .'

'Yes.'

'Now it is important that you concentrate and listen to everything that happens during the case. If something occurs to you that you haven't told me about then call me over or pass me a note. But be sensible about it. You may have already told me about it or it may be something that I have already thought of.'

'So how do I know when to pass you a note?'

'Just be sensible about it. I need to know everything, but if you pass me notes all the time it will be difficult for me to concentrate on what is going on and keep my train of thought going.'

'OK.'

'After the officer has been cross-examined, the prosecutor will call the next witness in the same way and each police witness will give evidence in this way.'

'Right.'

'The reality is that we win a case like this on the cross examination. Usually if you haven't shown the police to be wrong by the end of the prosecution case you've had it.'[1]

'Great. Cheer me up.'

'But that doesn't mean your evidence isn't important. It is very important. When you are being questioned, either by me or by the prosecutor, listen carefully to each question and think about it before you give your answer. Have you got that?'

'Yes I think so.'

'Don't give your answer until you are sure you have understood the question and have sorted out what you are going to say. Have you got that?'

'Yes. What are we going to do if William White doesn't turn up, Rachel?'

'Billie. I am telling you something very . . . very important and you are not listening to me.'

'I am listening, Rachel, but I'm worried about him.'

'We'll deal with him in a moment. Tell me what I have told you about how to answer questions.'

'You said I had to listen to the questions and answer them.'

'No. You must listen to the questions and not answer them until you are sure you have worked out in your mind what it is you want to say in answer.'

'Right.'

'A careless answer could lose us the case.'

'OK.'

'In a case of mine at the Old Bailey this skatty youth was being tried for armed robbery. At the end of his evidence-in-chief the barrister said to my client, "And so Mr X, did you commit this armed robbery?" X had stopped listening properly. He said "Yes." I think he's due out Christmas two years time.'

---

1 The high point of the defence tends to be at the end of the prosecution case. If the prosecution witnesses have not been fatally shaken by then, it is unlikely that the defence will win. The process of the defendants and their witnesses giving evidence very often has the effect of reducing the strength of the defence case unless they are particularly good witnesses and well able to stand up to cross-examination.

'OK, Rachel, I've got the point.'

'Another reason why you need to wait before you answer is that you will find that your mind, such as it is . . .'

'Thanks Rachel.'

'. . . will throw up one answer immediately, and then having thought about the implications of the question further, throw up another answer which may completely contradict the first answer. If both these answers have escaped from your mouth, you will at the very least look a complete pratt.'

'Yeah.'

'Also you need to give yourself time to work out exactly what is meant by the question. For example, when I was interviewing you I asked you whether the copper who had arrested you said anything to you in the van and you first of all said, "No", and then told me a great string of things that he had said. Now I think you did this not because you're a complete dumbo . . .'

'Thanks again, Rachel.'

'. . . but because you interpreted my question as being, "Did he say anything to you that *you* consider of importance in the case?" Don't do that. Listen to what the question actually says and not what you think it ought to say. OK?'

'Point taken.'

'When you give your answer . . .'

'Jesus Christ, Rachel, this is some lecture.'

'I know. But it's for your own good. I don't want you wrecking our case by not realising what is going on. You may not take any notice of what I am saying . . . and I'm sure you aren't . . .'

'I am.'

'Good . . . now, when you answer a question, keep your answer good and short and don't argue with the prosecutor. If he needles you, and in all honesty I have to say he seems the sort of prosecutor who will needle us all, don't let it get to you. Just keep your answers polite and short. If he puts allegations to you which are not true, just say they aren't true. Leave the argument about why they can't be true to me. OK? This is important. Nothing looks worse than the witness who, when asked if he did something, begins his answer, "I couldn't have, could I, because . . ." Just say "No. I didn't".'

'OK.'

'Watch the way the police do it. The most difficult ones to cross-examine will be the ones who keep their answers short and give away as little as they can.'

Beryl Black arrived at Heeling Magistrates' Court at about 9.35 am. She had meant to be there much earlier but had got lost. She had been in a complete panic for the past hour. It was her first summary trial. In fact it was her first contested hearing of any sort other than one easyish bail application. She was wracked with nerves. The brief had not been helpful in preparing the case. It told her that she represented Terry Turquoise on charges of interfering with motor vehicles and assault on police and little else, other than that the two incidents appeared to have been on different occasions. The brief said there might be a witness at court for the defendant, but that this witness had refused to give a statement to Terry's solicitors in advance. Beryl was urged to do her best in the rather unpromising circumstances.

Bewildered and disturbed, Beryl had consulted an older pupil in her chambers. 'Oh, don't worry,' he had said airily. 'The less there is in the brief the less work you have to do in advance.'

'Yes, but I am going to look a complete fool. And how can I work out in advance how to do the case unless I have more information? It's my first one, for God's sake!'

'Don't fret yourself, old girl. It is the tradition and spirit of the English criminal Bar to be able to perform miracles with no information in advance.'

'That's reassuring. So when I leave court wishing the earth would swallow me up, I am acting in the spirit of a long and hallowed tradition, am I?'

'You certainly are. And each time you do it you will get better at it. I am afraid you have yet to learn a fact of legal life. We depend on solicitors for our instructions, and to a man and woman they are idle, stupid, incompetent and greedy.'

Beryl looked so downcast that the older pupil felt constrained to give her some encouragement.

'Look, don't take it to heart. The bugger you're representing almost certainly did what he's charged with. Otherwise he wouldn't have been charged. Just do your best. You can do no more. And when you get there, find the prosecutor. If he's a member of the Bar and you explain your predicament, I'm sure he'll have pity on you and tell you what the case is about.'

On arrival at Heeling Court, Beryl sought out Vernon Violet. He was sipping coffee in the police room.

'Hullo' said Beryl. 'I'm Beryl Black. I'm representing Terry Turquoise.'

'Morning,' said Violet breezily. 'Solicitor or counsel?'

'Counsel,' said Beryl hesitatingly. The strange and pompous expression did not come readily.

'I've some problems with my instructions in this case,' she said, 'and I wondered if there was any chance of seeing the prosecution statements?'

'Sure. Help yourself.' said Violet. 'Here's the file. Can I buy you a coffee? The matron here makes the best coffee in London.'

'Er, thank you very much. Perhaps I could look at the statements first and then have a coffee. Can I take them over to that table?'

'Help yourself. It's a tinpot little case. I intend to make sure it's over by lunchtime.'

'Oh, good.' she said unhappily. Beryl took the file over to the table and looked through it. She was not sufficiently experienced to be familiar with all the documents the file contained. She sought out the witness statements and read them through, making notes of the dates and times of the incidents. There were only 25 minutes or so until the court sat, so that once she thought she had grasped the gist of the case she gave Violet back the file and went off to find Terry and any witnesses he might have with him.

Terry was waiting disconsolately in the hall.

Beryl called out, 'Terry Turquoise?'

'Yeah, that's me' said Terry.

'Hullo, Mr Turquoise, I'm Beryl Black. I am the barrister representing you.'

'Oh right.'

'Have you any witnesses with you?'

'I'm expecting one, but he isn't here yet.'

'Well let's go and talk about the case. I think there's a conference room over here.'

Beryl pushed the door open revealing a group of people around a table. They all looked up. 'I'm so sorry' said Beryl.

She tried several more. They were all full.

'We'll just have to find a corner,' said Beryl, exasperated.

'Yeah.'

They went and stood by a window. Beryl balanced her papers and notebook on the sill.

'Right. Mr Turquoise. I've looked at the police statements. They say that on 22 April they saw you breaking into cars . . . at about ten o'clock at night. It was in a road called Arbuthnot Street in Heeling. They say they saw you again two weeks later in the High Street at about eleven o'clock. They chased you and you ran away. When the officer caught you, he says you attacked him. Now I've got this very short statement you gave Rose Madder, the solicitors, but it isn't very helpful.'

Terry looked at her blankly.

'Well, what do you say about all that?'

'No. No. It wasn't like that.'

'Yes?'

'It didn't happen like that.'

'How did it happen?'

'Which bit?'

'Well, the business with the cars on 22 April for a start.'

'I don't know about that . . .'

'Don't you know anything about it?'

'No. It's nothing to do with me.'

'What do you mean?' Beryl repressed an overwhelming urge to seize Terry by the throat and bang his head repeatedly against the wall. It was a sensation experienced by many of Terry's friends and acquaintances.

'The copper chased me, grabbed me and dragged me back to where Billie was. I didn't attack him. How could I? He had my head tucked under his arm and kept hitting me with his fist.'

'Don't worry about that bit for the moment. Were you interfering with motor cars in Arbuthnot Street on 22 April?'

'I don't know where Arbuthnot Street is. I've never heard of it.'

'Were you interfering with motorcars anywhere?'

'No.'

'Do you know where you were?'

'Yeah, I was playing pool with a friend of mine.'

'Where?'

'In the Shrimp and Cucumber public house in Heeling . . . in Station Road.'

'Have you any witnesses to this?'

'Yeah. He's called Mervin Mauve. He's the mate I was with.'

'Well, we need him at court to give evidence.'

'He's coming. He can't get here until later. He's at work. He'll be here for about twelve.'

Beryl felt a surge of relief. 'Well at least something is sorted out. I just hope the case doesn't finish before he arrives. . . . What happened when you were arrested?'

'I was running down this road. . . . The copper came pounding up behind me. . . . He shouted, "You're fucking nicked so stop running". I kept going but I was completely knackered. . . . He caught me up, grabbed me collar and swung me round. I landed on me knees. He caught me round the neck and dragged me back to where Billie and the other copper were. On the way back he punched me in the face several times and told me I was a "fucking towrag".'

'Did you hit him?'

'Do us a favour. He had me round the throat. He was half strangling me. I was just trying to loosen his grip round me throat.'

At this point an usher came out of Court 4 and bawled, 'Case of Turquoise and Blue, Court 4.'

Beryl hurried over to him. 'I'm in that case.'

'Right, we're starting now. Could you come into court with your client, please.'

'Yes, oh, all right.'

Rachel and Billie appeared from one of the interview rooms. Rachel greeted the usher. 'Hullo, Horace. I'm in this one.'

'Hullo, Miss Red. Right you are. Mrs Yellow wants to start now. You're the only case in our list.'

Beryl looked at Rachel. 'I'm representing Terry Turquoise.'

'Oh hullo. We'd better have a word when we get the opportunity.'

Rachel pushed Billie through the doors of the court and Beryl followed her with Terry. The prosecutor, Vernon Violet, was already at his place. He had his papers in front of him and was staring at the door with an expression of aggressive boredom.

'Can I have your names, ladies, please. I'm sorry I didn't catch yours when we spoke just now.'

Rachel put down her papers on the desk and went over to speak to Billie who had gone into the dock. In her view it was important to establish relations with the prosecutor on her terms or not at all. Until she had the opportunity to assess for herself whether this was possible, she ignored prosecutors. In this instance she was not impressed by being shouted at and called, 'Ladies please'.

Beryl hurried over to Violet. 'My name is Beryl Black.'

'And you represent?'

'Turquoise.'

'And the charming and co-operative lady at the dock represents the other defendant?'

'Yes.'

'And her name is?'

'I don't know.'

'Excuse me, what's your name, you at the dock?' called Violet.

At this moment the magistrates came into the court, preceded by the clerk, who shouted, 'Stand please'.

The magistrates bowed uncertainly and awkwardly to the lawyers and sat down.

'The case of Terry Turquoise and Billie Blue, your worships,' called the usher.

'Are you Terry Turquoise?' asked the clerk.

'Yes.'

'Are you Billie Blue?'

'Yes.'

'Your worships,' the clerk continued, 'the defendants on the last occasion pleaded not guilty to two charges each, one of vehicle interference on 22 April and to a charge of assault on police on 6 May. In the case of Turquoise the assault is alleged to have been on PC Crimson and in the case of Blue on PC Orange. Were these offences alleged to have been on the same day?'

'No, Madam, the motor vehicle interference was on 22 April and the assaults when the defendants were recognised and arrested on 6 May', said Violet.'

'Right,' said the clerk. 'Do those pleas still stand?'

Rachel nodded firmly.

'Thank you and Miss Black?'

'Er yes.'

'Is there any objection to the charges from each occasion being tried together?'

'No,' said Rachel.

It had not occurred to Beryl that there was any question of this sort.

'Miss Black?'

Beryl thought feverishly. The only way round this was to have an adjournment. She didn't dare ask for one.

'No,' she muttered miserably. 'Oh my God,' she thought, 'this is going all wrong.'

Beryl needed more time with Terry to work out what the case was about and what his defence was in detail. However, the remorseless impetus of the case seemed to be sweeping her away. The moment for asking for more time seemed to have passed.[2]

'In any case', said Violet 'the prosecution would be seeking trial of all these charges together.'

'I dare say they would,' said the clerk. 'Well, let's get on.'

---

2 Making an application for an adjournment, even a short one, involves stopping the tide of the proceedings. Shyness and uncertainty deter the beginner.

Violet was already standing. He cleared his throat. 'Madam. I appear for the prosecution in this case. The defendant Turquoise is represented by my learned friend Miss Beryl Black and the defendant Blue by . . . my friend . . .'[3]

Violet leant over to Rachel and said in a stage whisper, 'I am afraid in spite of my requests you haven't told me your name.'

'I'll introduce myself, thank you,' said Rachel and turned round in her seat so that her back was to Violet.

'The bench knows Miss Red,' said the clerk.

'Well really . . .' said Violet to Rachel's back. 'I know you're a solicitor, but I would have thought you could have managed some of the more elementary courtesies nevertheless.'[4] He turned back to his papers, shaking his head. In the dock Billie and Terry were entertained by the exchange. It was part of Rachel's appeal for Billie that she stood up for herself and her clients at whatever cost, even to the extent of some spectacular rows both in and out of court.

'Yes, Mr Viola, perhaps we could get on with the case', said Mrs Yellow, the chairman of the magistrates.

'Violet, Madam, Violet.'

'I am so sorry', said Mrs Yellow.

10. The prosecutor's opening

Violet began his opening speech.

'Madam,[5] these two defendants, Terry Turquoise and Billie Blue, face two charges. They jointly face a charge of motor vehicle interference on 22 April of this year, and they each face a charge of assaulting a police officer in the execution of his duty on 6 May. In the case of Turquoise the officer the prosecution say Turquoise

---

3 It is a convention of the Bar that barristers are 'learned' and solicitors are not. Rachel Red takes great exception to this convention as having no basis in anything other than snobbery and a wholly unjustified sense of superiority.

4 Courtesies for Violet go one way.

5 It is a convention at the Bar that a bench of magistrates is addressed as if it consisted of the chair alone, 'sir' or 'madam'. Where, as in this case, one of the magistrates is not of the same sex as the chairman, it is very likely that that magistrate does not feel the form of address encompasses him or her. Rachel Red uses the form of address 'your worships' and makes a point of moving her gaze from one magistrate to the next so that all three feel that she is addressing them individually.

assaulted is PC Crimson, and in the case of Blue, Police Constable Orange.

'Madam, on 22 April these two officers, PCs Crimson and Orange, were on duty in a police patrol car in Arbuthnot Street in Heeling at about 10 pm, when they saw two males attempting to gain entry to a motor vehicle. The officers kept observation and saw one of the males, Blue, shake his head at Turquoise, the other male. They then moved on to another car and again tried the doors. This time the front passenger door opened. The officers decided to intervene to prevent any damage to the car . . . or theft from it. They got out of their vehicle and ran towards the men. Police Constable Orange shouted, "Stop, police! You are under arrest." Blue and Turquoise stood up and looked towards the officers, who were able to obtain a good look at their faces. The street was well lit at that point, you will hear. Blue and Turquoise thereupon took to their heels and ran away. The officers pursued them but they made good their escape.

'Madam, two weeks later, the same officers, Police Constables Crimson and Orange, were on patrol in a police vehicle driven by a third officer, PC Pink, in the High Street, Heeling when they saw these same two males, Turquoise and Blue, walking along the pavement towards them. The officers stopped their car, this time alongside the two defendants and jumped out. PC Orange shouted, "Stand still, you are under arrest for interfering with motor vehicles the other day." Again the defendants made off. But this time the officers were ready for them and caught them almost immediately. PC Orange caught up with Blue just around the corner in Doggett Road. As he caught up with Blue, PC Orange shouted, "Look, you can't get away. Just stop. You are making it worse for yourself." At that Blue stopped and turning round swung a punch at the officer's face. PC Orange managed to duck and the punch hit his helmet, knocking it from his head. PC Orange then got hold of Blue by the arm and arrested him. PC Crimson had in the meantime run past them and after Turquoise who had run on up Doggett Road. The officer caught him and grabbed him by the shoulder and swung him round. PC Crimson told Turquoise he was arresting him for vehicle interference two weeks before. At this Turquoise punched out at the officer. All the punches landed on the officer's arm. PC Crimson took hold of Turquoise by the neck and restrained him with a neck hold. PC Crimson then took Turquoise back to where PC Orange was restraining Blue. Both defendants were then taken to Heeling

Police Station where they were charged, making no reply after caution.

'Madam,' continued Violet, 'I propose to call the three officers to give evidence. That is, PCs Orange, Crimson and Pink. Before I do so it is my duty to remind you of the law in this case. Madam, the burden of proof in the case is simple. The prosecution brings this case. The burden is on the prosecution to prove the case beyond reasonable doubt. However, please remember that the prosecution witnesses in this case are police officers. I would suggest to you, Madam, that witnesses of that sort are substantially more worthy of belief than most categories of witness. I anticipate that the defence case will be to deny most of what the officers will say in evidence. I would ask you to consider carefully when you come to consider your verdict whether such witnesses would be capable of extensive deception of this court. I would ask you to bear in mind particularly that when on the second occasion the officers challenged the defendants and attempted to arrest them, their immediate reaction was to flee. I cannot see that the defendants are going to be able to maintain that they did otherwise. To run away from the police officers does not sound like the actions of innocent parties.[6]

'Finally, Madam, I would remind you of the ingredients of these two offences. The first is that of "vehicle interference" under section 9 of the Criminal Attempts Act 1981. The section defines the offence as, "(1) A person is guilty of the offence of vehicle interference if he interferes with a motor vehicle or trailer or with anything carried in or on a motor vehicle or trailer with the intention that an offence specified in subsection (2) below shall be committed by himself or some other person. (2) The offences mentioned in subsection (1) above are: (a) theft of the motor vehicle or trailer or part of it; (b) theft of anything carried in or on the motor vehicle or trailer; and (c) an offence under section 12(1) of the Theft Act 1968 (taking and driving away without consent); and, if it is shown that a person accused of an offence under this section intended that one of those offences should be committed, it is immaterial that it cannot be shown which it was."

'The second offence is that of assaulting a police constable in the

---

6 This is the sort of point the prosecutor might more easily make in a closing speech. However, as this is a summary trial, the prosecutor does not have a closing speech and has to try and put all the points he may wish to make into his opening.

execution of his duty. That offence is created by section 51(1) of the Police Act 1964, which simply reads, "Any person who assaults a constable in the execution of his duty . . . shall be guilty of an offence." The ingredients of this offence are that the assault takes place on the officer and that at the time of the assault the officer is in the execution of his duty.

'I would urge upon you, Madam, that if you accept the officers' evidence it is clear that the offences charged will have been made out. It is inconceivable that these defendants can have been attempting to gain access to these cars for any purpose other than theft or perhaps taking without the owner's consent . . . equally it will be apparent that the officers were in the execution of their duty when the arrests were effected on 6 April and they were assaulted.'[7]

11. Police Constable Crimson's evidence-in-chief

'Madam,' Violet continued, 'I will now call the prosecution evidence. Usher, please call Police Constable Cuthbert Crimson.'

'Yes sir.' The usher left the court and his muffled call could be heard from the hallway, 'Police Constable Crimson?'

A police officer entered the courtroom and strode into the witness box. He picked up the testament from the box and held it high above his head. 'I swear by Almighty God that I shall tell the truth, the whole truth and nothing but the truth . . .'

'Officer, could you give the court your full name and rank?' asked Violet.

'Yes sir. I am Police Constable three three four Cuthbert Crimson stationed at Heeling Police Station, your worships.'

Violet began his questioning. 'Officer, were you on duty on 22 April this year?'

'I was, your worships.'[8]

'Do you wish to refer to any notes?'

'If I may, sir.'[9]

'When did you make them up, officer?'

---

7 This is a competent opening. All the parties to the trial are better off for it. In particular, the defence benefits from a proper opening, as the magistrates will have grasped the basics of the case.

8 It is a convention in the Metropolitan Police that the answers to questions should be given to the bench and not to the advocate.

9 This convention frequently slips, particularly in moments of stress.

'I wrote them in the canteen as soon as possible after the incident.'

'Were the matters still fresh in your memory?'

'Oh yes indeed, sir.'

Violet turned to the magistrates. 'May he refer to his notes, Madam?'

The chairman looked at the defence advocates. 'Do you have any objections?'

Beryl Black shook her head.

'He hasn't said when he wrote them,' said Rachel Red, rising to her feet briefly.

The chairman turned to the officer. 'When did you write them?'

The officer scanned his notes. 'It must have been about half an hour after I got back to the police station.'

'When did you get back to the station?' enquired Violet, slightly impatient.

'I suppose that must have been about half an hour after the incident,' said PC Crimson.

'All right?' the chairman enquired of Rachel Red.

'Thank you, I have no further comment at this stage,' Rachel said with a slight emphasis on the 'this'.[10]

'Right, officer, can you tell the court what happened on 22 April?'

'Yes sir. At about 10 pm I was on duty in full uniform in a marked police vehicle with Police Constable Orange. We were driving down Arbuthnot Street . . .'

Rachel rose to her feet. 'Your worships. Mr Violet has the advantage of the officer's statement, which is no doubt identical to the officer's evidence. I wrote to the Crown Prosecution Service asking for copies of the officers' statements and was refused them.[11] I consequently have to note the officer's evidence in full. He is giving his evidence far too fast for me to note it. No doubt your learned clerk is having the same difficulty . . .'

'I am,' said the clerk. 'He is going far too fast for me.'

'Mr Violet . . .' said Mrs Yellow.

'Yes, Madam,' said Violet, irritated. 'Please, officer, give your evidence more slowly.'

---

10 Rachel Red says this so as not to suggest that she accepts the notes as legitimately written up.

11 There is no harm in seizing the opportunity to show the magistrates how unreasonable the Crown Prosecution Service has been.

'I suggest you watch the clerk's pen,' suggested Mrs Yellow helpfully.

'Yes, carry on with your evidence . . . but slower, officer,' said Violet.

'Certainly, your worships . . . We saw a car parked on the nearside of the road . . . It was under a street light . . . On the offside of the car we saw a male. He was standing by the driver's door with his hand on the door handle which he was trying to open . . . and on the nearside we saw another male standing with his hand on the front passenger door which he was trying to open . . . We stopped the police car and watched the two males. It was clear that neither door could be opened . . . The two males looked round them and then moved up the road to the next car . . . where they repeated the exercise . . . This time the male on the nearside was able to open the front passenger door . . . Fearing that the car would suffer damage at their hands, we both got out of the police vehicle and started across the road. As we went Police Constable Orange shouted, "Stop, police, you are under arrest." . . . At this the two males looked up and we were able to see their faces clearly. The male at the driver's door was the defendant Terry Turquoise and the male at the front passenger's door was the defendant Billie Blue . . .'

'You're a fucking liar,' shouted Terry Turquoise.

'You pig bastard,' added Billie.

Beryl Black leaped panic stricken to her feet.

'Quiet,' shouted the clerk, outraged.

The chairman looked at the defence advocates. 'I think you had better warn your clients that they do themselves no good by such outbursts.'

'Oh yes. I'll have a very strong word with him,' declared Beryl Black in an agony of embarrassment and hurried over to the dock where she whispered loudly and vehemently at Terry.

'I'm sure he won't do it again,' said Rachel Red. Rachel turned and winked at Billie and then sat down and concentrated on her notes.[12]

'As you were saying, officer . . .' said Violet.

'Er, yes sir . . . The male at the driver's door was the defendant

---

12 Rachel takes the view that as Billie's advocate she is responsible for his case but not for his behaviour. If Billie wants to shout out in court, that is his affair and decision, not Rachel's. Rachel feels that it is patronising and unwarranted to try to dictate to Billie on this subject.

Terry Turquoise and the male at the front passenger's door was the defendant Billie Blue.'

'Which is Turquoise and which Blue, officer?'

'Blue is the one in the dock nearest me and Turquoise is the other one, sir.'

'Was it dark at that time, officer?'

'It was after dark but it wasn't particularly dark in that road.'

'And why was that, officer?'

'Well sir. It's a particularly well lit road and there was street lighting that shone directly onto the defendants' faces as they looked at us.'

'Yes.'

'As we made our way to them, the defendants slammed the car doors and Blue shouted to Turquoise, "It's the Old Bill. Run, Terry!"'

'And what did they do then?'

'They ran away, your worships.'

'And what did you do?'

'We ran after them.'

'Did you catch them?'

'No, sir. Unfortunately not.'

'Did you see the defendants again?'

'Yes, sir.'

'And when was that?'

'Two weeks later, on 6 May in the High Street, Heeling.'

'Tell the court what happened.'

'At about 11pm I was in a marked police car with PC Orange again and another officer, Police Constable Percy Pink . . .'

'Slower please,' Rachel muttered.

'. . . PC Pink was driving the police car, your worships . . . We were driving down the High Street when we saw the defendants . . . PC Pink stopped the police car and we jumped out. . . . I shouted, "Stand still, you are under arrest for interfering with motor vehicles the other day." . . . The defendants again made off up the road and turned into Doggett Road . . . I and PC Orange pursued them. PC Orange caught Blue just after he had run into Doggett Road . . . I heard PC Orange try to arrest Blue and saw Blue punch at PC Orange . . . I saw PC Orange duck and the punch struck him on the helmet knocking the helmet off PC Orange's head . . . I ran on past them and after Turquoise. I caught up with him and grabbed him by the shoulder, swinging him round . . . I told Turquoise I was arresting him for vehicle interference two weeks before . . . At this

Turquoise punched out at me several times . . . All the punches landed on my arm. I took hold of Turquoise by the neck and restrained him with a neck hold . . . I then took him back to where PC Orange was restraining Blue . . . Both defendants were then taken to Heeling police station, where they were charged, making no reply after caution.'

'Is that your evidence in this case, officer?'

'Yes, your worships.'

'Please stay there. I am sure there will be some more questions for you to answer.'

'Certainly will . . .' Rachel muttered to herself.

12. Beryl's cross-examination of PC Crimson

'Miss Black? Do you have any questions?' enquired the chairman.

'Er yes, thank you, Madam.' Beryl rose slowly to her feet studying her notes feverishly. Panic rose inside her. No sensible question would form in her mind. What should she ask this forbidding-looking policeman? He was not even looking at her.

'Good morning, officer.'[13]

Police Constable Crimson looked at Beryl in some surprise and looked back at the magistrates.

'Good morning your worships.'[14]

'What were you doing in Arbuthnot Street on 22 April, officer, when you found yourselves in the road . . .?'

'We were on general patrol, your worships.'

'No one had reported any. . . any. . . break in to any car in the . . . in Arbuthnot Street?'

'Not that I am aware of, your worships.'

'And you just saw the defendants? You say? You just saw them? Just by the car?'

'Yes, your worships.'

'Are you sure you saw them?'

'Yes, your worships.'

13 Panic produces the most extraordinary comments in the novice advocate. While it is rigid and unimaginative to formulate the whole of a cross-examination in advance, formulating the first question avoids absurdities like this.

14 Metropolitan Police Officers particularly try and direct their answers to the magistrates during cross-examination. Hence this bizarre exchange.

'Quite positive?'[15]
'Quite positive, your worships.'
'Might you not be mistaken?'
'No, your worships.'
'It was dark?'
'Not particularly, your worships.'
'But it was night-time.'
'Yes, your worships.'
'Isn't it dark at night, officer?'
'Not necessarily. In this case there was very adequate street lighting. This lead to the street not being dark . . . your worships.'
'Were the street lights nearby?'[16]
'Yes, your worships.'
'Where were they, then?'
'I don't recall exactly where they were, your worships.'
'And you ran across the road towards the defendants?'[17]
'Yes, your worships.'
'Yet you didn't catch them?'
'No, your worships.'
'Why not?'
'They ran away, your worships.'
'But didn't you run after them, officer?'
'Yes, your worships.'
'Then why didn't you catch them?'
'They ran faster than we did, your worships.'
'Don't you run fast, officer?'
'Quite fast, your worships, but in this instance the defendants ran into a dark alley and by the time we got there they had gone.'
'Then on 6 May you say you saw them again?'
'Yes.'
'How can you be sure it was the same two young men?'
'I recognised them, your worships. They have very distinctive

---

15 Questions of the 'Are you sure?' type are pointless, having the adverse effect of enabling the witness to affirm his evidence. It is verbal marking time while the advocate waits for some worthwhile thought to come to mind. It is better to mark time in silence.
16 This form of leading questioning is easy for the witness to deal with. The answer the advocate hopes for is obvious.
17 This form of non-question which involves reciting back to the witness his evidence-in-chief for his confirmation is pointless. Again it is verbal marking time while the advocate waits for inspiration.

haircuts, your worships. And they were wearing the same hooped rugby shirts, your worships.'[18]

'But you can't be sure that it was the same two young men after two weeks, can you, officer?'

'Yes, your worships.'

'I suggest to you that you are wrong.'

'No, your worships.'

'Were you cross that they had got away from you on the first occasion?' Next to her Beryl ignored Rachel's sharp intake of breath. Indeed so absorbed had Beryl become in the fascinating exercise of devising questions that she did not notice it.

'Yes, your worships.'

'Was that why you chased them and arrested them on the second occasion?'

'No, your worships. We chased them and arrested the defendants because we recognised them as persons we had seen committing offences on 22 April in Arbuthnot Street by attempting to interfere with motor vehicles, your worships.'

'I suggest to you that you are mistaken, officer.'

'About what? Your worships?'

'About recognising the defendants.'

'Recognising the defendants when? Your worships?'

'When you saw them.'[19]

'On the second occasion I was not mistaken. When the defendants were taken to the police station they gave their names as Terry Turquoise and Billie Blue, which are, I understand, their names. Your worships.'

'I mean when you first saw them.'

'What about when I first saw them? Your worships?'

At this point the chairman intervened.

'I think that what Miss Black means is that you were mistaken when you said you recognised the defendants when you first drove up in the High Street, officer. Is that what you mean, Miss Black?'

---

18 There is an interesting line of cross-examination opened up here. It might be that the officers recognised the shirts, not the persons wearing them. Unfortunately Beryl Black does not notice this point.

19 Beryl Black is not really keeping a grip on her questions and has become confused. One of the consequences of inexperience is that the advocate is liable to concentrate on the mechanics of devising the questions to the exclusion of all else, including remembering the salient features of the case or even listening to the answers.

'Yes, Madam.'

'I am so sorry, your worship. How stupid of me. No, I was not mistaken. Your worships.'

'I suggest you are quite wrong when you say my client hit you, officer.'

'Unfortunately I am not wrong, your worships. I wish I had been.'

'Was it painful?'

'Yes indeed, your worships.'

'How many times were you hit?'

'I really can't say, your worships.'

'You must know. Was it once, twice, three times or what?'

'I don't know. Your worships.'

'You must know. People know how many times they have been hit. You must know.'

'Have you ever been hit, Miss Black?'

'Well no . . . it is not for me to answer your questions . . . I am here to ask them. It is for you to answer them. How many times were you hit officer?'

'I don't know.'

'This is absurd. You must know.'

'Miss Black, I think the officer has answered your question. You may not like the answer, but you can't force him to change it.'

'Yes, Madam. Well, officer, I suggest to you that my client did not hit you.'

PC Crimson stood gazing at the wall.

'Well officer?'

'I'm sorry, was that a question, your worships?'

'I think that Miss Black was putting her case to you, officer' said the chairman.

'Yes, your worship. Well your client did hit me . . . several times . . . your worships.'

'And you took him by the neck?'

'Yes, your worships.'

'Why?'

'To stop him from hitting me.'

'I suggest that you took him by the neck as soon as you caught him. You ran up behind him and grabbed him and put him in a neck hold.'

'That is not true, your worships.'

Beryl Black stood staring at her notebook and leafing through the pages as if looking for further points. In fact she was not taking anything in from the text. The page was a blur. She was just wondering what to do next. Eventually, with no further questions coming to mind, she subsided into her seat. She had no idea whether she had asked all she needed to, but she could think of nothing further.

'Is that everything, Miss Black?' asked the chairman.

Beryl leapt up again. 'Yes, Madam.'

13. Rachel's cross-examination of PC Crimson

'Miss Red, do you have any questions?' asked the chairman.

Rachel stood up slowly. She looked at her notebook for a time, but in an unruffled manner.[20] She then looked up at PC Crimson who was staring fixedly at the wall behind the magistrates.

'Officer, may I ask you about your notes?'

'Er yes.'

'When did you make them up . . . perhaps I should say . . . compile them?'

'Which ones?'

'All of them.'

'Er, your worships, I wrote the notes relating to 22 April, as I said, about an hour after I got back to the police station . . . about an hour after the incident . . .'

'Yes?'

'Sorry?'

'Is that all the notes you have been referring to?'

'No. I have also been referring to notes for 6 May.'

'When did you write those notes up?'[21]

PC Crimson examined his notebook for several seconds before answering.

'I don't seem to have recorded when I made those notes up.'

'Have you been referring to your notes when you gave evidence about what happened in the High Street on 6 May?'

'Yes.'

---

20 A well organised and competent cross-examiner has an indefinable disconcerting quality which can be used to advantage against a witness.

21 Rachel tries to keep her questions as simple and short as she can. She tries to avoid leading the witness so that he gets no help in devising his answers. The witness has little idea of the answers Rachel is hoping for because her questions are largely sterile and non-leading.

'I don't recollect that you were given the permission of the court to refer to those notes.'

'I thought I was given permission at the beginning of my evidence.'

'That was in relation to the notes you made on 22 April.'

'Oh, I'm sorry.'

'Well when did you make up the notes for 6 May?'

'I suppose it must have been when I got back to the police station.'

'When?'

'When? I don't really know exactly. . . it must have been within the hour.'

'Did you make those notes up on your own or in conjunction with other officers?'

'On which occasion?'

'Both occasions.'

'Well on the first occasion I wrote my notes with PC Orange.'

'And on the second occasion?'

'I don't really remember. I think again that it must have been with PC Orange . . . PC Pink may have been there as well.'

'And where did you make the notes up?'

'On which occasion?'

'Each.'

'Well I think that we probably made the notes up in the canteen on both occasions.'

'Did you confer with any other officer while you were making up your notes on either occasion?'

'Yes, with PC Orange on each occasion.'

'Any other officer?'

'PC Pink may have been there on the second occasion.'

'Can you not remember whether he was there or not?'

'I think that he was.'

'On the second occasion, on 6 May, when did you come on duty?'

Violet stood up. 'I am entirely unable to see the relevance of that question, Madam. Cross-examination needs to be relevant and I would ask that Miss Red confines her questions to relevant matters.'[22]

The Chairman looked at Rachel . . .

'Your worships. I am not responsible for Mr Violet's inability to understand the case.'

---

22 Violet can see that the officer is in difficulty and needs a helping hand.

Violet stood up again. This time instead of revealing a super-cilious disdain his voice was shaking with rage.

'That is highly offensive . . . '

'Your worships,' said Rachel. 'I have asked one question in furtherance of my cross-examination. All my earlier questions were simply establishing when the officer wrote his notes. A subject on which he has clearly misled the court and on which Mr Violet has failed to discharge his duty to the court. I think Mr Violet is displaying a remarkably intolerant attitude in challenging my cross-examination after one question.'

'One question . . . ' expostulated Violet.

'Mr Violet. I think that we should allow Miss Red to continue her cross-examination.'

'Thank you, your worships. Officer, when did you come on duty?'[23]

'I imagine it must have been about 6 pm, your worships.'

'And what did your duties involve prior to 11 pm?'

'I and the other two officers were patrolling Heeling in the area car, your worships.'

'Where had you come from when you saw the defendants?'

'From the station at the end of the High Street, your worships.'

'Where were you going?'

'Along the High Street, your worships.'

'For what purpose?'[24]

'Just general patrolling, your worships.'

'On that journey did you stop before this incident?'

'I don't recollect, your worships. I think that we did, but I can't remember.'

'Where were you in the car?'[25]

'I was in the back seat, your worships.'

'At what sort of speed were you driving?'

'Not very fast. Perhaps twenty miles an hour, your worships.'

'And what happened?'

'We saw the defendants, your worships.'

'How far away from them were you?'

---

23 It is a useful technique to be able to remember the question asked before an interruption and present it again in as near the original form as possible when the questioning resumes.

24 These questions are not good ones. Rachel is establishing where it would be a good idea to start her 'question sweep'.

25 This is the beginning of Rachel's questioning proper.

'Perhaps twenty metres, perhaps a little further, your worships.'
'Who saw them?'
'How do you mean?'
'Which of you saw them?'
'We all did.'
'How do you know?'
'Well, I saw them.'
'What happened then?'
'What do you mean?'
'What did you do?'
'I jumped out of the car and ran after the defendants.'
'Who was driving?'
'PC Pink.'
'Why did he stop the car?'
'I suppose he must have seen the defendants.'
'What were they doing?'
'As soon as they saw us they ran away.'
'But before they ran away.'
'They were just walking along the pavement.'
'In which direction?'
'I'm not sure. Away from us, I think.'
'In which case how did you recognise them?'
'They must have been walking towards us.'
'Did you see them trying any car door handles or interfering with any cars?'
'Yes, on 22 April.'
'I am referring to the night you arrested them.'
'No.'
'Were they next to a car?'[26]
'No. There wasn't a car in the High Street at that point.'
'Were did PC Pink stop the police car?'
'As near as possible to the defendants.'
'Next to them?'
'Just about.'
'Did they turn round to run away?'
'I don't know. I only know that they ran away.'
'What happened then?'
'PC Orange and I got out and ran after them.'
'Where were they when you started running?'

---

26 This is a leading question, but the answer is of little importance.

'Not far. A few metres along the pavement.'

'How far did you chase Terry Turquoise before you caught him?'

'About twenty metres. Just around the corner.'

'When did he start running?'

'I suppose as soon as we got out of the police car and I shouted at him.'

'Do you play any sport?'

'Yes, hockey for the Division.'

Violet stood up again. 'Really, Madam, I cannot see that this can be relevant to the . . . '

'So you're fit?'

'Yes.'

'You didn't have any difficulty in catching Terry Turquoise, did you, officer?'

'I had a little more difficulty than PC Orange had in catching Blue, but not really, no.'

'How far did you have to run in the High Street?'

'About twenty metres.'

'As you ran up the High Street, how far behind the defendants were you?'

'Just a few metres.'

'Did you lose sight of them after they had gone around the corner.'

'No.'

'Why not?'

'Because we didn't. They took the corner wide and we were right behind them.'

'How fast were you running?'

'Fairly fast.'

'When you say right behind them, how close?'

'A few feet.'

'When you ran round the corner into Doggett Road, where were you in relation to PC Orange?'

'I was slightly behind him.'

'How far behind him?'

'Just a couple of feet.'

'So PC Orange grabbed Billie Blue and you ran on after Terry Turquoise?'

'Something like that.'

'Why didn't you help PC Orange with Billie Blue?'

'Because I wanted to catch the other one.'

'How far did you have to run down Doggett Road to do that?'

'About forty metres.'

'How fast were you going during that time?'

'Fairly fast.'

'As fast as you could?'

'I don't know. Fairly fast.'

'How did PC Orange stop Blue?'

PC Crimson looked at his notebook. 'PC Orange caught Blue just after he had run into Doggett Road. I heard PC Orange try to arrest Blue and saw Blue punch at PC Orange. I saw PC Orange duck and the punch struck him on the helmet, knocking the helmet off PC Orange's head.'

'Yes. I heard that before when you read it out. What I am asking you is how he stopped him.'

'I don't follow you.'

'Well, officer, the position is that you have a man, Billie Blue, running away from a police officer, PC Orange, with the apparent intention of evading arrest. Yes?'

'Yes.'

'Both are going in your words "fairly fast". Yes?'

'Yes.'

'In those circumstances if the following officer grabs the fugitive it is unlikely that they will both instantaneously and tidily stop and have a conversation. Tell us in as much detail as you can what happened.'

'As I say PC Orange caught Blue just after he had run into Doggett Road. I heard PC Orange try to arrest Blue and saw Blue punch at PC Orange. I saw PC Orange duck and the punch struck him on the helmet knocking, the helmet off PC Orange's head.'[27]

'Did Billie Blue fall over when he was grabbed?'

'No. He punched at PC Orange.'

'Did they run along for a distance until they could stop. After all, they must have had quite an impetus from running so fast. They couldn't stop dead. Could they?'

'I don't know. All I can say is that PC Orange caught Blue just . . . '

'Yes, thank you. Please don't read that again. Can I suggest to you that whatever happened between PC Orange and Billie Blue at that point, you couldn't have seen it because you were pelting down the

---

27 The officer's way of dealing with this tricky point is to return to his notes. Rachel tries to coax him away from his notes.

pavement after Terry Turquoise as fast as you could to catch him . . .
That's right isn't it?'[28]

'No.'

'Can I ask you this. Is your account in your notebook identical
with the account in PC Orange's notebook?'

'I don't know.'

'You don't know?'

'No.'

'Now I don't represent Terry Turquoise so I shan't ask you any
questions about your arrest of him . . . '

'I am surprised,' said Violet *sotto voce*.

'I see the learned prosecutor is relieved at that . . . But can I ask
you this. Had you ever spoken to Terry Turquoise before?'

'Before that night?'

'Yes.'

'No, I hadn't.'[29]

'When you got Terry Turquoise back to where PC Orange was
with Billie Blue, what was going on?'

'Nothing . . . We just waited for the van to take them back to the
police station.'

'How long did you have to wait?'

'Not long.'

'How long?'

'I don't remember.'

'You must be able to give us some sort of estimate.'

'I suppose about five minutes, perhaps ten.'

'What happened while you were waiting for the van?'

'Nothing.'

'Was there any conversation?'

'If there was, I can't remember what it was.'

'You can't remember what it was?'

'I don't remember there being any conversation.'

'You had arrested Terry Turquoise for what?'

'Interfering with motor vehicles.'

'And PC Orange had arrested Billie Blue for . . . ?'

---

28 This is the sort of problem that arises when a police officer tries to ensure that
his notes corroborate another officer's evidence.

29 Rachel needed to be sure this would be his answer before asking a question
which might have led the magistrates to find out that Terry had previous
convictions.

'I don't know what he had arrested him for.'

'I think you ought to consider what you have just said, officer.'

'I knew he had arrested him for the same offence I had arrested Turquoise for but I hadn't heard him say it.'

'But I thought your evidence was that you heard him arrest Billie Blue before you ran after Terry Turquoise.'

'I heard him arrest him but I didn't hear him say what he was arresting him for.'

'Are you telling the court the truth, officer?'

'Of course, your worships.'

'What was the offence you had arrested Terry Turquoise for?'

'Interfering with motor vehicles.'

'When?'

'On 22 April.'

'Right, you had arrested Terry Turquoise and PC Orange had arrested Billie Blue for interfering with motor vehicles on 22 April. Surely one of you said something to them about that alleged offence. Didn't you?'

'I don't remember.'

'You don't remember. Officer, can I jolt your memory. Didn't you accuse the two of them of interfering with a motor vehicle not on 22 April but at the moment that you had drawn up in your police car that very night, the motor vehicle being the car parked in front of where you stopped your police car?'

'No, your worships.'

'Didn't you say to Terry Turquoise, "I saw you in that car, you dirty little thief"?'

'No, your worships.'

'And didn't Terry Turquoise say to you, "I weren't in no car. We've just come out of the pub. We were just going for some chips"?'

'No, your worships.'

'And didn't the two defendants start denying that they had been in any of the cars parked there and asked members of the crowd to see if any of the car door handles were open?'

'No, your worships. Nothing like that was said.'

'Did you ask the defendants why they had run away from you?'

'No, your worships, I don't recollect anything like that being said.'

'You say you had arrested Terry Turquoise for interfering with a vehicle on 22 April?'

'Yes, your worships.'

'Did you explain to him what you thought he had done?'

'Yes, your worships when I arrested him.'

'What did you say to him?'

'I told him I was arresting him for vehicle interference two weeks before, your worships.'

'What did you say to him?'

'Exactly that.'

'Exactly what?'

'That I was arresting him for vehicle interference two weeks before.'

'Could you put into direct speech what you said to him.'

'No, your worships. I can't remember exactly what I said.'

'How did you identify to Mr Turquoise when this vehicle interference was meant to have occurred?'

'I imagine I said something like "two weeks ago".'

'Did you ever go into any more detail with him than that?'

'I didn't, your worships, no.'

'When you had Mr Turquoise back at where PC Orange was waiting with Billie Blue, didn't you explain to them more precisely when this offence was meant to have occurred?'

'No.'

'Why not?'

'I didn't see any need to. I felt I had given Mr Turquoise as much information as he needed, your worships.'

'You and PC Orange asked the two defendants why they had run away from you, didn't you?'

'I don't recollect anything like that being said. As far as I was concerned, it was obvious.'

'Why was it obvious?'

'Well . . . we were chasing them.'

'I'm sorry, officer, just because two people run away from you doesn't make it obvious why they are running.'

'Well we had seen them at a car . . . I mean we had seen them at a car during the incident two weeks before. And PC Orange shouted out to them that was why they were being arrested.'

'Your first answer is nearer to the truth, isn't it, officer? That you thought you had seen them near a car that evening.'

'No, your worships.'

'When did you find out Billie Blue's name?'

'At the police station as I recall, your worships.'

'How did you get to the police station?'

'I went in the police car as I recall.'

'Didn't you travel in the back of the van?'

'I may have done, your worships.'

'You did, didn't you?'

'Now I think about it, yes, your worships.'

'What was said in the van?'

'In the van, your worships? . . . Nothing . . . . It was a very short journey.'

'What happened at the police station, when the defendants arrived there?'

'At the station? Well, the defendants were taken before the custody sergeant . . . '

'Yes?'

'I told the custody sergeant why Turquoise had been arrested and he was put into a cell.'

'What did you tell the custody sergeant?'

'I don't remember, your worships.'

'Well, what does the custody sergeant have to decide?'

'He has to decide whether to authorise the custody of the detained person.'

'What information does he decide that on?'

'On what the arresting officer tells him about the arrest.'

'That happens with every arrested person brought to the police station?'

'I believe so, your worships.'

'You're being very coy about this, officer. You know very well that this happens with every arrested person brought to the police station. Yes?'

'Yes.'

'So what did you tell the custody sergeant about why you had arrested Terry Turquoise?'

'That he had been arrested for motor vehicle interference . . . '

'On . . . ?'

'On 22 April.'

'Going back to your notes. Do you have the notes for these two incidents in one notebook?'

'No, your worships. I have my notes in two incident report books.'

'Why?'

'We are required to use separate books for each incident.'

'Can I ask you to look at the notes you have made for the incident in Arbuthnot Street on 22 April? How have you spelt the name Turquoise?'

'I have spelt it T.U.R.Q.U.O.Y.S.E, your worships.'

'Is that the way you have spelt it each time it is written?'

'In which notebook, your worships?'

'The Arbuthnot Street book.'

'I have only written in Turquoise once in that notebook and that is how it is spelt.'

'Only that once? How does the sentence read?'

'The sentence? . . . It reads "I saw the two males go to a second car. I saw one male *I now know to be Terry Turquoyse* at the driver's door . . ."'[30]

'And you have spelt Turquoise T.U.R.Q.U.O.Y.S.E?' Rachel bent over her notebook writing industriously.

'Yes, your worships.'

'Why did you go to Arbuthnot Street that evening, officer?'

'Which evening?'

'On 22 April.'

'We were on duty and patrolling the area.'

'So there was no specific reason for going down that street?'

'Not that I recollect, your worships.'

'Were you going anywhere?'

'Not particularly, your worships.'

'So what happened when you drove into Arbuthnot Street?'

'We saw the two defendants interfering with motor vehicles, your worships.'

'Could you describe the road?'

'No, not really.'

'From which end did you drive into Arbuthnot Street?'

'From the north . . . the bus station end.'

'Is it a busy road?'

'Just average.'

'Is it wide?'

'Not particularly, your worships.'

'Are there trees in it?'[31]

'I believe there are, your worships.'

'How many?'

'I wouldn't know, your worships.'

'Are there houses?'

---

30 Rachel is interested in the words in italics in the notebook. The rest of this series of questions about how the officer spelt Turquoise is camouflage.

31 Rachel could not expect to obtain any useful answers from questions of this sort.

'Yes, your worships, down each side. It's a normal suburban road.'

'What was the lighting like that evening?'

'It was good, your worships. That was how we were able to identify the two men as the defendants.'

'Well what is the lighting?'

'As I recollect there is regular lighting down each side of the road. And in particular there was a light by the second car that the defendants went to.'

'What sort of spacing is there between the lights?'

'I suppose fifty metres.'

'It was dark. You wouldn't have been able to identify the men at the cars if they hadn't been by a light.'

'I don't know, your worships. They were by a light and I could see them in that light.'

'How far down the road did you go until you saw the two men?'

'I suppose about half-way down the road.'

'How long is it?'

'I suppose it's about one hundred and fifty metres, something like that.'

'What sort of speed were you doing?'

'Not very fast.'

'Who was driving?'

'I was.'

'What did you see?'

'I saw two men on each side of a car.'

'Oh four men.'

'No, your worships. Two men . . . one on each side of the car.'

'What did you do?'

'I pulled into the side of the road.'

'What, without warning.'

'There was no other traffic.'

'Which side did you pull into?'

'The near side.'

'And which side were they on?'

'They were on the same side as us.'

'Did they see you pulling in?'

'I don't think so. There was a number of parked cars between us and them.'

'How many?'

'I don't know.'

'Just one?'

'No, more than one.'

'Two?'

'No, more than two.'

'How many?'

'I don't know.'

'Three?'

'Well really,' expostulated Violet. 'This is not cross-examination. It's just a ludicrous form of badgering.'

'Well how many, officer? Answer my question sensibly and I'll stop badgering you.'

'Probably three or more, your worships.'

'And having parked what did you do?'

'We sat and watched them.'

'Did you get out of your car?'

'Not at this stage.'

'How far were the two men from you?'

'It's hard to say.'

'Well try.'

'I really don't know.'

'Were they at the end of the road?'

'Oh no. They were well into the road.'

'Ten metres from the end of the road?'

'No, further than that.'

'Twenty metres from the end of the road?'

'Perhaps.'

'Twenty metres from the far end of the road?'

'Perhaps. It's hard to say.'

'It's not hard to say if you're trying to tell the truth, officer.'

Violet stood up. 'That is an outrageous comment. I have sat here and listened to Miss Red's cross-examination. I have restrained myself from interrupting. But this is too much . . . '

'I am most gratified that Mr Violet has restrained himself from interrupting my legitimate cross-examination. It shows that perhaps he is beginning to absorb some manners from somewhere . . . '

'Well really . . . I . . . '

'Now Ladies and Gentlemen, please' said the chairman. 'Can we get on without insults, please.'

Violet sat down. In his indignation he had forgotten the reason for his interruption.

Rachel continued. 'How far from the end of the road were they? Twenty metres?'

'Yes.'

'Right. The road is one hundred and fifty metres in length?'

'Yes.'

'You were half-way down it?'

'About.'

'So you were seventy-five metres from the far end of the road. The two men were twenty metres from the end of the road. They must have been about fifty metres from you. Yes?'

'I don't know.'

'With several parked cars in between?'

'Yes.'

'There are a number of large trees along the edge of the curb in Arbuthnot Street, aren't there, officer?'

'Yes. I believe there are.'

'And it makes it particularly difficult to see along the road and makes it particularly dark. Doesn't it?'

'As I said your worships. When the two defendants moved onto the next car they were right under a street light.'[32]

'So what happened then?'

'As soon as we saw they had opened the nearside front door we got out of our car and ran towards them and Police Constable Orange shouted, "Stop, police! You are under arrest".'

'Where did you each run?'

'I ran down the middle of the road.'

'Where did PC Orange run?'

'I didn't see.'

'Well, was he in the middle of the road?'

'He may have been, I don't know.'

'What happened then?'

'They both looked round and Blue shouted to Turquoise, "It's the Old Bill! Run, Terry". Then they both ran away.'

'Did you hope to catch these two men?'

'Of course, your worships.'

'Then why not wait until you'd caught them before shouting at them?'

'It wasn't me who shouted at them. I rather agree it was stupid to shout at them at that stage. I had a right go at PC Orange afterwards.'

'So what happened then?'

---

32 Rachel is manoeuvring the officer into a position where the evidence of Mr Ochre will have the greatest impact.

'By the time we got to them, they had gone down an alley. We searched it but we couldn't find them.'

'How long did you look for?'

'Perhaps ten minutes. We knew they had escaped fairly soon after we started looking.'

'Did you call for assistance from other officers?'

'No.'

'Why not?'

'There didn't seem any point.'

'What did you do then?'

'We went back to our car and continued patrolling.'

'For how long?'

'I think we were out for the rest of our shift. It was a quiet night other than that one incident.'

'So what time would it have been that you went back to the station?'

'I suppose about midnight. We went back for our break.'

'Did you check the cars you say they had been tampering with?'

'Yes, I expect we did.'

'What were the numbers of the cars?'

'I don't have any note of the numbers.'

'Did either of you take the numbers?'

'I don't know if PC Orange took them. I didn't.'

'Why not?'

'I didn't see any reason to take them.'

'What if something had been stolen from them?'

'Well, we looked in them and there didn't appear to be anything missing.'

'Officer, how can you tell if there is something missing from a car?'

'Well, put it this way, there hadn't been any time for the one who got the door open to get anything out and we didn't see that they were carrying anything when we were chasing them.'

'You must have walked straight past the cars on your way back to your car.'

'No. We went down to the end of the alleyway the defendants ran down and came out in Arbuthnot Street further up the road just by our car.'

'You drove off then?'

'Yes.'

'Did you turn round?'

'No, we just carried on up Arbuthnot Street.'

'So you drove past the two cars and could have got their numbers.'

'I suppose we could have done. I didn't consider it necessary.'

'One final question, officer. Without that street light, would it be fair to say that you wouldn't have been able to see the two defendants so as to recognise them when you saw them two weeks later in the High Street?'

'No.'

Rachel sat down and started writing up her notes. Violet rose to his feet.

14. The re-examination of PC Crimson

'I have just one or two questions in re-examination. Have you any doubt that the two men you saw in Arbuthnot Street were the two men you arrested in the High Street and who stand in the dock today?'[33]

Rachel sighed.

'No sir. None whatever.'

'How were you able to see them in Arbuthnot Street?'

'They both looked round in our direction at the first car and then again at the second car. Then when PC Orange shouted at them they looked round again and Blue shouted to Turquoise, "It's the Old Bill! Run, Terry". I had a good look at them.'

'Yes, thank you, officer. Do you or your colleagues have any questions, Madam?'

The chairman looked at the other magistrates. Mrs Beige leant forward and whispered in her ear.

'Yes . . . all right,' said the chairman. 'My colleague wonders what steps you took to try and find out who the two men were after the Arbuthnot Street incident, officer.'

'None,' said PC Crimson.

'Why not?'

'There didn't seem to be any steps we could take except wait until we saw the two men again. Which we did, your worships.'

'Yes, thank you officer.'

---

33 The prosecutor has no more right to lead his witness in re-examination than he has in evidence-in-chief, but Rachel feels it is more trouble to object than it is worth as the questions are of little significance.

'Madam, may this officer be released from the court so that he can return to his duties?'

'Yes, by all means.'

'Thank you your worships. I will remain, if I may.'

Police Constable Crimson sat down at the back of the court.

'Police Constable Orange, please, usher,' called Violet.

The usher left the court.

'Police Constable Orange . . . ' the usher could be heard shouting in the hall.

15. Police Constable Orange's evidence-in-chief

The door opened and a second police officer strode into the court. He made his way to the witness stand, leaping into it with a long stride. He raised the testament and announced the oath.

' . . . I am Orlando Orange, Police Constable four four five nine of the Metropolitan Police stationed at Heeling, your worships.'

'Officer,' said Violet. 'Were you on duty in Arbuthnot Street in Heeling on 22 April?'

'Yes, your worships, I was.'

'Do you wish to refer to any notes on what took place?'

'Yes, your worships, I do.'

'When did you make up those notes?'

'On return to the police station.'

'And when was that?'

'Oh, about an hour after the incident.'

'And were the matters still fresh in your mind?'

'Yes, your worships, they were.'

The chairman looked at the two defence advocates. 'Do you have any objections?'

Beryl Black stood up. 'No, madam. I have no objections.'

'I have no comment on them at this stage, your worship,' said Rachel.

'Officer, on 22 April you were in Arbuthnot Street. What happened?'

'Yes sir. Well at about 10 pm I was on duty in full uniform in a marked police vehicle with Police Constable Crimson. . . . '

'Officer, I must ask you to take your evidence a little slower, as there are various people taking notes of it,' said Mrs Yellow.

'Yes, your worships . . . we were driving down Arbuthnot Street. We saw a car parked on the nearside of the road . . . It was under a street light. On the offside of the car we saw a male . . . He was standing by the driver's door with his hand on the door handle which he was trying to open and on the nearside we saw another male standing with his hand on the front passenger door which he was trying to open . . . We stopped the police car and watched the two males . . . It was clear that neither door could be opened. The two males looked round them and then moved up the road to the next car . . . where they repeated the exercise . . . . This time the male on the nearside was able to open the front passenger door . . . Fearing that the car would suffer damage at their hands, we both got out of the police vehicle and started across the road . . . As we went I shouted, "Stop, police! You are under arrest." . . . At this the two males looked up and we were able to see their faces clearly. . . The male at the driver's door was the defendant Terry Turquoise and the male at the front passenger's door was the defendant Billie Blue, your worships . . . '

'How were you able to see their faces?'

'We were able to see their faces, your worships, because Arbuthnot Street is a well lit street . . . and . . . '

'Yes?'

'They were just under a street light at the time that they looked up from the second car and looked in our direction.'

'What happened then, officer?'

'As we made our way to them the defendants slammed the car doors and Blue shouted to Turquoise, "It's the Old Bill. Run, Terry." . . . Both of the men then made off down an alley at the side of the road and made good their escape.'

'Did you see them again?'

'No, your worships.'

'I mean did you see them again ever?'

'Oh yes. At about 11pm on 6 May I was in a marked police car with PC Crimson and Police Constable Percy Pink . . . PC Pink was driving the police car, your worships . . . We were driving down the High Street, Heeling when we saw Billie Blue and Terry Turquoise . . . PC Pink stopped the police car and we jumped out . . . PC Crimson shouted, "Stand still, you are under arrest for interfering with motor vehicles the other day." . . . Blue and Turquoise again made off up the road and turned into Doggett Road. PC Crimson and I pursued them . . . I caught Blue just after he had run into Doggett Road. I told Blue that I was arresting him . . . As I did so Blue threw a punch at my head . . . I ducked and the punch struck me on the helmet knocking the helmet off my head . . . I then

secured Blue and waited for PC Crimson who had run on past me
after Turquoise . . . PC Crimson then returned with Turquoise. Both
defendants were taken to Heeling Police Station, where they were
charged, making no reply after caution. That is my evidence, your
worships.'

'Thank you, officer. Just one final question. Have you any doubt
that the two men you arrested in the High Street were the same men
you saw in Arbuthnot Street on 22 April?'[34]

'None whatsoever, your worships.'

'Yes, thank you.'

Violet sat down.

16. Beryl's cross-examination of PC Orange

Beryl stood up.

'But officer, I thought you arrested my client in the side road . . .
Doggett Road?'

'Yes, that's right.'

'But you have just said that you have no doubt that the men you
saw in Arbuthnot Street were the ones you arrested in the High
Street?'

'A slip of the tongue, your worships. It was a mistake.'

'How much else in your evidence is a slip of the tongue?'

'None of it, your worships.'

'But you knew you had arrested him in the side road?'

'Yes, your worships. It was a mistake.'

'Your counsel said this question to you and you just agreed with
it, when you knew it wasn't right?'

'It was a mistake.'

'But you are prepared to agree with things even when you know
they are not true?'

'No.'

'But you did just now.'

Violet stood up. 'Look. I really must object. It doesn't seem that

---

34 This is a classic example of how an advocate can put his own witness in difficulty
by leading him. The witness assumes the question must be correct as it comes
from his side and so doesn't listen to it properly. The message is clear that he is
expected to agree with the question, so he does. The question has been prefaced
with an introduction that signals to the witness that the question is of little
significance and so the witness is even less on his guard . . .

there is any dispute as to where m'friend's client was arrested, is there?'

'That's not the point.'

'It seems to me to be very much the point.'

'The point is that this officer is prepared to say things that are not true.'[35]

The chairman intervened. 'I think we have the point, Miss Black. You can move on now.'

'Yes, Madam. Officer, it was pitch dark when you drove into Arbuthnot Street, wasn't it?'

'No, your worships. It was ten o'clock at night. There is good street lighting in the road.'

'But you couldn't possibly have seen the faces of men fifty metres away from you. Could you?'

'Fifty metres?'

'Well they were fifty metres away from you, weren't they?'

'No.'

'Well, Police Constable Crimson said that was the distance they were.'[36]

'I don't think they were that far away, your worships. They were certainly close enough for me to see their faces clearly.'

'A fleeting glance?'

'I beg your pardon.'

'A fleeting glance? That was all you got of them, a fleeting glance?'[37]

'No, your worships. The defendants turned towards us when they were at the first car and we saw their faces. When they were at the second car they turned towards us again. They were in the full beam of the street light and we got another good look at them. So much so that when I saw them again in the High Street, I immediately

---

35 It's quite a neat point, but Beryl ruins it by overdoing it.

36 It is an error to reveal to this witness what his colleague has said in his earlier evidence. Uncertainty for the witness is the life-blood of effective cross-examination.

37 Beryl is trying to pin the *Turnbull* test on the officer that a 'fleeting glance' is insufficient identification to support conviction without other evidence: *R v Turnbull* [1976] 3 WLR 445, CA, guideline (6). He would have to be very inexperienced or stupid to fall for a ploy like that. Beryl would do much better to coax time estimates from the officer and then try and convince the magistrates in her closing speech that the timings meant the view was a 'fleeting glance'.

recognised them. It was much more than a fleeting glance . . . much, much more.'

'Had you ever seen them before?'

Rachel muttered at Beryl in spite of herself, 'Steady. . . dangerous ground.'[38]

'No, your worships.'

Rachel breathed a sigh of relief.

'I must put it to you that you are completely mistaken and that you simply could not have recognised anyone again after looking at them for such a short time in the dark.'

'Are you asking me or telling me?'

'I am asking you.'

'Well the answer is that I am not mistaken . . . your worships.'

'I put it to you that the man you saw in Arbuthnot Street was not my client.'

'I am sorry, which one is your client?'

'Terry Turquoise.'

'Oh indeed he was. I remember the other man, Blue, shouting at him, "It's the Old Bill, Tel . . ." I believe your client is known as Tel.'

'And then you say you saw my client in the High Street? . . . the next time . . . on the 22 April?'

'I did see your client.'

'Yes . . . and you say that you chased him?'[39]

'No. I chased and caught Billie Blue, your worships.'

'Did you see my client hit Police Constable Crimson?'

'No, your worships, I was concentrating on securing Mr Blue.'

Beryl searched through her notes and turned briefly to look at Terry.[40] Finally she said, 'I have no more questions', and sat down.

17. Rachel's cross-examination of PC Orange

Rachel stood up and looked at the far wall for a time.

'Officer, what time was it that you drove into Arbuthnot Street?'

---

38 Rachel trusted herself to have assessed the dangers in asking a question like this, but not a novice. Advocates always trust themselves and not other advocates.

39 This form of recitation of the witness's evidence-in-chief does not amount to cross-examination. It elicits no information and does not put the witness under any pressure as he only has to agree or disagree.

40 Displaying to all clear signs of uncertainty and indecision.

'About ten o'clock, your worships.'

'What sort of vehicle were you in?'

'The area car, your worships.'

'How would you describe the road?'

'Arbuthnot Street or the roads generally?'

'Arbuthnot Street.'

'Well . . . it's a residential street, average width, with trees on each side . . . '

'Length?'

'I would say it's about three hundred metres long.'

'Lighting?'

'Yes. It's well lit.'

'How many lights?'

'I wouldn't know. But there are lights the usual distance apart.'

'Parked cars?'

'Yes. There were parked cars down each side. Not a lot but some.'

'How far had you gone down the street before you saw the men by the car?'

'I don't really know.'

'Give us some idea.'

'It's very hard.'

'Why?'

'Well it's some time ago now.'

'So that's the best you can do is it? It's very hard?'

'I suppose perhaps a quarter of the way down the road . . . something like that.'

'So about seventy-five metres down the street?'[41]

'I don't know about that.'

'Well, your estimate of the length of the road was three hundred metres. A quarter of the way down would be seventy five metres. Yes?'

'Perhaps.'

'Well, have you got a different measurement?'

'No.'

'When you stopped how far away from you were the two men . . . people[42] by the car?'

---

41 The aim of Rachel's cross-examination is to commit the officer to facts. The aim of the officer is to avoid committing himself.

42 This is a deliberate error to emphasise Rachel's view that if this incident took place the officers probably could not even see whether the suspects were male or female.

'It's hard to say.'

'Give their worships[43] an estimate.'

'I don't think I can.'

'You are telling this court that although you say you could see their faces, you are unable to give any estimate of any sort of how far they were away from you. Is that what you are saying, officer?'[44]

'I suppose they were between twenty and forty metres from us.'

'On which side of the road?'

'Who?'

'You and the men. Which side of the road were each of you?'[45]

'We stopped on the nearside and the men were on the far side.'[46]

'What sort of car were you in?'

'I don't recollect now.'

'Were you in uniform?'

'Yes.'

'What sort of police vehicle have you and PC Crimson used together during this year? And if you can't help us, we can always bring your operations Chief Inspector to court this afternoon to tell us.'[47]

'I am fairly sure it was the area car we were using that night.'

'Describe the area car to us.'

'Describe it?'

43 An ironic use of the officer's technique.

44 A quick summary to show how absurd the cumulative effect of the officer's refusal to remember has become. The aim is to shame the officer into an answer.

45 It is essential that these questions are 'sterile'. Lax wording in the notebooks has left the officers vulnerable on this issue. The officer is searching the questions to see what answer Rachel seems to be expecting. Orange knows it is likely that PC Crimson has already given an answer on this point. He does not know what that answer was. If he can identify what Crimson said he can give an answer that is likely to be safe. His best chance of finding out is from the phrasing of the advocate's questions, if the advocate is incautious and fails to deploy 'sterile questions'.

46 Rachel deliberately gives the officer no indication as to whether this is a safe answer or not. She goes straight on to another topic. The officer is left in a state of uncertainty and therefore vulnerable in further cross-examination.

47 Rachel knew that Orange was pretending not to remember what sort of car he was driving. Police officers avoid any involvement by senior officers in cases of this sort. It was easier to answer the question correctly than to run the risk that this was not a bluff. In fact the type of car was not sufficiently important to disrupt the trial with the effort required to identify the operations chief inspector and bring him to court.

'Yes.'

'Well it's a Rover saloon . . . it's white with police markings.'

'Does it have orange stripes down the side and an emergency blue beacon unit on the roof?'

'Yes.'

'It would have been hard not to notice such a car stopping in the street twenty to forty metres from you, wouldn't it?'

'They may have been further from us than that.'

'How far?'

'Now I come to think it over carefully, I think that they may have been as far as sixty to seventy metres from us.'

'OK. What were they wearing?'

'I don't recollect.'

'Didn't you make a note of their descriptions that night?'

'No.'

'Did you see what they were wearing when you saw them that night?'

'I don't believe I did. At least not clearly.'

'Did you transmit an alert to other officers about these two when they had escaped from you?'

'I don't remember.'

'I understand that police radio messages are taped at New Scotland Yard. Perhaps we could check.'

'Yes. I don't think we did radio any message about them.'

'What? Two persons committing crime had escaped from arrest after a chase and you didn't even mention them to the other officers in the area?'

'They hadn't escaped from arrest. We hadn't been able to arrest them.'

'I thought that you had shouted at them, "Stop, police! You are under arrest."'

'Oh yes. I am sorry, your worships. I had indeed arrested them.'

'But no message about them to other officers over the radio?'

'I don't think so.'

'That seems very strange. Is it because this incident never happened?'

'No, indeed the incident did happen as I've described it. It may be that there were no other officers in the area that night, your worships.'

'But you didn't check.'

'I don't remember, your worships.'

'Did you complete a crime report about the incident?'

'No. I don't believe I did.'

'Why not?'

'Well the other officer . . . Police Constable Crimson may have done.'

'But it was your arrest.'

'Yes. But it still may have been he who completed the report.'

'So far as you know, did anyone complete a crime report?'

'Not so far as I know, no.'

'It should have been, shouldn't it?'

'Yes. It should have been. It may have been.'

'But not by you.'

'No.'

'Did you check whether the collator at the police station knew any local called Tel?'[48]

'No.'

'Going back to Arbuthnot Street, you say now that they were about seventy metres from you when they were at the first car.'

'Yes.'

'What did you see them do?'

'They were trying the car door handles.'

'Where were you when you saw them do that?'

'We were stopped by the road side.'

'Well, why did you stop then?'

'Stop? We stopped because we saw them behaving suspiciously by the car.'

'What were they doing?'

'Trying the handles.'

'But you have just said you were already stopped when you saw them trying the door handles.'

'Yes?'

'Well what made you stop?'

'We saw them behaving suspiciously.'

'What did you see them doing?'

'It's hard to say, your worships. Sometimes when you are on

---

48 This is an extraordinarily dangerous question to have asked. The officer might well have given an answer that showed that Terry Turquoise had criminal convictions. Terry Turquoise was not Rachel's client. Rachel was taking a risk. It may be that she assessed from the way the officer was giving evidence that it was not a danger in the circumstances. However the little advantage, if any, that the point gave her did not really outweigh the risk or the discourtesy in trespassing on Beryl's territory.

patrol you see people you think are behaving suspiciously so you stop and watch them. Sometimes they then commit a crime and sometimes they don't. It's what policing is all about, your worships.'[49]

'Yes, officer. But when I asked you what the suspicious behaviour was you said it was trying car door handles. Yet you also said you were already stopped and watching them when they tried the car door handles.'[50]

'Well the position is, your worships, that we saw them behaving in a suspicious manner . . . how I cannot really now say . . . we stopped and then they tried the door handles.'

'Ah, so they waited until the police had arrived and were sitting watching them before carrying out the crime?'

Violet leaped up. 'I object to that remark. It is comment and not a question.' Mrs Yellow looked at Rachel and nodded. 'Yes, I think it was, Miss Red.'

'Did you have your lights on?' Rachel resumed.

'I don't know. I think we had only had the side lights on anyway. I don't know if PC Crimson turned them off when we stopped.'

'Which doors were they trying?'

PC Crimson looked at his notebook. 'I wasn't able to see which man was at which door at this stage.'

'What happened then?'

'They moved on to the next car.'

'Going in which direction?'

'Moving away from us.'

'How far away was this next car from you?'

'It was just beyond the first car, so it was probably about sixty-five to seventy-five metres from us.'

'On which side of the road?'

'On the same side as the first car.'

'Which side was that? I'm sorry.'

'On the . . . on the left side . . . our nearside.'

Rachel turned round quickly just in time to see PC Crimson with

---

49 This is a creditable 'bale out' answer. Rachel deals with it by dragging the witness back to what he originally said.

50 Rachel has overdone this point. The officer manages to get off the hook quite neatly in his next answer.

his left arm draped over the back of the seat next to him. He quickly put his arm to his side.[51]

'Earlier on in your evidence you said that the men were by a car on the other side of the road from where you were stopped. Why have you changed your evidence?'

'Did I say that? I'm sorry I must have been mistaken.'

'Did the fact that PC Crimson had his left arm raised over the back of the chair next to him help you to correct your mistake, officer?'

'No. Certainly not.'

'So you saw that PC Crimson had his left arm raised, officer?'

'No. I didn't, your worships. I was not looking at PC Crimson.'

The clerk stood up and spoke to the chairman.

'Yes, we agree, Madam Clerk.' Mrs Yellow looked at PC Crimson. 'Officer, we think it would be better if you sat entirely still so that there can be no further misunderstandings.'

Violet stood up. 'If there is any problem, it might be better if the officer waited outside the court.'

'I believe you have another officer outside waiting to give evidence,' said Rachel.

'Er yes. That's true.'

'In which case either PC Crimson stays in court or he leaves the building entirely.'

Violet glowered at Crimson and then sat down. Rachel turned back to the witness.

'So which side of the road were the two men?'

'On the same side as we were.'

'So how did you get to them?'

'We just ran down the road.'

'The same side?'

'Yes.'

'Officer, could you read out what you have written in your notes at this point.'

'In my notes?'

'Yes.'

---

51 If an advocate is concentrating, it is not difficult for the advocate to sense when the witness's attention has been drawn to an unusual part of the courtroom. Crimson should have sat still. His quick movement of his arm off the back of the chair was an involuntary and highly suspicious reaction to Rachel turning and looking at him.

'Where?'

'At the point where you say you went towards the two men.'

There was a pause.

'Yes, I've done that.'

'Now read that passage out loud, please.'

'It says . . . "Fearing that the car would suffer damage at their hands, we both got out of the police vehicle and started across the road . . ." '[52]

'Yes. You've written "started across the road" . . . now you say you didn't have to cross the road.'

'I don't think I meant in my notes that we crossed the road.'

'But you've written " started across the road". Doesn't that mean you crossed the road?'

'I don't read it that way.'

'What do you say that passage "started across the road" means?'

'I take it to mean we ran down the road. That's what I meant when I wrote it.'

'I suggest you have just made that up to try and explain the major discrepancy between what you have said in evidence just now and what you said in your notes and in your evidence-in-chief.'

'No.'[53]

'Officer, what happened then?'

'At the second car, they were under a street light so we were able to get a good look at the two of them when they looked round. The male at the driver's door was the defendant Terry Turquoise and the male at the front passenger's door was the defendant Billie Blue.'

'Which way was this car facing?'

'In the same direction we were facing.'

'Were there any other parked cars on this side of the road?'

'Yes, there were. We were, however, able to see in spite of those cars because the road is slightly crescent-shaped.'[54]

'And what happened?'

'The male at the front passenger door, Terry Turquoise, opened the door he was trying.'

---

52 It is an infinitely more telling technique to make the witness read the target passage from his notes than for the advocate to call for the note book and read it out. The witness will often sound reluctant and hesitant.

53 That is as far as the point can be taken in cross-examination without losing the sympathy and interest of the magistrates. The witness has made a major mistake which should substantially damage his credibility.

54 The witness is trying to anticipate possible cross-examination.

'Yes?'

'We then got out of the police car and ran towards them. As we got near them I shouted, "Stop, police! You are under arrest."'

'Where were you when you shouted that?'

'Quite close to them. Nearly up to them.'

'But why shout at all if you were trying to catch them? Why warn them you were coming?'

'They could see us coming. I wanted them to know we were police and to stay there . . . not to run off . . . escape.'

'But if you shout at them something that tells them you are police, they are more likely to run off, aren't they?'

'Not necessarily.'

'How close to them were you when you say you shouted at them?'

'I don't remember.'

'Well officer, you were either so close that they couldn't get away, which would seem the sensible time to shout . . . in which case how did they escape? . . . or you were sufficiently far away for your warning to have given them ample time to escape, which seems somewhat absurd. One of those must be so, mustn't it? . . . which?'

'Well, your worships . . . they escaped . . . I can't say whether I shouted too soon or too late.'

'What do you mean too late?'

'Obviously I shouted too soon . . . as they did escape.'

'How do you explain that?'

'They nipped down an alley that I did not know existed. It took us a little time to find it and once we had, they had gone.'

'Weren't you immediately behind them?'

'No. I would say we were about thirty metres behind them.'

'Doesn't that mean you were thirty metres away when you shouted at them, perhaps further away as you were already running and they had to build up speed?'

'I don't think I was that far away when I shouted at them.'

'What did PC Crimson think of you shouting out like that?'

'I don't know what he thought.'

'Did he say anything about it?'

'When?'

'At any time.'

'Not that I can recollect.'

'So they ran from you and at first you couldn't find where they had gone?'

'That's correct.'

'Did you have any clues as to their identities?'

'No, none at all.'

'How long were you out of your car for?'

'I should think about ten minutes.'

'When you got to the spot, where did you find the two had gone?'

'Up an alleyway.'

'What did you do?'

'Well, we looked up and down the alleyway and then we went back to our car and drove on.'

'Did you report what you were up to over the radio?'

'I don't remember.'

'Could you give us the numbers of the two cars the suspects were interfering with please?'[55]

'I don't have a note of them.'

'Did you make any sort of record of the numbers of the cars you say they were interfering with that night?'

'I may have done.'

'If you did, what did you do with that record?'

'I don't remember.'

'Did you check the cars?'[56]

'I believe we did on our way back to our car.'

'What did you find?'

'The car we had seen the defendants at before they ran off was indeed unlocked.'

'So what did you do?'

'We locked it and left it.'

'Did you find out from your control room who the registered owner was?'

'I don't believe we did.'

'Why not?'

'Well, we had made the car secure and we did not think that anything had been taken from it, so it did not seem necessary.'

'How could you be sure that nothing had been taken from it?

---

55 Rachel knows that he does not have the numbers. It is an effective technique to assume that something has been done, particularly if, as in this case, it would have been done if the prosecution was an honest one.

56 Rachel could have asked the officer to describe in detail what he did rather than go straight to the point. Clearly she felt that the points to be made following on from the officer saying he had checked the cars were good ones so as to make it worthwhile prompting the officer into saying that he had checked them rather than trapping him into admitting that he had not.

Surely if this had really happened you would have tried to contact the owner and warn him.'

'No, not necessarily.'

'What if the man opening the passenger door had had the opportunity to remove a wallet with credit cards? Surely you would have taken a substantial risk in not notifying the owner.'

'I didn't see it that way.'

'What other cars did you check?'

'Just the two.'

'But, officer, you had arrived to find these two, as you say, 'behaving suspiciously'. That must raise the possibility that they had been in other cars before you arrived . . . If what you are telling this court is correct . . . Didn't you check to see if that had happened?'

'No, your worships. We did not think that likely.'

Rachel felt that this point could not be taken further but wanted it to sink in with the magistrates. She leafed through her notebook shaking her head for a few seconds.

'When did you write up your notes about this incident?'

'About an hour later in the canteen back at Heeling police station.'

'Does it surprise you that your evidence-in-chief is virtually word for word the same as PC Crimson's evidence?'

'No, your worships. We wrote our notes together.'

'Why did you do that?'

'It is the usual way to write up notes.'

'Yes. I understand that. But how did your two sets of notes come to be identical?'

'I don't think they are identical.'

'Well where you did something your notes say "I" and PC Crimson gives your name and vice-versa. Am I right?'

'Yes.'

'So with that reservation your notes are identical. Yes?'

'Possibly. I haven't seen PC Crimson's notebook.'

'Well, take it from me that his evidence was identical to yours and he read his evidence out of his notebook just as you have. So how did that happen?'

'Well, we made sure that we had the same details correct of what had happened.'

'So it was a pooled recollection?'

'I suppose it was.'

'So the account contained things that you had remembered and things that PC Crimson had remembered?'

'Yes . . . maybe.'

'So it follows, doesn't it, that the account in your notebook contains things you didn't remember and PC Crimson's notebook contains things that you had remembered but that he hadn't?'

'No. My notebook contains only what I remembered.'

'But there are things in PC Crimson's notebook that only you remembered?'

'No, I don't think so.'

'Officer, surely the result of producing a pooled recollection is that the standard account will contain recollections of the persons contributing to the pool.'

'I don't know what you mean.'

'Well it comes to this, doesn't it? You and PC Crimson got together and decided what you were going to say in evidence and wrote it up in your notebooks. And the evidence you have given today is not what you really remember as happening that night but is simply a reading of the notes you two made up.'

'No.'

'Well, can I put it to you that you did not see anyone interfering with motor vehicles in Arbuthnot Street that night?'

'I beg your pardon?'

'You have made up this account of seeing two men interfering with cars in Arbuthnot Street on 22 April.'

'I resent that suggestion.'

'I am sure you do. It's true nevertheless, isn't it?'

'No.'

'What's more you didn't even write your notebook that night as you have claimed.'

'I did, your worships.'

'All right, officer. Please read out the first reference in your notebook to the defendants by name.'[57]

'One moment, your worships . . . "At this the two males looked up and we were able to see their faces clearly. The male at the driver's door was the defendant Terry Turquoise and the male at the front passenger's door was the defendant Billie Blue . . . "'

'Is that exactly what you have written in your notebook, officer?'

---

57 Rachel has had the questions that follow carefully planned following the questioning of PC Crimson over the spelling of Turquoise in his notes.

'That is what I saw, your worships.'

'Is that exactly what you have written in your notebook?'

'That is what I saw.'

'Officer. I am asking you to read out the first reference in your notebook to the defendants by name.'

'I don't understand, your worships. That is how it is written.'

'May I see your notebook please, officer?'[58]

'Yes.' The usher collected the notebook and took it to Rachel who examined it briefly and handed it back to the usher.

'Officer, please read out the first reference in your notebook to the defendants by name and please read it out word for word.'

'" . . . at this the two males looked up and we were able to see their faces clearly. The male at the driver's door was a man I now know to be Terry Turquoise and the male at the front passenger's door a man I now know to be Billie Blue . . . "'

'Thank you, officer, at last. Now could you please explain to their worships how you came when you wrote your notebook to describe the first man as "a man I now know to be Terry Turquoise" and the second man as "a man I now know to be Billie Blue" when at no time during that night did you have the first idea who they were?'[59]

There was a long pause while the officer stared at his notebook.

'I can't.'

'Is it because your evidence is a fabrication from start to finish, officer?'

'No.'[60]

'All right, let's move on to 6 May, then. On that night you saw the two defendants in the High Street on the pavement. That's correct, isn't it?'

'Yes.'

'And you formed the view that they either had been or were

58 Rachel tries to cross-examine without asking to see an officer's notebook. Sometimes however it is unavoidable. Calling for a notebook is in itself a declaration of the officer's lack of honesty. It if turns out there is no point to be made on the notebook, the advocate loses ground.

59 Rachel, having identified this coup, had the problem of whether to use it at the end of the cross-examination or at some other stage. She decided to use it here, at the end of her cross-examination on the first incident in the expectation of discrediting the officer's remaining evidence and unnerving him.

60 Although this is a devastating point, there is nothing more that can be said in cross-examination. It is a matter for strong comment in Rachel's closing speech.

actually interfering with motor vehicles . . . cars . . . in the High
Street . . . that night. Correct?'

'No.'

'Which way were you travelling?'

'We were going east to west down the High Street.'

'And what were they doing?'

'They were walking along the pavement.'

'Which side?'

'On our nearside.'

'Which direction were they going in?'

'In the same direction as us . . . east to west.'

'In his opening, Mr Violet told the court that they were walking
towards you. Which of you is correct, officer?'[61]

'My recollection is that they were walking in the same direction,
your worships.'

'What happened?'

'We recognised them and stopped the police car.'

'How far were you from them when you recognised them?'

'I don't know. I or PC Crimson told PC Pink to stop the car and
he stopped it just behind them.'

'How far from them?'

'Not far. Perhaps ten metres.'

'Why not alongside them?'

'I think there were parked cars.'

'So if PC Pink stopped the police vehicle[62] at a point ten metres
behind them, after you had told him to stop, you must have decided
that it was necessary to stop at a point perhaps twenty metres plus
behind them . . . allowing for the time to make the decision . . . tell
PC Pink to stop . . . PC Pink to apply the brakes . . . the vehicle to
stop?'

'I don't know.'

'So why did you decide to stop?'

'We recognised them.'

'How did you do that?'

'I think they must have looked round at us.'

---

61 A telling point. This is why it is essential to listen carefully to the prosecutor's
opening address and to take a full note of it.

62 This officer is skilled at disrupting cross-examination by 'misunderstanding' the
question. It is therefore essential that important questions are put without any
possible ambiguity, hence: 'PC Pink stopped the police vehicle' and not 'He
stopped the car'.

'What, both of them?'

'I think so, yes.'

'They both looked round at the same time?'

'I suppose they must have, yes.'

'Why do you think they did that?'

'I don't know, perhaps they realised there was a police car behind them and they had guilty consciences.'

'But there was traffic in the High Street, wasn't there?'

'Yes.'

'So how could they tell a car was a police car?'

'I don't know. Perhaps they were looking behind them a lot after what they had done on 22 April.'

'Oh I see. It's your thesis that they spent the following two weeks walking around looking over their shoulders in case you were following them?'

'Why not? They did run away, didn't they?'

'Which one did you recognise?'

'I recognised both of them.'

'You recognised both of them from Arbuthnot Street?'

'Yes.'

'And PC Crimson did the same?'

'I don't know who he recognised.'

'But you wrote up identical notes. When you were writing up your notes you must have told each other that you both recognised both of them.'

'I don't know what PC Crimson wrote in his notes.'

'Yes, you do. He wrote exactly the same thing as you wrote in your notes.'

Violet stood up. 'Madam, I must object. I cannot see how it can be right to question this officer on what another officer wrote in his notebook.'

The chairman looked at Rachel. 'Well Miss Red? It seems to us a rather compelling objection.'

'Your worships, if we were dealing with two witnesses who had committed to note form their own unadulterated recollection, I would agree with you wholeheartedly and I would not have dreamt of following this line of questioning. In fact we are dealing with a very different situation. In this case these two officers have sat down and put together an account to give to this court in evidence-in-chief. Each officer has then written into his notebook his version of this account. These two accounts are identical except for the necessary variations to allow for the fact that one is being presented to the court by one officer and the other by the other officer. It is my case that this account is almost wholly false and is certainly designed to mislead this court. At the very least there must be features of the account that were put in by the other witness. If that is so, this officer is giving evidence about matters that are not part of his recollection. However I do not think that the question I have put needs to be taken any further, so I will move on.'

'Thank you Miss Red.'

Violet grunted irritably and sat down.[63]

'What were they doing when you saw them?'

'Walking along the pavement.'

'And what were they doing when you stopped?'

'Walking along the pavement.'

'What happened?'

'What when we stopped?'

'Yes.'

PC Orange looked at this notebook. 'I shouted, "Stand still, you are under arrest for interfering with motor vehicles the other day." Blue and Turquoise again made off up the road and turned into Doggett Road. PC Crimson and I pursued them.'

'How far were you from the corner of the High Street and Doggett Road when you got out of the car?'

'I don't know.'

'Give the court some sort of estimate.'

'I really can't remember.'

'You are unable to give any sort of estimate to the court?'

'I suppose somewhere between twenty and thirty metres, your worships.'

'When did the defendants start running?'

'When we got out of the car.'

'Was it clear that they were running away from you?'

'Oh yes.'

'How far in front of you were they when you started running after them?'

---

63 Rachel has used Violet's objection to put a major defence point to the magistrates. Provided the magistrates are bright and alert, and Rachel has put it well enough, the magistrates will now have this criticism of the officers' notebooks in the forefront of their mind. Violet knows that his objection has been exploited in this way and wishes he hadn't made it. Opportunities to put features of the defence case to the magistrates are likely to crop up in unexpected ways like this throughout the trial. Rachel tries to be ready for them.

'Not far, perhaps ten metres.'

'Surely if you shouted at them, you would have just shouted something like "Stop police!"?'

'I did.'

'Yes, but you say you shouted out about interfering with motor vehicles the other day.'

'Yes. I shouted that as well.'

'They were already running by then.'

'No. I don't believe they were. I think that I shouted that at them and then they started running.'

'So you are saying that until you mentioned interfering with motor vehicles the defendants showed no signs of running away?'

Violet started to rise to his feet. He was about to object to Rachel putting words in the officer's mouth, which she certainly was, when the officer said, 'Yes.'

'If your evidence about the incident in Arbuthnot Street had been true and you did shout that before they started running as you claim and they had heard it, you must have known that on past form they would run away. Isn't that so?'

'I don't follow you.'

'Isn't it police practice, and a very sensible practice it seems to me, to make sure that you are as close to a suspect as possible and in a position to secure them before revealing to the suspect what he is suspected of doing and that you are arresting him?'

'It is not always that easy to secure a suspect, as the defendants showed on the two occasions.'[64]

'That is not quite the point. The two men had no reason to know that you were the officers who had chased them on 22 April, even on your account. Correct?'

'They may have done.'

'But you had no reason to believe that they would know you were the same officers.'

---

64 It is a common technique for deflecting an awkward question to direct the answer to an unimportant detail of the question rather than the real sting. The hope is that the advocate will be satisfied by this answer and forget that the central question has not been answered. It is to counter this sort of tactic that it is necessary for the advocate to keep in mind the central question and repeat it in the same form until it has been fully dealt with and ruthlessly to avoid being side-tracked by the diversionary answer. Repeating the question in exactly the same words emphasises to the court the advocate's view that the witness has not answered the question.

'That may be right, your worships.'

'If you had simply approached them and then when you were face to face with them told them you were arresting them and why, they might not have been able to run away. Isn't that right?'

'Yes, but they might still have run away.'

'Yes, but by shouting at them with the information as to why you wanted to speak to them and that you were arresting them . . . if you did, you were making it almost certain that they would run away. Weren't you?'

'I don't see the point.'

'The point is, officer, that your account is not truthful. It is inconceivable that you as a police officer would have shouted out, in the way that you claim, that you were arresting them and the reason for the arrest before you had got as close to them as you could without alarming them into running away. That is why your account simply cannot be true.'

'Your worships. I do not understand what Miss Red is getting at.'[65]

'What she is saying, officer,' said Mrs Yellow, 'is that you would normally not have shouted out at a suspect that you were arresting him until you came up to him.'

'In normal circumstances that is probably right, your worships.'

'So what is different here?'

'I didn't want them to walk off, your worships.'

'I don't follow that. You did precisely what was most likely to cause them to walk off as you say . . . or so you claim.'

'I don't agree. I expected them to stop and allow me to speak to them.'

'Very well . . . What happened then, officer?' said Rachel.[66]

PC Orange turned to his notes. 'Blue and Turquoise again made off up the road and turned into Doggett Road. PC Crimson and I pursued them. I caught Blue just after he had run into Doggett Road. I told Blue that I was arresting him. As I did so, Blue threw a punch at my head. I ducked and the punch struck me on the helmet, knocking the helmet off my head. I then secured Blue and waited

---

65 Which of course is not true. He simply cannot see how to get round it.
66 Rachel has made as much as she can of the point without boring the magistrates and causing the point to tell against her.

for PC Crimson who had run on past me after Turquoise. PC Crimson then returned with Turquoise.'[67]

'How far into Doggett Road did you catch Billie Blue?'

'I suppose it was about twenty metres.'

'Where was PC Crimson while you were running after Billie Blue?'

'He was just behind me.'

'How far?'

'I don't really know. I didn't look back.'

'Was Billie Blue running fast?'

'Not as fast as I was, your worships.'

Violet chuckled loudly.

'But as fast as he could?'

'I expect so, your worships.'

'What happened when you grabbed him?'

'He tried to punch me in the face, your worships.'

'But he was going fast. You were going fast. When you grabbed him you could not have just stopped immediately.'

'I think we did.'

'It is more likely that you ran for a distance holding him while you slowed him down.'

'No. He stopped and turned and punched at me.'

'And what did PC Crimson do?'

'He ran on after the other defendant, Turquoise, your worships.'

'Where did you get hold of Billie Blue?'

'In Doggett Road, your worships.'

'Where on his body?'

'By the collar at the back of his neck, your worships.'

'What happened to that hold?'

'I maintained the hold until he had calmed down and I then took him by the arm.'

'Could you describe what happened after you had taken hold of his collar?'

'Yes, your worships. I told Blue that I was arresting him. As I did

---

67 The officer, whenever he can, gives evidence from his notes. He reads the narrative as far as possible in the hope that this will carry the cross-examination to the point where he stops reading. Rachel ignores this and takes the narrative back to where she had got to.

so Blue threw a punch at my head. I ducked and the punch struck me on the helmet knocking the helmet off my head.'

'What did you say to Billie Blue when you arrested him?'

'I said, "I am arresting you for interfering with motor vehicles."'

'Didn't you say to him, "Got you, you bastard . . . you're fucking nicked"?'

'Er no, your worships. That is not the way I would arrest a member of the public.'

'When you say he punched at you, did you let go of him?'

'No, your worships.'

'Did he try and strike you again?'

'No, your worships.'

'What did you do?'

'Nothing, your worships. He very quickly calmed down.'

'Did you say anything to him?'

'I may well have uttered an unguarded expletive, your worships.'

'Didn't you tell him why he was being arrested?'

'Yes, your worships. I told him I was arresting him for interfering with motor vehicles.'

'Didn't you give him more information than that about the offence?'

'I had already told him that as I got out of the car.'

'But you couldn't have been sure that he heard that and took it in, could you?'

'Yes, your worships. That was why he ran away.'

'But once you had secured him and he had calmed down, didn't you tell him why he was being arrested?'

'All I did further was to caution him.'

'Is that in your notes?'

'No, your worships.'

'Why not?'

'It was an oversight, your worships.'

'At the time did you consider that Billie Blue had assaulted you?'

'Yes.'

'Why didn't you arrest him for that offence as well?'

'I didn't consider it necessary.'

'But you are under an obligation to arrest a suspect for every offence he has committed, are you not?'

'Yes.'

'And you didn't arrest him for assaulting you?'

'No.'

'Did you ever arrest him for assaulting you?'[68]

'No, your worships.'

'How did you get them to Heeling Police Station?'

'In the van, your worships.'

'How long was it before the van arrived?'

'Not long, your worships, perhaps a couple of minutes.'

'Was there any conversation during that time about why they had been arrested?'

'Not that I recollect, your worships.'

'Did you hear PC Crimson say to Terry Turquoise as he brought him up to you, "I saw you in that car, you dirty little thief."?'

'I don't remember him saying that.'

'Do you remember Terry Turquoise answering him and saying, "I weren't in no car. We've just come out of the pub. We were just going for some chips"?'

'No, he didn't say that, your worships.'

'Was there any conversation as to what they had done that evening?'

'Who, your worships?'

'Billie Blue and Terry Turquoise.'

'I didn't hear any.'

'Did you ask them why they had run away?'

'No, your worships. It was obvious why they had run away. It was because they knew we had recognised them from the incident in Arbuthnot Street.'

'I suggest to you that that is exactly what PC Crimson did say to Terry Turquoise . . . he said, "Why did you run away?", and Terry Turquoise said, "Just for a laugh." Isn't that right?'

'No, your worships.'

'And then you said, "So you just run for a laugh?" Isn't that what you said?'

'No, your worships.'

'And then Billie Blue said, "Yeah honest, it was just for a laugh. We haven't touched no car." Didn't he say that, officer?'

'No, your worships.'

---

68 While this is in a way a telling point, the fact is that neither common assault nor assaulting a police officer under the Police Act 1964 s51 is an arrestable offence. On the other hand there is a parallel provision under a Metropolitan Police Act which creates an offence of assaulting a constable in the execution of his duty in London and carries a power of summary arrest.

'And PC Crimson then said, "Well you're both fucking nicked anyway." Didn't he say that?'

'No, your worships.'

'And Billie Blue said, "Well which car are we meant to have been in?" Didn't he say that?'

'No, your worships.'

'And you then said, "Just you shut up. We'll sort that out down the nick." Didn't you say that?'

'No, your worships.'

'And Billie Blue then said to you, "No. If you say we were in a car, you show us which car we were in and see if it's open." Didn't he say that?'

'No, your worships.'

'And you and the other officer said, "Just shut up and get in the panda". Didn't you say that?'

'No, your worships. We had arranged for them to be taken to the station in the van.'

'But both Billie Blue and Terry Turquoise kept saying, "No, if you say we were in a car, you show us which one." So you said, "We'll have to get the van." Isn't that what was said?'[69]

'No, your worships. We had arranged for them to go to the station in the van. We were not in a panda. We were in the area car and there was not enough room for the three of us and two prisoners. In any case, we would not take two prisoners in the area car in these circumstances.'

'Was there a crowd around the four of you?'

'There were a number of people, yes. I think they were pleased to see that we had arrested two persons who had been interfering with cars. It is a very troublesome offence for the residents of Heeling, your worships.'

'Did Billie Blue and Terry Turquoise start shouting at the crowd asking them to try the car doors and see if any of them were open? And did several of the crowd start trying car doors finding that none of them were open? Is that what happened?'

'Not so far as I am concerned. There was no question of cars being interfered with that evening. We were solely concerned with

---

69 It is not technically required to put the defence case to the prosecution witnesses in any form in summary proceedings. However it is essential that the magistrates are told the defence case in detail as soon as possible. This is the earliest opportunity to do this.

the offences committed in Arbuthnot Street on 22 April, your worships.'

'Well, officer, can I put it to you that until you got to Heeling police station, so far as you were concerned the only offence you thought Billie Blue might have committed was in the High Street, that night. Isn't that right?'

'No, your worships.'

'Officer, what happens to an arrested person on arrival at a police station?'

'He is put before the custody sergeant, your worships.'

'And then?'

'The custody sergeant decides what steps to take with that person, your worships.'

'On the basis of what information?'

'The information given him by the arresting officer.'

'And is there a document completed with that information?'

'Yes, your worships. The custody record.'

'Is it right that the custody sergeant is a sergeant who spends his shift solely dealing with the prisoners in the station?'

'I believe so. Not being a sergeant I have no direct experience of the job, your worships.'

'So his only source of information about what a prisoner has been arrested for is the arresting officer?'[70]

'Possibly, your worships.'

'Well, could the custody sergeant have obtained information about Billie Blue from anyone else?'

'Probably not, your worships.'

'Would you look at this document, officer.'

The usher took the document Rachel was holding out and took it over to PC Orange, who looked at it as if it was a copy of the Sheehy Report.

'What is that, officer?'

'It appears to be a copy of Mr Blue's custody record.'

'Whose handwriting is it in?'

'It has my signature in one place. Otherwise it appears to be in the custody sergeant's writing.'

---

70 To obtain maximum impact for the content of the custody record, Rachel has to make sure that the magistrates appreciate exactly what the custody record is. Rachel does this by making the officer desribe the custody reception procedure in his evidence. He does this reluctantly.

'In the top left corner there is a box marked "reasons for arrest"?'

'Yes. It says. "Interference with motor vehicles".'

'Who would have given the custody sergeant that information?'

'Me.'

'If you turn over to the second page there is a narrative section beginning . . . well could you read it out please, officer?'[71]

'It says . . . "Relevant time begins 12.04. DP arrested interfering with motor vehicle, chased and arrested."'

'What decisions does the custody sergeant have to make?'

'He has to decide whether to detain the arrested person pending charging or not.'

'Well, isn't it that he has to decide whether there is enough evidence to charge the person for the offences for which he has been arrested?'

'Yes.'

'Doesn't that entry sound as if the custody sergeant thought Billie Blue had been arrested for interfering with motor vehicles just before his arrest?'

'No.'

'It says DP (which I take to be detained person) "arrested interfering with motor vehicles". Doesn't that mean that he was arrested while interfering with motor vehicles?'

'No. It means arrested after interfering with motor vehicles.'

'That's how you read it, is it?'

'Yes.'

'Well perhaps the court will see it in another light . . . Did you interview Billie Blue?'

'No.'

'Why not?'

'I wasn't told to.'

'Did you not decide to interview him on your own initiative?'

'No.'

'But look, it was decided to charge him with theft. Correct?'

---

71 Where a telling point is expected from a document it is more effective to require the witness to read out the passage than for the advocate to read it to him. However the witness reads it and however innocent the passage, it is likely to sound shifty. On occasions the witness will read it out incorrectly in order to conceal some feature. This will usually show in the witness's voice and the witness can be further discredited by requiring him to read it as many times as are required before he reads it correctly.

'Yes.'

'At no time had you put to Billie Blue that he had been stealing from cars on 22 April, did you?'

'Yes.'

'But not face-to-face in a form where you could see what he had to say about it . . . and you had not used the expression "theft". You had simply said "interfering with motor vehicles" . . . you didn't say "theft".'

'No.'

'Did it not occur to you that he might be entitled to have the specific allegation put to him and a record made of what he had to say about it?'

'I conferred with the custody sergeant and he did not think it necessary to interview him.'

'Is that because the custody officer thought that the vehicle interference had taken place at the time of Billie Blue's arrest, as he has recorded in the custody record?'

Violet stood up. 'I object to that question. The officer specifically stated that he did not think the entry in the custody record said that.'

'Well, I've made the point. I don't require the officer to answer the question. Officer, what in fact happened is this . . . you for some reason thought that Billie Blue and Terry Turquoise had been interfering with motor vehicles that night in the High Street. Isn't that correct?'

'No, your worships.'

'You chased them and caught them and accused them of being in a car, which they hotly denied. That's correct isn't it?'

'No, your worships.'

'When they were initially at the police station you were still accusing them of interfering with motor vehicles that same night in the High Street. That's correct isn't it?'

'No, your worships.'

'You then decided to change it because you didn't think that the charge of interfering with motor vehicles that night would stick. That's correct isn't it?'

'No, your worships.'

'So you decided to accuse the two of them of interfering with motor vehicles on 22 April, an incident that hadn't occurred. That's correct isn't it?'

'No, your worships.'

'And for good measure the two of you threw in the assaults on police that hadn't taken place. Didn't you?'

'No, your worships.'

'Back at the police station on the night of 6 May you made up your notes for both occasions in two separate incident report books and included the names of the two defendants, Billie Blue and Terry Turquoise . . . when if you had made up your notes for the incident in Arbuthnot Street on 22 April as you claim, you could not possibly have known the names of the persons you claimed to have seen in order to put them in your notes . . . That's correct is it not, officer?'

'No, your worships.'

'Well, what is your explanation for having their names in your notes for the incident on 22 April?'

'I haven't one.'

'But you must have some explanation, officer . . . they are your notes . . . you wrote them.. How did you come to put in the names of two persons at a time when you have admitted you did not know their names? . . . How?'

Violet rose to his feet. 'I think the officer is being quite unfairly hounded on this point.'

'I don't propose to pursue this point any further in evidence . . . ' said Rachel. 'One final matter, officer. You say that Billie Blue punched you when you grabbed him.'

'Yes, your worships.'

'Any particular reason why the custody sergeant hasn't mentioned that in the custody record?'

'I don't know, your worships.'

'Did you tell him about it?'

'Perhaps not. I can't remember, your worships.'

'Is that because it didn't happen?'

'No, your worships.'

'Assaulting a police officer in the execution of his duty is a serious offence, isn't it?'

'Yes, your worships.'

'Yet you didn't mention it to the custody sergeant?'

'I'm not sure.'

'He'd have written that down if you told him about it, wouldn't he?'

'Yes.'

'I have no more questions of this officer. Thank you, your worships.'

Rachel sat down.

Violet stood up. 'Officer, who makes the decision as to whether a
prisoner is interviewed?'

'In a case like this, the custody sergeant, your worships.'

'Who decides what to put in the custody record, officer?'

'The custody sergeant, your worships.'

Violet turned to the chairman. 'I have no further re-examination.
I don't know if you have any questions, Madam?'

Mrs Yellow looked at the other two magistrates who shook their
heads. 'No thank you, Mr Violet.'

'In that case I will call my last witness. Thank you, officer. You
may sit at the back of the courtroom . . . Police Constable Pink,
please usher.'

18. Rachel's cross-examination of PC Pink

The usher left the court and returned almost immediately with
another police officer who made his way to the witness box.

The officer took the oath.

'Officer, please give the court your full name, rank and station.'

'Yes sir. I am Police Constable five six six five Percy Pink,
stationed at Heeling police station.'

'Officer, were you on duty on 6 May with PCs Crimson and
Orange?'

'Yes sir.'

'Do you have notes you wish to refer to?'

'Yes please, sir.'

'When did you make those notes up?'

'About an hour after the incident.'

'Were the matters still fresh in your memory?'   .

'Yes, sir.'

'May the officer refer to his notes, Madam?'

Mrs Yellow looked at Rachel and Beryl who nodded.

'Yes, officer.'

'Madam, as the officer's evidence is purely corroborative of part
of the other officers' evidence, I tender him for cross-examination.'[72]

---

72 It is an unfortunate practice of some prosecutors to leave witnesses, particularly
police witnesses, to be cross-examined in this way without the essential advantage of being questioned by a friendly advocate before the rigours of cross-
examination. It must be of doubtful legality for the prosecutor to claim that a
witness is purely corroborative. The prosecutor is making assertions on the

Violet sat down leaving PC Pink looking distinctly ill at ease.

Beryl stood up hesitantly. 'I have no questions of this witness, Madam' and sat down.

Rachel stood up. 'Officer, did you make your notes up alone or with other officers?'

'With other officers.'

'Who?'

'PCs Orange and Crimson.'

'Where did you make them up?'

'In the canteen at Heeling Police Station.'

'Did the other officers tell you what to put in your notes?'

'No, your worship.'

'Why was it necessary for you to make up your notes together?'

'It wasn't necessary exactly. It's just that that is the way it is always done.'

'But why?'

'Well it is important to record what happened accurately.'

'How?'

'I beg your pardon?'

'How do you go about it?'

'Go about what?'

'Well, you are all there in the room intending to make up your notes together. What happens?'

'I don't follow you.'

'What actually happens?'

'Well, we discuss what occurred.'

'Yes?'

'Then we write it down.'

'In the same words?'

---

witness's evidence that are quite unjustified. It is a different matter where the prosecutor tenders a witness for cross-examination without any comment as to the content of the witness's evidence. However, the same criticism is to be made of the practice so far as the witness's ability to cope with the questioning is concerned. It is a paramount obligation of an advocate to ensure that the witnesses he calls are given the best opportunity to cope with the ordeal of giving evidence. In some instances there is a countervailing argument for the prosecutor in that a witness that has given no evidence-in-chief is more difficult to cross-examine effectively. The defence advocate may have to carry out the role of examiner-in-chief, at least in part, in order to set up the features of evidence for cross-examination.

'Well, no.'

'Very similar words?'

'Yes. I suppose very similar words.'

'What happens if you don't agree over something?'

'I don't follow you.'

'Well you are all discussing what happened. That's right, isn't it?'

'Yes.'

'What happens if two of you think that different things happened?'

'Well they would put different things in their notes.'

'So what's the point of writing your notes together?'

'I suppose to try and get them the same as far as possible.'

'Who decides what goes into the note?'

'We each decide.'

'What do you mean by that?'

'I don't know. We just discuss what happened and then write our notes.'

'Do you mean that some of you remember some features and some remember others?'

'Perhaps.'

'So your notes contain things that the other officers remembered but that you didn't?'

'No. My notes only contain what I remembered.'

'So why do you need to make your notes up with other officers then?'

'I thought I had explained.'

'The truth is, officer, that you write your notes together to make sure the accounts you each give are completely consistent regardless of what you remember of the incident. That's right, isn't it?'

'No, your worships. That isn't correct.'

'Were you in the High Street that evening with PCs Orange and Crimson in a police car of which you were the driver?'

'Yes.'

'How did you get back to the police station?'

'I drove back.'

'Anyone with you?'

'Yes, I believe that PC Orange came back in the car. I think that PC Crimson went back in the van.'

'When you got to the police station, where did you go?'

'I joined the other two officers in the canteen.'

'Did you go into the custody suite where the prisoners were?'[73]

'No.'

'Could you read out the beginning of your notes on this incident please . . .'

'Certainly. . . "On 6 May at about 11 pm I was driving a marked police car with PC Orange and PC Crimson as passengers. We were driving down the High Street when I saw two men I now know to be Billie Blue and Terry Turquoise walking on the footway. PC Orange told me to stop the car which I did. PCs Orange and Crimson got out of the car and ran after the two men who had run down the High Street. I heard PC Crimson shout, 'Stand still, You are under arrest for interfering with motor vehicles the other day.' The two men and the two officers then disappeared into a side road. After I had parked the car and radioed for assistance I left the police car and went into the side road. I there found the other two officers with their prisoners. I remained with them until the prisoners were placed in the van . . ."'

'Thank you, officer, that is all I ask you to read. Did you hear any conversation between the officers and the men they had arrested when you joined them?'

'No. I don't recollect anything being said.'

'What, nothing at all?'

'No. The van arrived very quickly and the prisoners were put inside.'

'May I repeat my earlier question. Did the other officers tell you what to write in your notes?'

'No.'

'Well, how were you able to put names to the two men whom you describe as "two men I now know to be Billie Blue and Terry Turquoise"?'

'I must have got it from the custody record.'

'When?'

'I don't know.'

'How did you get the names from the custody record?'

'Well, I would look at the custody records and get the names from them.'

'How?'

'Well by looking at the custody records in the custody suite.'

---

73 Following her own technique Rachel should not have led the officer on this point.

'But I thought you went straight to the canteen?'

'I may have gone to the custody suite first.'

'What? To look at the custody records?'

'Yes.'

'But you said in your evidence that you went straight to the canteen.'

'I may have been mistaken.'

'If you did go to the custody area, how did you know which custody record to look at?'

'How do you mean?'

'If there were three prisoners in the cells and you found three custody records, how would you know which custody records referred to the two men you saw in the High Street?'

'It would be obvious.'

'It would be, or was obvious, officer?'

'It was.'

'Why?'

'I don't recollect. It just was obvious.'

'This is not true, is it officer? The other two officers told you the names of the men they had arrested and you just put the names in your notes. You described them as "whom I now know to be" when you didn't have the first idea who they were. That's right, isn't it?'

'No. I got their particulars from their custody records, your worships.'

'Officer, could you tell the court how you have spelt the names of the defendants in your notes?'

'Spelt them? Well I have spelt Billie Blue . . . B.I.L.L.I.E . . . B.L.U.E . . . and Terry Turquoise T.E.R.R.Y . . . T.U.R.Q.U.O.Y.S.E, your worships.'

'Officer could you look at this document . . . What is it?'

'It is Mr Turquoise's custody record, your worships.'

'How is Mr Turquoise's name spelt there, officer?'

'It's spelt T.U.R.Q.U.O.I.S.E, your worships.'

'Officer, you spelt Turquoise in your notes with a Y instead of an I. That is how PC Crimson and PC Orange spelt it in their notes. If you had been taking the name from the custody record you would have spelt it with an "I", don't you agree?'

'Not necessarily, your worships. I must have misread it.'

'I suggest to you that you spelt it that way because you took the spelling from PC Orange or PC Crimson and not as you now claim from the custody record, officer.'

'No, your worships.'

'I have no more questions of this officer,' said Rachel and sat down.

'I have no re-examination, thank you officer,' said Violet. 'May this officer be released, Madam?'

Mrs Yellow nodded.

'Madam,' said Violet. 'That is the case for the prosecution.'

19. Beryl's submission of no case to answer

Beryl had been shuffling through her notebook during the evidence of PC Pink. She now stood up. 'Madam, I wish to make a submission of no case to answer'.

'Yes, Miss Black,' said Mrs Yellow.

'The reality, Madam, is that it is impossible for you to say that there is a case to answer in this case . . . The evidence is completely . . . completely impossible to accept. The officers claim that they saw my client in the dark . . . in this street while running towards them . . . they can only. . . only have seen them for a second at the most. It is quite impossible for them to have recognised them from that, when they saw them again in the High Street weeks later . . . I submit that it is nonsense. Madam, you and your colleagues will be aware of the case of *Turnbull* on identification. If ever I have seen one, this is a case of a fleeting glimpse, which *Turnbull* says is completely inadequate for a conviction. I would therefore submit that the case ought to be dismissed at this stage on the basis that there is simply no case to answer . . . and so far as the assault on police is concerned . . . I would ask you to throw that out as well. Clearly if the officers' evidence is unsatisfactory on the interference charge, it can hardly be relied upon for the assault part.'[74]

'Yes,' said Mrs Yellow and looked at Rachel.

'I have no submission to make, other than to support Miss Black,' said Rachel.[75]

---

74 One of the most difficult features of advocacy for the beginner is to express views as opposed to recounting facts. Inexperience and nervousness prevents the thoughts in the mind from appearing through the mouth in a form that has the meaning intended by the advocate.

75 This is not a case in which a submission of 'no case to answer' should have been made. There clearly is a prima facie case. The submission has no chance of success and gives the competent prosecutor the opportunity to make a further speech to the magistrates after he has heard some of the defence points. However, Rachel cannot disclaim the submission entirely by making no submission at all.

Violet rose to his feet. 'Madam. If I may answer Miss Black's eloquent submission. The position at this stage in the case is that you have only to decide whether there is a case to answer. You do not have to decide questions of guilt or innocence. The heavy burden on the prosecution of proving the case beyond reasonable doubt is not to be considered at this stage. All the prosecution have to do to establish a case to answer is to call evidence that shows on its face that the offence has been committed by the defendant in relation to the charge under consideration. I would say that this the prosecution clearly has done. PCs Orange and Crimson have told you in evidence that they saw these two defendants in Arbuthnot Street interfering with motor vehicles. The presumption from the circumstances in which these two defendants were seen by the officers, trying the doors of two cars in a street, not, as you will see from the charge sheets, their places of residence . . . at a late hour and in the dark, and while doing so looking furtively round them . . . and when challenged by the police running away and escaping. The presumption has to be that they were in the course of committing an offence in relation to those cars . . . probably one under the Theft Act . . . trying to take the vehicle without the owner's consent or theft of the contents . . . Miss Black urges you that this is a fleeting glimpse case. That is manifestly not so. These officers stopped their vehicle and watched these defendants for some time. They had the opportunity when approaching the defendants to see them at close range. It would be hard to think of a more convincing opportunity to observe and commit to memory the features of criminals at work. At the very least, Madam, this is a very convincing case to answer . . . Miss Black does not restrict herself to the first charge, somehow she uses her attempted impeachment of the first charge to challenge the charge of assault on a police officer. I suppose she would say that this was on the basis of a "fleeting glimpse". Madam, Mr Turquoise hit this officer several times. The officer has said so in evidence. I can think of no more compelling case to answer. Miss Red wisely says nothing in support of this submission. Madam, there is clearly a case to answer on all the four charges against these two defendants.'

'Thank you, Mr Violet, we will retire to consider the submission.'

'Coffee,' muttered the usher, just audibly.

Ten minutes later the magistrates returned.

'Please stand up,' said Mrs Yellow to the two defendants. 'We find that there is a case to answer on all the charges. You can sit down, now . . . Miss Black?'

20. Terry Turquoise's evidence-in-chief

Beryl stood up uncertainly. 'I'll call Mr Turquoise, if it pleases you, Madam.'[76]

Terry Turquoise left the dock and went over to the witness box. The usher handed him a testament. 'Please read the oath on the card, Mr Turquoise,' said the clerk.

Terry peered at the card and read out the oath.

'Thank you,' said the clerk.

'What is your name?' said Beryl.

Terry looked at her. 'Terry Turquoise.'

'Mr Turquoise, were you in Arbuthnot Street on 22 April?'[77]

'No.'

'Where were you?'

'I was playing snooker with my cousin at his place.'

'Are you sure?'

'Yes.'

'Where were you doing that?'

'At his place.'

'Where is that?'

'I don't know the address. It's just round the corner from the chip shop in the Broadway.'[78]

'Oh right. What time did you get there?'

'About seven . . . no about six-thirty.'

'How long did you play snooker for.'

'A long time. All evening.'

'Right. Were you stealing from cars in Arbuthnot Street that night?'

'I said I was playing snooker.'

'Yes, I'm just asking you that to make it clear.'

'Oh right. No, I was not stealing from cars.'

'Now, on 6 May were you in the High Street with Billie Blue?'

'6 May?'

'Yes.'

'When was that?'

---

76 'If it pleases you' is one of the more absurd but harmless platitudes wheeled out by the Bar.

77 Beryl should have put some more inconsequential questions to Terry before moving onto the important topics in order to allow him to become accustomed to giving evidence.

78 Beryl should have ironed out this sort of difficulty before the case started.

'The night you were arrested.'

'Yeah. That night I was in the pub with Billie. Then we went down to the chip shop.'

'Yes, and did you see the police?'

'We saw the Old Bill coming and we run.'

'Why?'

'I don't know.'

'Why did you run?'

'I don't know, I said . . . I don't know . . . We just did.'[79]

'Did the policeman catch you?'

'Yeah.'

'Did you hit him?'

'Me hit a copper? No way.'

'Did you see Billie hit the policeman?'

'No. We had no reason to go hitting no policeman.'

Beryl looked down at her notebook leafing through it. Eventually she looked up. 'I have no more questions, Madam.'[80]

21. Cross-examination of Terry Turquoise

Mrs Yellow turned to Rachel. 'Do you have any questions, Miss Red?'

'No thank you, your worships.'

'Mr Violet?'

Violet rose slowly to his feet and stared at Terry. 'Mr Turquoise, you are a thief . . . you steal from cars . . . you were in Arbuthnot Street that night to steal from cars. Weren't you?'[81]

'No, I wasn't.'

'Why were you there, then?'

---

79 By failing to go through his evidence with him before the case started Beryl has not given herself and Terry the opportunity to ensure they are on the same wavelength.

80 Beryl's examination-in-chief of Terry is pitiful. The preparation for the case has been so inadequate that Beryl has almost no knowledge of what Terry's defence is. In addition Beryl's inexperience prevents her from filling in the gaps from her general knowledge of similar cases.

81 This is an illegal but very effective opening question. The comment (and it is not permitted to make comment while cross-examining) 'you steal from cars' suggests that Terry has previous convictions for theft from motor vehicles, but the question itself is entirely legitimate: 'You were in Arbuthnot Street that night to steal from cars . . .?'

'I . . . you're trying to catch me out . . . I wasn't there at all.'

'Oh really well where were you?'

'As I've said I was at my cousin's playing snooker.'

'At what address?'

'As I've said. I don't know the address, but I could take you there.'

'What is your cousin's name?'

'Mervin Mauve.'

'And is he here to give evidence for you?'

'Yes.'

'He is?'

'Yes. He is outside.'

'How often do you go to his home?'

'Often.'

'But you don't know his address?'

'No. I just go there. I don't write him letters or nothing.'

'How often do you go there?'

'Often . . . once a week . . . twice a week . . . something like that.'

'And what do you do when you go there?'

'I sometimes have a meal off of his mum . . . sometimes we play snooker . . . sometimes we play cards . . . sometimes we go down the pub . . . it all depends.'

'What time did you go round there that evening?'

'Six-thirty . . . seven . . . seven-thirty . . . always about that time.'

'And what time did you leave?'

'I expect we went and had a drink before closing time . . . then his mum makes us a sandwich and I goes home late.'

'What time did you leave?'

'Probably around eleven . . . eleven-thirty, something like that.'

'Did you stay in your cousin's flat that evening?'

'Yes . . . I think we did. I don't think we went down the pub.'

'What did you do while you were there?'

'Like I said . . . we probably played snooker . . . I don't remember that clearly.'

'If you don't remember that clearly, how do you know you were there that evening?'

'I just do.'

'Did you go to Mervyn's last week?'

'Yeah.'

'Which day?'

'Wednesday and Friday.'

'Do you know what date it was last Wednesday?'

'Yeah. Today is 15 July so last Wednesday must have been 10 July.'

'Why didn't you tell the officers who arrested you that you had been with your cousin Mervyn on the night they said you were in Arbuthnot Street interfering with motor cars?'

'They didn't say anything like that. The first I knew was when I was charged.'

'Why didn't you tell the officer charging you that you hadn't been there and that you had been at your cousin's?'[82]

Rachel looked at Beryl to see if she would object to this question. Beryl made no move.

'I didn't realise which night he was talking about. I had to think hard to realise that 22 April was a Wednesday and that I must have been at my cousin's that night. By then I had been charged and I was being released.'

'Why didn't you mention it when you did realise?'

'They were busy throwing us out of the nick. No one was interested in us except to get us out.'

'Now really, that is absolute nonsense, Mr Turquoise, and you know it. All you had to say to the custody sergeant was, "Sergeant, I have an alibi for that night", and he would have noted it down. Perhaps you wouldn't be here now, Mr Turquoise . . . that is if it had been truthful . . . The reason you didn't mention your alibi was that you hadn't thought it up by then. Had you? And in fact you did not have an alibi because it was you in Arbuthnot Street, stealing . . . or trying to steal from cars. Yes?'

'That's not true. They simply weren't interested in us. The sergeant read the charge as quick as he could and then went off for his dinner. It was another copper who released us.'

'Now on 6 May, you were in the High Street with Mr Blue. Weren't you?'

'Yes.'

'And you saw the police car?'

'Yes.'

'The car stopped?'

'Yes.'

---

82 Until recently this would not have been a permissible question. On being charged the defendant is cautioned that he does not have to say anything in answer to the charge. See however comments on the Criminal Justice and Public Order Act 1994 below pp 241–245. Practically, if the first time Terry heard the date was when the charge was read out, it is not surprising he did not say anything even if it turned out that he had an honest alibi.

'Police officers got out and when you saw them you ran away. Didn't you?'

'Yes.'

'Why, Mr Turquoise?'

'I don't know.'

'Come now, Mr Turquoise. Why did you run away when the officers got out of their car?'

'I just don't know. I suppose it was for a lark.'

'No, Mr Turquoise, I'll tell you why you ran away. When the officers got out of the car they shouted at you, didn't they?'

'Yes they may have done.'

'What did they shout, Mr Turquoise?'

'I don't know, do I?'

'Yes you do. Mr Turquoise. The officer shouted, "Stand still, you are under arrest for interfering with motor vehicles the other day." That's what he shouted, didn't he, Mr Turquoise?'

'I don't know.'

'So he may have shouted that?'

'I don't think so.'

'But I thought you said you didn't know what they shouted, Mr Turquoise?'

'I don't think it was that.'

'I thought you said you didn't know what they shouted, Mr Turquoise?'

'No. But I don't think it was that.'

'Mr Turquoise are you telling this court the truth?'

'Yes. I am.'

'Mr Turquoise, if you don't know what the officer shouted how can you say that you don't think it was, "Stand still you are under arrest for interfering with motor vehicles the other day"?'

'I just don't.'

'Well I suggest to you Mr Turquoise that the real reason you ran away was that as soon as you heard the officer shout, you realised that they had recognised you from Arbuthnot Street and you ran away just as you had on 22 April. That's right isn't it, Mr Turquoise?'

'No.'

'You ran away from the officers because you wanted to escape from them, didn't you, Mr Turquoise?'

'No.'

'Oh I see. You ran away from them but you didn't want to escape from them. Is that what you are saying, Mr Turquoise?'

'Not exactly.'

'You wanted to escape from them, didn't you, Mr Turquoise?'

'Well I suppose so in a way, yes.'

'So when the officer caught up with you and caught hold of you, you still tried to escape from him.'

'I was still trying to escape from him?'

'That is what you were trying to do, weren't you?'

'Yes . . .'

'And when the officer caught hold of you, you tried to get out of his hold, didn't you, by punching at him several times.'

'No. I didn't punch him at all.'

'Well, what did you do to try and escape from him?'

'Nothing when he had stopped me.'

'Well, I put it to you that that is not true. You punched Police Constable Crimson several times, Mr Turquoise.'

'No.'

'Now Mr Turquoise, you heard the evidence given by the police officers . . . in this court . . . this morning. Didn't you?'

'How do you mean?'

'You were listening to the officers' evidence. Weren't you?'

'Yeah.'

'You heard them say they saw you in Arbuthnot Street on 22 April trying to steal from two cars . . . you heard that?'

'Yes.'

'And that you ran away. You heard that?'

'Yes.'

'And that they saw your face clearly in the light given by the street light. You heard that?'

'Yes.'

'Now do you say the officers were lying when they gave that evidence?'

Rachel looked at Beryl to see her reaction to this question. Beryl made no move.

Terry looked at Violet. 'How do you mean?'

'Are you saying that these two police officers were lying in their evidence about you?'

'I don't know.'

'You don't know what you are saying?'

'No . . . I don't know whether they were lying.'

'Well are you saying that they were telling the truth?'

'No . . . I don't know what they were doing. All I know is that I wasn't in Abberthot Street or whatever it's called.'

'Well let's look at this carefully. The officers each said that they saw your face clearly lit up by the street light and for a sufficient length of time to recognise you easily when they saw you in the High Street on 6 May. That's what they said. Yes?'

'Yes . . . I suppose so.'

'Not you suppose so. That is what they said, isn't it, Mr Turquoise?'

Rachel wrote out a note and pushed it over to Beryl. It read, 'You ought to object to this line of cross-examination.' Beryl looked at her unhappily.

Terry nodded to Violet's question.

'Speak please, Mr Turquoise. This is a court of law not a mime class.'

'Yes.'

Rachel wrote out another note. 'You can't let him treat your defendant like this.'

'You'd never seen these officers before had you, Mr Turquoise?'

'No.'

'And so far as you know they had never seen you before. Had they?'

'No.'

'Now. . . Mr Turquoise . . . why should these two officers make up an account like this about you? . . . why should they give this evidence about you? . . . why should they do that? . . . unless, Mr Turquoise . . . and the explanation is quite simple . . . the officers' evidence was true and correct evidence . . . That is the real explanation, isn't it, Mr Turquoise? . . . On 22 April you were in Arbuthnot Street stealing from parked cars, weren't you, Mr Turquoise?'[83]

'Why would I be doing that?'

'Thank you, Mr Turquoise.' Violet sat down and pointedly turned round to talk to the two PCs who were by then sitting behind him.

---

83 This is unfortunately a not uncommon form of illegal questioning by prosecutors. Rachel has encountered it frequently and has the technique for scotching it as it starts. Beryl, while unhappy about it, cannot think why it is illegal and on what basis to object. Violet has a problem in this case. He wants to give the court, and in particular the police officers, a display of virtuoso savage cross-examination, but where the defence is substantially one of non-presence, there is little to cross-examine on, so he resorts to forensic bullying. The only way to stop him is through well argued objections.

Terry made his way back to the dock. Beryl turned to the usher. 'Mervin Mauve, please.'

The usher went to the door. 'Mister Mervin Mauve, please,' he called.

22. The evidence of Mervyn Mauve

Beryl's witness appeared hesitantly at the door and looked round the court.

'Please go into the witness box, Mr . . . er Mauve . . . thank you,' said Mrs Yellow.

Beryl was examining some scrawled notes she had taken during the coffee break. She looked up at her witness in the box. 'What is your name?'

'My name? . . . Mauve . . . Mervin Mauve . . . M...A...U...'

'Yes. I've got that,' said the clerk.

'Do you have any other names?' asked Beryl.

'Er well Godfrey, but I never use it . . .'

'Where do you live?'

'46a Wilf's Parade . . . Heeling.'

'That's it,' called Terry from the dock. Mrs Yellow glowered at him.

There was a long pause, during which Beryl staring at her notebook wondered how to start the questioning of this alibi witness who had been sprung on her with no notice or any opportunity to work out what he would say.

'Was Terry Turquoise at your flat on 22 April?'

Violet rocketed to his feet.

'Yes' said Mauve quickly before Violet could speak.[84]

'Madam. I object. That is the most blatant piece of leading of a witness it has been my . . .'

'. . . my pleasure to hear . . .' muttered Rachel under her breath.

'. . . my misfortune to hear, Madam . . . It is outrageous. My learned friend should know better . . . a member of the Bar . . .'

---

84 In addition to being a leading questioning, this is the classic way to lead an alibi witness and possibly the rest of the defence case into extreme difficulties. Beryl should have moved heaven and earth to ensure she had the opportunity to talk over Mauve's evidence with him before calling him. Beryl is insufficiently experienced to be aware of the pitfalls of alibi evidence.

Mrs Yellow looked at Beryl over her pince nez. 'Yes. Could you put it some other way, Miss Black?'

'Yes, Madam.'

Violet gave an explosive snort.

'Mr Mauve, do you know any of the men standing behind me . . .'

The witness looked at the usher.

'. . . in that dock there . . . the two men?'

'Yes,' said Mauve. 'That's my cousin Terry and his friend Billie.'

'Where were you on 22 April?'

Violet snorted again.

'I was at home.'

'All day?'

'No. I was at work during the day and at home in the evening.'

'Was anyone with you?'

'Yes. My cousin Terry. That geezer there.'

'When was he with you?'

'Oh from about six, seven, seven-thirty to some time late.'

'What did you do?'

'I should think we were playing snooker. We usually do. Or watch TV and we usually go to the pub.'

Beryl's sigh was almost audible as she sank down onto the bench. 'I have no further questions, Madam.'

'I have no questions of this witness, thank you, your worships,' said Rachel.

Violet rose to his feet. Rachel could hear the metaphorical grinding of teeth and sharpening of knives.

'Mr Mauve. You are Terry Turquoise's cousin?'

'Yes.'

'You have come to court to say anything that you think might get your cousin out of trouble. Is that right?'

'Anything truthful, yes.'

'What day of the week was 22 April, Mr Mauve?'

'. . . er . . . Tuesday, was it? . . . I don't really remember . . . Thursday? . . . Yes Thursday.'

'It's no good looking at Mr Turquoise. He doesn't know which day it was either.'

'Right, well I think it was a Thursday.'

'Mr Mauve, it was a Wednesday.'

Silence.

'Any comment, Mr Mauve?'

'No.'

'You don't know from one day to the next who was with you, or where you were a week before, let alone two weeks, do you, Mr Mauve?

'Yes.'

'Did you see Mr Turquoise at your home last week?'

'Yes.'

'When?'

'I . . . don't . . . Wednesday . . . he came round Wednesday.'

'Any other days?'

'Yes . . . Thursday . . . I think he came round Friday as well . . . We went to the Rose and Thistle.'

'That's not what Mr Turquoise says.'

'Well, I can't help that.'

'Would it surprise you to hear that Mr Turquoise said he came round to your address on Wednesday and Friday last week? He made no mention of Thursday.'

'Perhaps he forgot the Thursday.'

'Perhaps you made it up, Mr Mauve.'

'No. I didn't make it up. The Wednesday and Friday were right, weren't they?'

'When did Mr Turquoise tell you that he needed you to come to court and give evidence for him?'

'Last week.'[85]

'He told you last week?'

'Yeah. So I made the arrangements to have the day off work.'

'And did you go and see his solicitors and give them a statement?'

'No.'

'Well did they come and see you?'

'No. No one took a statement off of me.'

'No one took a statement off of you . . . and the first time you were asked to come to court was last week. Is that correct, Mr Mauve?'

'Yes.'

---

85 While this is strictly correct, Terry had told his solicitors about the alibi witness some weeks before, but nothing had been done about interviewing him. Mauve had known he was to give assistance in the case in some form for some weeks, but not that he had to come to court to give evidence orally until the week before, when Terry told him he had to come. Beryl's instructions are so inadequate that she is not aware of the true position and her inexperience means that she fails to spot the implications of Mauve's answer and the impression given to the magistrates, which is that he did not know of his role in the alibi defence until the week before the trial.

'The truth is that you have no idea whether Mr Turquoise was with you that night or not. That's right, isn't it, Mr Mauve?'

'No.'

'You've come to court to say anything you think might get your cousin Mr Turquoise out of trouble. That's right, isn't it?'

'No.'

'Thank you, Mr Mauve. I have no further questions.'

Beryl stood up again uncertainly. She stared at her notebook and then looked up.

'Do you have any re-examination, Miss Black?' asked the clerk.

'Er no . . . yes please, Madam . . . Mr Mauve . . . you say were asked to come court last week . . . but when did you first say you would be a witness?'

Violet leapt to his feet. 'I object to that question.'

'And why?' asked the clerk.

'It cannot be relevant to the case when the witness first said he would be a witness . . .' said Violet.

'No,' said Beryl. 'You asked . . . I should say my learned friend asked Mr Mauve when he was first asked to come to court. I am just establishing that when he was asked to come to court was not the occasion when he first . . . Mr Mauve first put himself forward as a witness, an alibi witness for Mr Turquoise . . . The suggestion was that he had made his evidence up quite recently . . .'

'I said no such thing.'

'Well you suggested it.'

'Madam,' said the clerk to Mrs Yellow. 'It seems to me that Miss Black's question is perfectly proper if it is to establish the point as to when Mr Mauve first became a witness in the light of Mr Violet's cross-examination.'

'About six weeks ago,' said Mauve.

'Thank you, Madam. I have no further questions,' said Beryl.[86] 'Thank you, Mr Mauve . . . That is the case for Mr Turquoise, Madam,' said Beryl.

'Thank you, Miss Black. Miss Red?'

---

86 Thanks to the whollly inadequate preparation of Terry's case Mr Mauve's evidence has been a disaster. Beryl retrieves what she can of his evidence in re-examination.

23. Billie Blue's evidence-in-chief

Rachel stood up. 'Thank you, your worships. I will call Billie Blue to give evidence.'

Billie went over to the witness box and took the oath.

'What is your full name?'

'Billie Blue.'

'And your address?'

'33 Claribel Mansions, the Glen, Heeling.'

'How long have you lived there?'

'All my life . . . twenty-six years.'

'What is your work?'

'I am a panel beater.'

'Who do you work for?'

'I work for XYZ Panel Beaters, 13 Wingnut Crescent, Heeling.'[87]

'Now you recollect the 6 May, which was the night you were arrested?'[88]

'Yes.'

'Where did you spend most of that evening?'

'I spent it in the pub, the Dog and Bone in Heeling High Street, with Mr Turquoise there.'

'What time did you get there?'

'I should say we got there at about eight o'clock . . . sometime around then.'

'And when did you leave?'

'Some time around closing time.'

'What time was that?'

'Around eleven.'

'And where did you go?'

'We walked up to the chippy. . . the chip shop in the High Street.'

'What were you going to do there?'

'Get some chips to eat . . .'

'Did anything happen?'

'Yes. We were walking along the pavement when Terry said, 'Run! Old Bill!''

---

87 These initial questions are of almost no significance to the case, but they enable the witness to settle down and become used to dealing with questions with confidence before the important topics are reached.

88 While strictly this is a leading question, there can be no objection to it as Billie's presence in the High Street on that night is not in issue. There has to be a leading question of some sort to begin the evidence.

'Yes. What happened then?'[89]

'I looked round and I saw this Bill car pulling up alongside us. So I started running.'

'Why did you run?'

'I was a bit drunk. It was mainly for a lark. I can't really give any other reason. We were pissing with laughter . . . I beg your pardon, your worships . . . we were laughing a lot as we ran. I think that's why they caught us so easy.'

'What happened?'

'The officer ran up behind me, grabbed me by the neck and swung me round. He said something like, "Got you, you bastard . . . you're f...ing nicked."'

'What happened then?'

'He just held me while the other officer chased Mr Turquoise. I heard a scream and then the other officer brought Mr Turquoise back. I heard him saying to Mr Turquoise, "I saw you in that car you dirty little thief."'

'Yes. Then what happened?'

'I heard Mr Turquoise say, "I weren't in no car. We've just come out of the pub. We were just going for some chips."'

'Yes?'

'Then the officer said, "Well why did you run then?"'

'Yes?'

'Mr Turquoise said, "Just for a laugh". And the officer who had hold of me said sort of sarcastically, "So you just run for a laugh?"'

'Yes?'

'And I said, "Yeah, honest it was just for a laugh. We haven't touched no car."'

'Yes?'

'Then the second officer said, "Well you're both nicked anyway." And I said, "Well, which car are we meant to have been in?"'

'What was said then?'[90]

'The first officer said, "Just shut up. We'll sort all that out down at the police station."'

'Yes?'

'I said, "No. If you are saying we were in a car, we want you to show us which car we were in. We want to see if it's open."'

89 This is the right sort of non-leading question to keep the narrative moving.
90 This is about as far as Rachel can legitimately go to remind the witness that there is more conversation to be recounted.

'And then what was said?'

'The officers told us to shut up and get in the panda . . . We were saying, "No, if you say we were in a car, you show us which one." So they decided to radio for a van for us. We stood there waiting for the van. Quite a crowd gathered.'

'Yes?'

'So me and Terry started shouting at the crowd, "These coppers say we were in a car over there." And we told them to try the car doors and see if any of them were open. And several of them started trying car doors and none of them were open.'

'What happened then?'

'The van arrived and a sergeant came out of it and we started on at the sergeant.'

'What were you saying?'

'We were saying, "These officers say we were in a car in the High Street but we weren't." We tried to get him to try the car door handles and I believe Mr Turquoise said he wanted him to finger-print all the cars in the High Street and see if our fingerprints were on any of them.'

'What did the sergeant say?'

'He didn't say anything, he just said, "Put them in the van." And we were taken down to the station.'

'What did the two officers do?'

'One of them come in the van with us.'

'Which one?'

'It was the one who nicked . . . arrested Mr Turquoise.'

'Was anything said in the van on the way to the police station?'

'We just kept saying to him that he couldn't have seen us in a car because we hadn't been in one. Then he said, "Well you run and I know why you run, it's because you were the ones my mate caught breaking into cars last week."'

'Yes?'[91]

'We said we hadn't been breaking into cars and if he had seen us why hadn't he arrested us.'

'And what did he say?'

'He said it was because we had run away like we had tonight.'

'What was said then?'

---

91 Billie is a good witness. Rachel has been over the case with him enough times for Billie to have a good grasp of how to describe what happened in full. Rachel uses the slightest of questions to keep him moving. He leaves almost nothing out.

'Nothing. We got to the police station by then.'

'Did he tell you where he and the other officer had seen you in the cars and when?'

'No.'

'Did he say what happened when they had chased you?'

'No. We were just taken into the charge room.'

'What happened in the charge room?'

'The sergeant behind the desk took our particulars. When he took mine he asked the first officer why I had been arrested and the officer said, "Breaking into cars, Sarge."'

'Did you ask anyone what you were being held for?'[92]

'Yeah. I asked the officer who had been in the van with us.'

'What did you say to him?'

'I said, "What are we being charged with?"'

'And what did he say?'

'He said, "I'll think of something."'

'When did you find out that you were being charged with theft from cars on 22 April?'

'When I was charged.'

'What was your reaction to that?'

'I was a bit confused. If a date is just given to you like that, it takes a bit of time to work out what's going on.'

'Yes?'

'Well we were thrown out of the nick soon after we were charged.'

'Were you in Arbuthnot Street on 22 April trying to break into cars?'

'No.'

'Do you know where you were?'

'Not really. There are a number of places I could have been, but I haven't been able to remember what I was doing that night, for certain.'

'Going back to the time of your arrest, did you punch the officer when he arrested you?'

'No, I didn't.'

'Stay there please, there will be further questions for you.'

Rachel sat down. Beryl stood up.

---

92 This is strictly a leading question, but it is the sort that is not likely to be objected to.

'Um, Mr Blue, you say you were not in Arbuthnot Street on 22 April?'

'Yes.'

'And you don't know where you were?'

'No, not really.'

'And you didn't hit the officer when he arrested you?'[93]

'No.'

'Did Mr Turquoise hit the officer who arrested him?'

'I didn't see Mr Turquoise hit anyone.'

'Yes . . . right . . . but the officers were accusing you of trying to get into a car?'

'They said we were in a car.'

'Yes . . . I have no further questions.'

Beryl sat down.

24. Cross-examination of Billie Blue

Vernon Violet stood up.

'Mr Blue. When you saw the officers in the High Street on 6 May your reaction was to run away. That's right isn't it?'

'I ran away, yeah.'

'You ran away after the officers had got out of their car, didn't you?'

'I don't know when it was exactly.'

'Police Constable Crimson shouted at you saying he was arresting you for interfering with motor cars on 22 April and you ran away. Didn't you?'

'We ran, yeah.'

'And you ran because you knew it was you who had been interfering with motor vehicles on 22 April in Arbuthnot Street and you were afraid of being arrested for it. That's right, isn't it, Mr Blue?'

'No.'

'We'll look at it piece by piece. PC Crimson shouts at you, doesn't he?'

'Yeah.'

---

93 Beryl has no real idea whether she has any worthwhile questions to put to Billie. She is mentally marking time to see if any inspiration comes to her. These questions are pointless.

'And he shouts at you that he is arresting you for interfering with motor vehicles on 22 April, doesn't he?'

'He may have. I didn't hear what he said.'

Rachel stood up. 'Your worships, I hesitate to interrupt Mr Violet's most eloquent cross-examination, but if he examines his notes with care he will see that Police Constable Crimson said nothing of the sort. PC Crimson said he shouted at the two defendants: "Stand still, you are under arrest for interfering with motor vehicles the other day." He said nothing about where or when.'[94]

Violet looked distinctly put out. 'It amounts to the same thing.'

'It most certainly does not,' said Rachel. 'Mr Violet is basing his cross-examination on the thesis that the officer told Mr Blue why he was being arrested and for what offence and that the fact that Mr Blue then ran away shows that he had a guilty conscience about that particular offence. If the officer did not in fact specify the offence, Mr Violet's thesis is destroyed.'

Mrs Yellow turned to Violet. 'Miss Red has a point, doesn't she, Mr Violet?'

'I don't concede that at all, Madam. However I see that the court's sympathies are with my friend, so I will move on.'[95]

'Mr Blue, you ran away because you wanted to get away from the police officers, didn't you?'

'Yes.'

'So when the officer caught up with you and grabbed you, you still wanted to get away from them, didn't you?'

'No. When he caught me I just stopped.'

'No, you didn't, Mr Blue, you struggled with the officer and punched him, didn't you?'

'No, I didn't.'

'And the punch was aimed at his face, wasn't it?'

---

94 Rachel is able to use this inaccuracy by Violet to torpedo a developing effective cross-examination. Violet should have been more careful. He should have known that with an advocate of Rachel's experience and ability he could not get away with an inaccuracy of this sort, if it was an inaccuracy rather than a deliberate deception.

95 This comment born of pique is not well judged. The magistrates challenged in this way are likely to lose whatever sympathy they had remaining for Violet and by implication the prosecution case. Prosecutors like Violet are often in a more delicate position than they appreciate. While to some extent overawed by the Bar, lay magistrates tend to consider their local practitioners to be part of the local team and take rudeness to them badly. It is a short step for the awe to become irritation.

'No.'

'Well where was it aimed?'[96]

'It wasn't aimed anywhere. I didn't punch at him.'

'Well, Mr Blue, I put it to you that you struggled and punched the officer because you were worried that he was arresting you for the offences you had committed in Arbuthnot Street on 22 April. That's right isn't it?'

'No.'

'You say you weren't in Arbuthnot Street on 22 April.'

'No. I say I wasn't interfering with motor cars in Arbuthnot Street on 22 April.'

'Is there a difference?'

'Yes. I don't know where I was on 22 April. I often drive down Arbuthnot Street. I can't say I didn't drive down it on 22 April. I just wasn't interfering with cars.'

'So you know Arbuthnot Street well?'

'Not well. No. I just know it.'

'You know it's a residential street?'

'Yeah. Like every other street in Heeling.'

'And you know there are cars parked there at night.'

'Yeah.'

'You went there on 22 April to steal from parked cars, didn't you?'

'No.'

'You were there with Terry Turquoise. You tried one car while unknown to you there were police officers watching you. And then you tried another car and managed to get into it. That's right isn't it?'

'No.'

'You then moved on to the next car which you managed to open. But you were then disturbed by the officers running down the road. That's right, isn't it?'

'No.'

'You ran off down an alleyway and made your escape, but not before the officers had had a good look at your faces by the street lighting. That's right, isn't it, Mr Blue?'

'No.'

'You knew the officers had seen you and could recognise you again and that's why, when you saw the same officers in the High

96 Rachel thought to intervene but saw that Billie was well able to deal with the question.

Street, you were panic-stricken and ran away. That's the reason, isn't it, Mr Blue?'

'No.'

'Mr Blue, you heard the evidence the officers gave . . . They said they saw you in Arbuthnot Street on 22 April trying two cars and opening the doors of one of them. . . . You heard that, didn't you?'

'Yes.'

'Well, are these officers lying? Have they made all this up about you? . . .'[97]

Rachel was on her feet. 'Your worships, I object to that question. It is not permissible for an advocate to invite one witness to comment on the evidence of other witnesses . . .'

'Of course I can . . .' said Violet. 'That is the purpose of cross-examination.'

'No. The purpose of cross-examination is, like all other questioning, to obtain evidence. Billie Blue's opinion of the officer's evidence is not admissible evidence, it is inadmissible opinion. It is for your worships to decide whether the officer's evidence is correct or not. And if your worships feel you need to make a decision as to an officer's motives in giving incorrect evidence . . . if you decide he has . . . then again it is for you and not this witness.'

The clerk stood up and turned to the magistrates. 'I agree with Miss Red. It is not permissible to ask Mr Blue why he thinks the officers gave the evidence they did . . .'

'Mr Violet, we accept the advice of our clerk.'

'Very well. In which case I have no further questions, Madam.' Violet sat down.

Rachel stood up. 'Mr Blue, were you in Arbuthnot Street stealing from cars on 22 April?'

'No.'

'Did you punch the officer when he arrested you on 6 May?'

'No.'[98]

---

97 This is a classic ham prosecutor's trap. If the defendant witness falls into the trap and says the officers are lying it leaves him open to having his convictions put to him. Even if this is not done (in public order cases the practice is not to put convictions to a defendant in these circumstances), it is not a ploy that a defence advocate should allow to proceed.

98 These questions and answers are not necessary in pure evidential terms. Billie had already given these answers to Rachel in his evidence-in-chief. However, it is Rachel's practice always to have the last word provided it is kept quick and to the point.

'Your worships, I have no further questions. I don't know if you have any questions of Mr Blue?'

Mrs Yellow looked at her colleagues. 'Yes, we have one question. Have you any idea where you were on 22 April, Mr Blue?'

'Well, I've thought hard about this. I think that I may well have been round my cousin's. That's Paula Purple. I've talked it over with her, but I go round her place that often that we can't be sure whether I was there that night or not. I think I was but as I can't be sure I didn't want to say it in evidence in case anyone thought I was trying to put one over on the court, your worships.'[99]

'Thank you , Mr Blue.'

Billie left the witness box and returned to the dock.

Rachel turned to the usher. 'William White, please, usher.'

25. The evidence of William White

Nipper White made his way to the witness box. At the clerk's direction he picked up the testament and took the oath. He then looked at Rachel and waited expectantly.

'Mr White, could you give your full name to the court please.'

'Yes. William White.'

'And your address?'

'Er, 47 Bluebell House, Heeling.'

'What's your work, Mr White?'

'I'm a guard conductor with British Rail.'

'How long have you done that?'

'Oh about five . . . six years.'

'Do you go to a pub in the High Street in Heeling, Mr White?'

'Yes. I use the Dog and Bone.'

'How often do you go there?'

'Two, maybe three times a week.'

'Do you know either of the men standing over there in the dock?'

'I know the one furthest away from me. I know him as Billie.'

'Do you know his surname?'

'I looked at the list outside the court, so I assume his surname is either Turquoise or Blue. I don't know which.'

'Have you seen Billie before today?'

---

99 This is a compelling answer. Much better than the badly concocted alibi evidence Billie tried to foist on Rachel.

'Yes. I saw him in the Dog and Bone one Friday about three weeks ago. Now I come to look at him I think that the other man over there was with him. At least I think so.'

'Did you speak to Billie?'

'Yes.'

'What was said?'

Violet leapt to his feet. 'This is going to be hearsay, Madam, and I object to it.'

'Madam Clerk?' said Mrs Yellow, looking down to the clerk.

'I think you should hear what Miss Red has to say about it, Madam,' said the clerk.

'Yes. Quite right. Miss Red? It does sound as if it is going to be hearsay.'

'Yes, your worships. It is going to be hearsay, but it is going to be fairly and squarely within one of the exceptions to the rule making hearsay inadmissible. The hearsay is going to establish the fact of what was said and not the truth of what was said. Mr Violet is going to want to know how this witness came to give evidence in this trial. This evidence shows how. What Mr White says is not designed to establish the truth of the hearsay but to show how he came to be giving evidence.'

'Well, how can that be relevant?' enquired Violet.

'If it isn't I don't expect you to cross-examine on it then,' replied Rachel.

'I really find it hard to see how this evidence can be relevant, Miss Red,' said Mrs Yellow.

'Very well, your worships. I will leave it. Mr White, did you see an incident in which men were arrested by police in . . .'

Violet was on his feet again, seething with indignation. 'Madam, this is the most blatant leading of the witness.'

Rachel waited for the chairman's reaction.

'It does seem to be a leading question, Miss Red . . .' said Mrs Yellow.

'Your worships. Every witness has to be introduced into his evidence by some form of questioning that is leading in some sense. In the case of this witness, he does not know the date when the incident took place, but he did see an incident which seems identical to the incident you are trying. I've got to be allowed to put to him some form of leading question to get him to the relevant point in his recollection. The only alternative to that is to get him to describe everything that has happened to him over the last six months. I think the court has better things to do.'

'I rather agree,' said Mrs Yellow. 'Carry on, Miss Red, but lead the witness as little as possible.'

'Of course, your worship. Mr White, did you see an incident in which men were arrested by police in the last few months?'

'Yes.'

'How many such incidents have you seen?'

'Well, several actually, but only one in Heeling High Street, which is the one I think you are referring to.'

'Yes. That is the one I would ask you to deal with. Are you able to say when it was?'

'No. It was some months ago.'

'Where did it take place?'

'Across the road from the chip shop at the junction of the High Street and Doggett Road.'

'Where were you when it happened?'

'I was outside the chip shop.'

'At what time did it take place?'

'I am not sure of the exact time, but it was soon after closing time. I had been in the Dog and Bone. I left and went to the chip shop to get some supper and I was just about to go in when I heard a commotion across the road.'

'Yes?'

'Well, I looked over and I saw two men running along the High Street and then turn into Doggett Road. They were being chased by two policemen.'

'Yes. Then what happened?'

'One of the policemen caught one of the men in Doggett Road. The other man ran on up Doggett Road and the second policeman chased him.'

'What happened then?'

'Well the first policeman took hold of the first man and they appeared to be standing talking.'

'Yes?'

'I didn't see what happened to the other man and the other policeman until they came back down Doggett Road to where the first policeman was standing with the first man.'

'Yes?'

'Well. I watched them for a bit. They just seemed to be talking. Then a police van arrived and I went into the chip shop to get my supper.'

'Did you see anything more?'

'No. When I came out they had all gone.'

'What were the first man and the first policeman doing before the other two came back down Doggett Road?'

'Nothing. They were just standing there. They may have been talking, but I couldn't hear anything from where I was.'

'Was there any fighting?'

'Not that I saw after the first policeman had caught the first man and grabbed him. There didn't seem to be any more physical confrontation. The officer was just holding the man.'

'Are you able to say who the various men and officers were?'

'No. I didn't recognise them and they were too far away to see easily.'

'Please stay there, Mr White, there will be some more questions.' Rachel sat down.

Beryl stood up. 'Mr White, did you see if there was any punching between Mr Turquoise and PC Crimson?'

'Mr Turquoise is the second guy, right? And PC Crimson is the second officer?'

'Yes. I'm sorry Mr White, yes Mr Turquoise is the second guy and . . .'

'This is leading the witness, Madam,' expostulated Violet.

'No, it's not,' said Beryl. 'I'm just trying to identify the men to the witness to help him.'

'Exactly,' said Violet. 'Leading the witness.'

'Madam, I am not leading the witness. I am just trying to identify to him who I am questioning him about,' said Beryl in indignation.

'. . . and anyway you're allowed to lead him,' muttered Rachel, 'you're cross examining him.'

'I didn't see anyone punch anyone,' said William White.

Violet sat down, muttering to himself.

'Well, I haven't any more questions,' said Beryl.

Violet stood up again. He was clearly irritated. 'Mr White. You use the Dog and Bone public house frequently, do you?'

'Yes. Quite frequently. The staff from the station go there a lot.'

'And you've seen these two defendants in the pub, have you?'

'Yes.'

'And they have asked you to come along and give evidence have they?'

'Yes. Well, one of them actually asked me.'

'And you said you would?'

'Yes.'

'And you're prepared to say anything to help your mates out, are you?'

'Sorry?'

'You're prepared to come to court and say anything for your friends to help them out of trouble.'

'They're not my friends and I'm not prepared to lie for them or anybody else.'

'Look at the facts, Mr White. Mr Blue and Mr Turquoise drink in the same pub as you. Yes?'

'I've seen them in the Dog and Bone once.'

'And they've asked you to come to court and give evidence for them.'

'One of them asked me to come. That's Billie.'

'And you discussed with him what you were going to say?'

'No I didn't. I just told him that I had seen the incident outside the chip shop and he took me to see his solicitor.'

'That's not true, is it Mr White? You've come here to tell lies to try and get Mr Blue and Mr Turquoise out of trouble. That's right isn't it?'

'No. That's not true and if I had known I was going to be spoken to like this I wouldn't have come.'[100]

'How did you know that road was called Doggett Road?'

'Because I live up it. That's how.'

'The incident was so far away from you that you couldn't recognise anyone?'

'Well, I didn't know any of them. If they were people I knew I think that I would have recognised them and taken more notice.'

'That's right, Mr White. You were so little interested in the incident that you went into the chip shop.'

'Well, only when I thought it had finished.'

'You couldn't see what was going on, could you Mr White?'

'I'm sorry.'

Rachel stood up. 'I think Mr Violet should make clear to the witness the basis of his cross-examination. Is he saying the witness is lying for his friends or is he saying that he couldn't see the incident? I think the witness should be told so that he can deal with the allegation.'

'I don't see why I should justify my cross-examination to Miss Red, Madam. Anyway I have no further questions to put.'

---

100 Violet made an assessment of this witness that was not borne out by his cross-examination. It is unlikely that the magistrates considered this a suitable way to cross-examine any witness.

Violet sat down.

'I have no re-examination,' said Rachel. 'Do your worships have any questions of Mr White?'

Mrs Yellow looked at her colleagues. They shook their heads. 'No thank you, Mr White.'

'Thank you, Mr White. Your worships, I have one more witness. Mr Ochre, please, usher.'

'Mr Ochre,' called the usher.

26. The evidence of Mr Ochre

Mr Ochre went into the witness box and took the oath.

'Please give the court your full name, Mr Ochre.'

'Yes. Certainly. I am Oswald Oliver Ochre.'

'And your address?'

'My professional address is the Highways Lighting Department, Heeling Borough Council.'

'Have you had cause to examine the street lights in Arbuthnot Street, Mr Ochre?'

'I have indeed.'

'And when was that last?'

'As a result of a complaint as to the lighting in Arbuthnot Street, I examined the lighting in that street on 10 April this year.'

'And what did you find?'

'I found that of the four lights in Arbuthnot Street, two lights were not working.'

'Which ones?'

'I have a sketch plan here. The two lights at the bus station end were working; the two at the other end were not.'

'When were these lights mended?'

'Unfortunately due to financial stringency they have not yet been replaced . . . one cannot . . . alas . . . mend a lightbulb.'

'Yes I'm sorry. Please stay there, Mr Ochre. There may be further questions.'

Violet stood up. 'Mr Ochre, none of this evidence has been put to the officers.'

'I'm sorry.'

'Madam, none of this has been put to the officers for their comment as it should have been.'

Rachel stood up. 'Your worships, there is no obligation to put evidence like this to any other witness. In any case the rule on putting the defence case to prosecution witnesses does not apply in the magistrates' court. Having said that, I have no objection to either officer being recalled to have this evidence put to them for their comment.'

'Perhaps you should finish your cross-examination of Mr Ochre first, Mr Violet,' said the chairman.

'Yes, Madam. Mr Ochre, did you yourself check these lights to see if they were working?'

'Yes. I make a practice of driving down roads where lights are reported out of order . . . on my way home . . . just to check that the report is correct.'

'When did you do that in Arbuthnot Street?'

'Oh I'm afraid I don't know. I remember doing it but not when exactly. It would have been in the week after the report came in.'

'And what did you see when you checked them?'

'The lights were out of action as reported.'

'Yes, thank you.'

Rachel stood up. 'Do your worships have any questions of Mr Ochre?'

'No thank you.'

'Could Mr Ochre leave the court?'

'If the officers are to be recalled to have this evidence put to them, perhaps Mr Ochre ought to remain in case any further points arise, Miss Red,' said the clerk.

'Certainly.'

Mr Ochre went to the back of the court and sat down.

'If I may, I would like to recall PC Orange to have this evidence put to him, as it should have been, Madam,' said Violet.

27. The recall of Police Constable Orange

PC Orange went back into the witness box.

'You are still under oath, officer,' said Mrs Yellow.

'Yes, your worship.'

'Officer,' said Violet. 'You have been in court and you have heard the evidence of Mr Ochre. What do you say?'

'I say that the defendants' faces were illuminated by the street lighting, your worships.'

'Thank you, officer . . .'

Rachel stood up. 'May I ask the officers some questions arising out of that, your worships?'

'Certainly, Miss Red.'

'Officer. You went to Arbuthnot Street on 6 May, after the defendants had been arrested and released, during the day, didn't you?'

'I expect we were in Arbuthnot Street as part of our duties, your worships.'

'No. You went back to decide what you were going to say the defendants had done.'

'No, your worships.'

'It was during the day so you were not able to see that that street light was not working.'

'No, your worships.'

'You decided what you were going to say and then . . . then . . . (Rachel waved her pencil at the officer) wrote up the notebooks dealing with the 22 April.'

'No, your worships.'

'And that is why your notebooks for 22 April describe the defendants as, "A man I now know to be Terry Turquoise and a man I now know to be Billie Blue". By then you did know them. That's what you did, isn't it?'

'No, your worships.'

'But what of course you couldn't know was that the street light you intended to rely upon so heavily in your notes and in your evidence was out of action. You didn't know that, did you?'

'That's not correct, your worships.'

'I have no further questions, your worships.'

'Do you want to recall the other officer, Mr Violet?' said Mrs Yellow.

'No thank you, Madam.'

'Miss Red, do you have any more evidence?'

'No, your worships, that is the case for Billie Blue.'

28. Criminal Justice and Public Order Act 1994 s35

'Madam,' said Violet, rising to his feet. 'Before m'friend addresses you, I have a submission to make.'

'Yes?' said Mrs Yellow.

'It's a submission under s35 of the Criminal Justice and Public Order Act 1994. . . . No doubt you are familiar with the provisions of the section. . . . Madam, the section reads: "Where, in any proceedings against a person for an offence, evidence is given that the accused (a) at any time . . . on being questioned . . . by a constable trying to discover whether or by whom the offence had been committed, failed to mention any fact relied on in his defence in those proceedings; or (b) on being charged with the offence . . . failed to mention any such fact, being a fact which in the circumstances existing at the time the accused could reasonably have been expected to mention when so questioned, charged or informed, as the case may be, subsection (2) below applies. (2) Where this subsection applies . . . the court or jury, in determining whether the accused is guilty of the offence charged, may draw such inferences from the failure as appear proper." . . . Madam, this provision applies exactly to this case. Each of these defendants has put forward an alibi in relation to the Arbuthnot Street charge on 22 April. Both defendants were charged with the offence of vehicle interference in Arbuthnot Street on 22 April at Heeling police station on 6 May. The wording of the charges made abundantly clear to these two defendants sufficient circumstances of the offence to enable them to give the charging officer the details of these alibis at the time of the charge . . . The charging officer gave each defendant the correct caution to bring s35 of the Act into play, as you can see from the custody record . . . Madam, this sort of situation is exactly what the provisions of the Criminal Justice and Public Order Act 1994 were brought in to combat . . . defendants waiting until the day of their trial before revealing a defence of this sort . . . a spurious defence of this sort . . . I would therefore submit to you that you should rule that this is a situation within the ambit of s35 in which the defendants should have revealed the circumstances of this defence to the charging officer at the time of charging and that secondly you should draw an adverse inference from their failure to disclose the alibis. . . . The inference I would ask you to draw is that the reason the alibis were not revealed to the charging officer is that at the time of charging the defendants had not yet concocted them . . .'

Violet sat down and turning to the officers gave them a brief wintry smile.

'Miss Black?' enquired Mrs Yellow.

Beryl rose to her feet. 'Madam. I would ask you to say that such an inference should not be drawn in this case. As you have heard, my client, Mr Turquoise did not understand what he was being charged with at Heeling police station on 6 May. He thought it was to do with the offences he was suspected of committing on that evening. I would ask you to say that it would be wholly unreasonable to expect him to give his alibi at that time. He simply hadn't had time to sort it out. . . .'

'Exactly,' said Violet.

'Miss Red?'

'Your worships. The provisions of this Act seem at first sight to be simple enough. When, however, they are looked at in detail they are extraordinarily difficult to apply. And there is a very grave danger of substantial miscarriages of justice unless they are applied with great care. The first consideration under s35 is whether there was any point raised in the defence that should reasonably have been made known to the charging officer . . . I would concede that an alibi is almost certainly capable of falling within such a category . . . It might be hard to find a point of defence that the section was more specifically designed to cover. Before the section comes into play, it has to be established whether it is reasonable to have expected the defendant to have revealed the feature of his defence at the time of being charged . . . I would urge your worships to say that it is not reasonable to have expected Mr Blue to have told the charging officer of his alibi . . . I would ask you to consider the facts that came out in evidence. And that is the evidence of both the prosecution and the defence . . . The first time Mr Blue was made aware of the specific date and place of the charge of interfering with motor vehicles in Arbuthnot Street was as the charge was being read out. This is common ground to both the prosecution and defence cases. Mr Blue has told you that he was charged and released from the police station in quick succession. There is no prosecution evidence to the contrary. He has told you in evidence that he had no time whatsoever to work out precisely when the charge related to or where he had been on that date. If Mr Blue had been interviewed, the position might have been different. He was not interviewed . . . I would ask you to say that it would be harder to find a case in which it could be more convincingly said that s35 should not come into play as Mr Blue could not reasonably have been expected to give the details he has given in evidence today . . .

'There is a second matter and that is that Mr Blue did not have the benefit of legal advice before the charge was put to him. He had of course been offered legal assistance on his arrival at Heeling police station. But at that time he was under arrest for different matters so far as he was concerned. Mr Blue told you that he thought he had been arrested for vehicle interference on the night of his arrest. I would urge you strongly that if the prosecution seek to bring s35 into play in relation to a charge, they must show that, in full knowledge of the charge that he faced, the defendant had been offered legal advice so that he could have had explained to him the implications of every important step he took or failed to take . . .'

Rachel considered quickly whether she should use the same arguments in urging the justices if they thought the section did come into play to draw no adverse inference. She equally quickly decided that this would dilute her main argument.

'That is my submission.'

Violet quickly stood up. 'May I answer Miss Red's point, Madam?'

'Yes, Mr Violet.'

'Madam, I am afraid that none of the points Ms Red makes meet the case in point. A defendant cannot be permitted to evade the consequences of the section by pleading ignorance either of the charge or the law. The fact that he receives no legal advice, for whatever reason, is no basis for evading the section. Otherwise every knowledgeable defendant would refuse legal advice and use this as a basis for escaping the effect of the section. In this case the two defendants when arrested were told that they were being arrested for vehicle interference two weeks previously. The fact that they claim not to have realised the day on which this is alleged to have occurred until the words of the charge were read out cannot assist them for this reason . . . Unless the defendants knew that they had been involved in an incident in which they had escaped from officers, they must have had in mind that they were going to put forward an alibi in evidence. They therefore could and should each have told the charging officer that they had not been present when the offences being put to them had been committed. . . . The reason of course that they did not is that at the time of being charged they knew they had been there . . .'

Violet sat down.

The clerk turned to Mrs Yellow and whispered extensively to her. Mrs Yellow nodded several times. Then she looked at the advocates.

'We have been advised that we should consider the questions under s35 of the Criminal Justice and Public Order Act when we consider the case generally. We will therefore now hear the defence speeches . . . Miss Black?'

29. Beryl's closing speech

Beryl tried to master her rising sense of panic. It was for her to address the magistrates first. She had spent the time during the evidence called by Rachel trying to sort out something sensible to say. The problem was that she was so inexperienced that she had little idea of how to put together a coherent speech. She had no idea of what sort of argument might sway the magistrates in their view of the case.

Beryl stood up and gave Mrs Yellow a sickly grin. 'It's for me to address you now on behalf of Mr Turquoise,' she said.

'Yes . . . Miss Black.' Mrs Yellow just managed to avoid calling the nerve-stricken advocate 'Dearie'.

'The prosecution have called their evidence in this case and it seems to me to be . . . to be evidence on which it would be impossible to say that the defendant . . . Terry Turquoise has committed any crime at all. He has specifically denied that he did anything wrong and in particular denies that he was there on . . . on . . . in Arbuthnot Street . . . Street when the police officers say he was. . . .'

Beryl rambled on for some minutes, staring with glazed eyes at the magistrates who sat looking at her in stunned silence.

'. . . and finally, Madam, I would remind you of the burden of proof in this case. You . . . the prosecution . . . you cannot convict Terry Turquoise of the offence . . . of either offence unless you are sure . . . that is . . . it has been proved to your satisfaction beyond a reasonable doubt that he committed the offence. I would remind you of the point in the evidence when the officer . . . Police Constable Orange . . . no, Police Constable Heselfig said that the arrest had taken place in the High Street instead of in the side road . . . Dogger Place, madam. I would ask you to accept that that answer colours . . . undermines the prosecution case so as to make it completely unreliable . . . and finally that the contradictions over the notes show the police officers to have completely fabricated the case against these defendants who should be aquitted.'

'Miss Red?' said Mrs Yellow after watching Beryl subside into her seat in relief.

30. Rachel's closing speech

'Your worships,' Rachel began. 'This is a most unfortunate case. Unfortunate because there is only one conclusion that your worships can draw from the prosecution evidence.[101] And that is that these officers, and in particular Police Constables Orange and Crimson have come to this court with the intention of deceiving your worships.[102] Both officers claimed that they had written their notes for the 22 April incident in Arbuthnot Street within an hour of the incident in the canteen at Heeling police station. That claim, your worships *was not true*. Your worships, each officer referred to the two defendants in those notes as *"a man I now know as Terry Turquoise"* and *"a man I now know as Billie Blue"*. They could not have written those notes on the night of 22 April, because they did not know the defendants' identities until 6 May when the officers arrested the defendants and took them to Heeling Police Station.

'In order to obtain your worships' consent to their referring to those notes, each of these two officers lied to your worships, saying they had written their notes that night, when they could not have done so. Where does that place the credibility of these officers? I would say that so far as this case is concerned it is quite impossible to say that anything these officers gave in evidence is proved beyond a reasonable doubt. Indeed, everything they said is riddled with very reasonable doubt.

'Even the evidence of Police Constable Pink, limited though his involvement is, has been tainted by the same techniques. PC Pink had

---

101 The fluency of the experienced and competent advocate looks like magic. In fact the explanation is prosaic. Experience means that the advocate has encountered many permutations of facts, circumstances and arguments. The experienced advocate has an armoury of rudimentary arguments and techniques. It is a simple matter to assemble an apt and compelling speech from them. But it is not so simple for the inexperienced advocate who does not have this armoury. Every point has to be painstakingly thought out and fitted together with its newly devised comrades.

102 This is a dangerous way to begin a closing speech. It may antagonise the magistrates. Even with the best benches, it can sometimes seem that the defendant has to prove his innocence. By making this bold assertion of lying by the officers, Rachel raises the burden of proof for herself. Rachel is aware of this. However she is determined to put her view of the police evidence exactly and boldly. Rachel takes steps to lower the burden of proof she faces later in her speech.

recorded in his notebook the names of the defendants when there was no way, on his initial evidence, that he could have known their identities unless prompted by the other officers.

'With that fundamental flaw in the officers' notes, I would ask you to look with great care at the rest of the evidence that they gave. You will recollect the incident in PC Orange's evidence when he initially gave the position of the second car in Arbuthnot Street as being on the far side of the road, in contrast to the evidence given by PC Crimson, which was that the car was on the same side as the police car. PC Orange then changed his evidence on the position of the car to his own side of the road. Your worships had a better view of the court and will have formed a more reliable opinion of how the officer came to change this feature of his evidence. I formed the distinct impression that PC Crimson raised his left arm at this point in the evidence and that PC Orange was looking at him when he did this . . . PC Orange's initial evidence was consistent with what he had written in his notes . . . Once he had changed his account . . . his evidence ceased to be consistent with his notes.

'Your worships, these officers' notes were identically worded in the descriptions recorded in them. I would urge you to look closely at what the officers claimed to have taken place. Dealing with the arrests in Doggett Road, Police Constable Orange described what he claimed took place when he arrested Billie Blue. It must be a matter of some surprise that Police Constable Crimson gave an identical description in his notes. The reality, your worships, even if Police Constable Orange was being truthful, must have been different. PC Crimson was a matter of feet behind PC Orange and running flat out to catch Terry Turquoise. Is it conceivable that he saw and took in so much of what happened between PC Orange and Billie Blue when he must have been past them in a matter of a second and on up the road? . . . I would ask you to say that it isn't . . .

'I would invite your worships to consider carefully what the custody sergeant wrote in the custody record later in the police station, recording, as PC Orange told you, what PC Orange had told him. He wrote, "*DP arrested interfering with motor vehicle, chased and arrested.*" The custody sergeant had to make decisions as to whether there was evidence on which to charge Billie Blue and PC Orange knew that. It is embodied in s37 of the Police and Criminal Evidence Act 1984. Section 37 is in Part IV of the Act, which deals with the very strict requirements of how a prisoner in police custody should be treated. The section reads: "*Where a person is arrested for an offence . . . the custody officer . . . shall determine whether he has before him sufficient evidence to charge that person with the offence for which he was arrested . . .*"[103]

'Your worships, it was essential that the custody sergeant was told everything relevant about the offences for which Billie Blue had been arrested. Yet the wording in the custody record gives the clear impression that the vehicle interference had taken place on the same night as the arrest. I would urge your worships that there is only one conclusion to be drawn from that. And that is that the officers at the time that that custody record entry was made, had not yet decided to make the allegation relating to 22 April in Arbuthnot Street. They still had in mind to allege that the vehicle interference had taken place immediately prior to the arrests . . . on 6 May. The first time the allegation of vehicle interference on 22 April in Arbuthnot Street was put in a proper and comprehensible form to the defendants was when they were charged . . .' (for the rest of the sentence Rachel tapped her pencil on the desk in rhythm to her words) '*even on the officers' own evidence.*[104]

'Your worships, is it believable that an officer of even moderate competence would tell an arrested person that he or she was being arrested for interfering with motor vehicles *the other day*, and not give any further details?

'Your worships, the defendants were entitled to an opportunity to

---

103 When an advocate reads from any form of text, statute, text book or law report, the tendency is for the voice to speed up, to rise in pitch and for emphasis to be levelled out. This conveys a clear signal to the listeners: 'This is boring and irrelevant, do not listen'. As this is not a conscious effect, deliberate steps have to be taken to give the reverse signal. When reading to a court, the advocate should increase the volume, lower the voice, slow down the delivery and exaggerate the emphasis. The advocate should look frequently at each magistrate to ensure that he or she is listening. If the text is really boring and irrelevant, it should not be read.

104 For most of the time Rachel tries to stand as still as possible in a stance that causes no distraction to her listeners. Violet has a habit of putting one foot on the seat beside him. This irritates Mr Magenta, who was a drill sergeant in the Coldstream Guards and likes people to stand properly. The two women magistrates, who are used to male gestures of dominance and self-satisfaction, take no notice. Occasionally Rachel uses her pencil to make a point, either in this way or by waving it at witnesses when making a particularly telling point in cross-examination. Rachel uses the pencil sparingly and the magistrates who know Rachel recognise that she considers something to be of particular significance when the pencil emerges.

explain themselves, and the police officers as they very well knew, were under an obligation to give the defendants the opportunity to explain themselves. Is it really conceivable that police officers would not have put such allegations in detail to the defendants when they arrested them, if they had them in mind? Or at the very latest when they got them to the police station? Isn't it the only plausible explanation that the officers did not have any other occasion in mind for the allegation of interfering with motor vehicles . . . other than that night . . . the night of the arrest? If that is so, what happens to the court's view of who is correct on the description of the arrests and whether the defendants put up any resistance, as has been claimed by the officers?

'I have given your worships my view of the truthfulness of the officers' evidence. But of course the officers' truthfulness is not the issue in this trial and it is the wrong way to approach the decisions that have to be made. The law requires[105] . . . that you look at the evidence in the case as a whole and not that you try and decide which side is telling the truth . . . that you decide whether on that evidence the prosecution have proved the case on each charge . . .' (pencil again) '*so that you have no doubt but that the defendant committed that offence.* Only if you have no such doubt does that defendant stand in danger of being convicted on that charge.

'I would urge your worships that in this case, there must at the very least be a doubt about the accuracy of the prosecution case . . . At the very least, your worships.

'May I end by reminding you of perhaps the only piece of wholly independent evidence. The two officers made it clear in their evidence to this court that it was the street light right by the car in Arbuthnot Street on 22 April that enabled them to identify the two men as the defendants. Mr Ochre from Heeling Borough Council Lighting Department, a witness with no knowledge of the case or any of the parties and witnesses to it, has told you that light was not working on that day . . . and is still not working. The officers said

---

105 Rachel has quite deliberately moved from the first person 'my view' to the third person, 'the law requires'. As she is a lawyer of repute in this court, the magistrates accept the change and are likely particularly to take note of what she then says. Over years of practice in this court Rachel has taken care to make sure that she is as accurate as possible in the legal opinions she expresses to the magistrates and they always find her opinions instructive and helpful. The change is also a rhetorical sleight of hand. She is now dictating to the magistrates rather than urging them. But she only does it briefly.

both in their evidence-in-chief and in cross-examination in answer to the specific point that without that light they could not have identified and subsequently recognised the defendants . . . Your worships, the light was not working on that night . . . I ask you to acquit Billie Blue of these two offences.'

Rachel sat down.

Mrs Yellow stood up. 'We will adjourn to consider our verdict.'

'Stand, please,' bawled Horace the usher. The magistrates gathered their notes and trooped out.

CHAPTER 16

The pleas in mitigation

Beryl came out of the courtroom. Terry and Billie were standing disconsolately in the hall.

Beryl went over to Terry. 'Look, I'm sorry about the result. I hope you feel I did the case as well as I could.'

Terry looked at her.

'It was my first contested case.'

'What? Your first contested case? How long have you been doing this?' said Terry.

'Just for two weeks.'

'*What?* You've been a barrister for only two weeks and those solicitors lumber me with you? I don't believe it! No wonder we bloody lost . . . Your first bloody case . . .'

Rachel came out of the court and stood on the edge of the group.

'Rachel here did a really good job for Billie . . . but you go and lose the case for us.'

Beryl was horrified by his unexpected reaction. 'I have been a barrister for much longer than that. It's just that I have only been able to do my own cases for two weeks.'

The courtroom door opened and Violet came out with two of the police officers.

'Well, cheerio,' called Violet affably to the officers.

'Yes sir. Thank you very much,' said PC Orange loudly to Violet.

'Pleasure, officer. Any time. Well, I'll be off. I just have to go and consult with the Crown Prosecution Service over the file.' Violet strode off down the corridor.

The officers passed the group as they made for the door.

'So long, Billie . . . Terry,' said PC Orange. 'Better luck next time, eh?'

'Fucking coppers,' said Terry bitterly after the officers had left the court. 'Come on, Billie.' He turned to Beryl. 'I'm going to tell   251 those solicitors what I think of you . . . and them.' He walked off and out through the door.

Billie spoke to Rachel. 'You did your best, Rachel. It's a pity everyone didn't. I'll see you in the office.' He gave Beryl a withering look and followed Terry.

'Don't take it to heart,' said Rachel. 'I don't think they were very fair to you. I'm not quite sure why they are blaming you.'

'I told them it was my first contested case.'

'Ah, well, that was a mistake. Terry was sore at losing and as soon as you said that, you gave him someone else to blame for losing other than himself. One of the first things you learn in this business is never to make admissions of weakness to anyone. If you'd kept quiet about it, Terry wouldn't have known and he would probably have been quite satisfied with you.'

'I was going to be a vet when I was doing my A levels. I wish I had stuck to that.'

'Beryl, every profession has its bad moments. Come on, let's go and have some coffee and talk over what happened.'

1. Pre-sentence reports

Rachel arrived at Heeling Magistrates' Court on 6 August at 9.30 am. Billie was nowhere to be seen. She went in search of the duty probation officer. Rachel finally tracked the officer down at 9.45 am as she hurried into the court with a pile of reports. Rachel extracted from her Billie's report and took it over to the advocate's bench. She had little time, as the bench that had tried Billie and Terry's case were sitting specially at 10 am to sentence them before dispersing to other courts around the building.

The probation report was a page-and-a-half long. Rachel's estimate of the bench was that they would not give Billie a custodial sentence if they could be given some convincing argument to impose a non-custodial one. It was Rachel's experience that the justices would normally accept a reasonably argued case in a probation report for a non-custodial sentence.

The probation report read:

Report on **Billie Blue**
Address: 33 Claribel Mansions, the Glen, Heeling, telephone number: 081 855 5656:
Date of birth: 14 February 1970.
Billie Blue has been found guilty of two offences:

1) Interfering with a motor vehicle with intent to steal from it on 22 April 1996 in Arbuthnot Street, Heeling.
2) On 6 May 1992 assaulting Orlando Orange, a constable of the Metropolitan Police in the execution of his duty.

Billie lives in council accommodation with his girlfriend, Noreen and their daughter, Cologna, aged six months.

The address is a one-bed roomed flat of which Noreen is the tenant. Billie has lived with Noreen for five months. Before that he lived with his mother and family at 35 Dresden Drive, Heeling.

Billie attended Heeling Comprehensive School, leaving at the age of 16 with GCSEs in art and technical drawing. He then went into his grandfather's panel-beating business as a trainee panel-beater. Billie is still employed there as a panel-beater. The business is called XYZ Panel Beaters of 13 Wingnut Crescent, Heeling. Billie earns around £100 per week net.

Billie has outgoings of: £35 per week rent, £5 per week fares. Billie contributes around £50 per week to the household bills and £5 per week on an outstanding fine of which £200 remains outstanding.

Billie's family consists of his mother and his sister Esmeralda. His father left home when he was 12 years old. The father now lives in Liverpool. The family does not see him.

Billie was in care for a year when he was 13 years old for a year, the reasons being that Billie was not going to school and his mother could not control him.

Billie has been convicted seven times, of which five were by Heeling Juvenile Court. In 1989 he was given a sentence of six months youth custody for several charges of vehicle interference. His remaining convictions are all for theft or interfering with motor vehicles or taking a motor vehicle without consent. Billie was on probation for one year from 1990. I was his probation officer. I had a good relationship with him. Billie worked hard while on probation and attended for appointments without trouble.

Billie is in breach of a conditional discharge for taking a motor vehicle without the owner's consent which was imposed on him on 25 August 1992. The facts of that offence are that Billie had been to play football at a club in Bedford. Billie phoned home and was told that his mother had been taken to hospital. He panicked and took a car to get to the hospital. Billie tells me that he left some money for the petrol in the car and that was why he was not given a custodial sentence.

The present offences

I understand from Billie that he pleaded not guilty to the two offences but was convicted. I have spoken to Billie about them and he still insists that he did not commit them. I do not therefore propose to comment on

254 Advocacy in the Magistrates Court / Chapter 16

them in detail. I understand that the first offence involved Billie in trying
car door handles with the intent to steal from the cars and on the second
occasion with resisting arrest and striking the officer who tried to arrest
him.

I have known Billie and his girlfriend for some time. I have on a
number of occasions met and spoken to Billie's grandfather for whom
he works. I know that Billie is an extremely hard-working and valued
member of his grandfather's company. His relationship with his girlfriend is a different matter. It is clearly a very fragile relationship and the
strains are considerable. I know from Billie's girlfriend that the previous
period of probation caused Billie to behave much better in every sphere
of his life, including his attitude and behaviour towards Noreen and the
baby.

I am inclined to think that Billie offends when with others. This does
not mean that he is easily influenced by anyone else, just that he behaves
badly when in company with other young men of a similar irresponsible
turn of mind.

My recommendation to the court would be a two-year period of
probation. I would seek to help Billie adopt a more responsible attitude
towards his girlfriend and his daughter and to structure his non-working
time more constructively. I believe that this would have an influence on
Billie and might well take him through his present irresponsible phase
into a more adult approach to life. During the period of such an order, if
one were made, I would expect to work on more constructive ways for
Billie to spend his spare time rather than with other criminally inclined
young men.

I do not believe that community service would be appropriate in view
of the hours that Billie is required to work.

Signed: Sid Silver, senior probation officer, Heeling Probation Office.

Rachel went out into the hallway. The crowd was considerable.
Billie was standing by the window. Rachel caught his eye and he
made his way over to her.

'Hullo, Rachel.'

'I've got the report, Billie.'

'What's it like?'

'It's all right.'

'Sid Silver is a good guy. What does he recommend?'

'Two years probation.'

'Two years? Whew! I'll be on his team till I croak.'

'It's better than prison.'

'You don't say! Am I in danger of prison?'

'You know you are. You're in breach of a conditional discharge
for taking a motor vehicle. Then bopping a copper gets a prison

sentence all on its own these days. And you've got quite a bit of form, including bopping coppers.'

'So what happens now?'

'I do my bit.'

'You do just that, Rachel and you get free resprays for your wings for life.'

'Tasty offer.'

Beryl came bustling over with Terry in tow.

'Hullo, Rachel . . . Hullo Mr Blue.'

'Mr Blue? . . . a bit formal ain't it?'

The usher appeared at Rachel's elbow. 'Miss Red, the court is ready for you in the cases of Blue and Turquoise.'

'Right, Horace.'

They went into court. To Billie and Terry's relief, there was no sign of Violet. As the sentencing had gone back into the general list, it was being dealt with by the regular Crown Prosecution Service prosecutor, Mr Scarlet. He peered in mystification at the file.

'Mr Scarlet, the bench is the same bench who tried the case,' said the clerk. 'They do not need to hear the facts.'

Mr Scarlet was visibly relieved. 'And the antecedents?'

'All given last time . . . just reports,' said the clerk.

Mr Scarlet sat down.

The duty probation officer handed the reports to the clerk who passed them back to the magistrates.

'Good morning, Miss Red, Miss Black,' said Mrs Yellow.

'Good morning your worships.'

'Would you wish us to read the reports or do you wish to address us first?' asked Mrs Yellow.

Rachel answered quickly: 'I would prefer you to read the reports first, please, your worships.'

'Very well,' said Mrs Yellow, standing up and leading the magistrates to the door.

'All stand', bawled the usher.

2. Beryl's plea in mitigation

Ten minutes later the magistrates returned.

'Yes, Miss Black?' said Mrs Yellow.

'If it please you, Madam. You have read the report on Mr Turquoise. I would now like to say a few words on his behalf . . . Can I start by reminding you that Mr Turquoise pleaded not guilty to these two charges . . . He denied them emphatically. You will recollect the nature of the evidence against him . . . It was the evidence of two . . . no, three police officers . . . whose evidence was of the most . . . the most . . . the most unbelievable sort . . . You will recollect that they had in their notebooks entries they said they made on the night of the first incident . . . I should say the first "alleged" incident . . . details of entries . . . they could not have put in if they made their notes up when they say they did . . .

'Of course you have found Mr Turquoise guilty . . . but at this stage I would ask you to say that the basis of the evidence against him is . . . was such that in spite of that finding the penalty should only be a nominal one[1] . . . The report has suggested a probation order . . . I would urge you to adopt that recommendation . . . Madam.'[2]

3. Rachel's plea in mitigation

Beryl sat down.

'Yes, Miss Red,' said Mrs Yellow.

Rachel rose. She knew the reactions of these magistrates fairly well. If they had been immediately impressed by the correctness of the recommendation, Mrs Yellow would probably have said so straight away. The fact that nothing was said meant that something nastier than probation was at least in their minds. This meant that Rachel would have to deploy all her troops.

'Your worships, can I start off by saying that neither I nor Mr Blue would seek to pretend that this is other than a serious case and that both I and Mr Blue realise what sort of sentence you will have in

---

1   At the end of a bitterly contested case there is always a great temptation for an advocate to allow the question of 'guilty/not guilty' to spill over into an address in mitigation. If this is to be done, it must be in such a way that the court is not directly challenged on its finding. Otherwise the address is in danger of being in aggravation of sentence, not mitigation.

2   The danger in a recommendation of this sort is that the court will view it as a nominal penalty and a let-off. The advocate therefore needs to bolster the impression that the reverse is so and that a probation order will not be a nominal order but will be arduous for the defendant, beneficial for him and in particular will benefit the community in preventing the defendant from offending again.

3   Unless the court specifically say they have a custodial sentence in mind it is best not to refer to such a sentence in terms in case the court did not have it in mind . . . that is until the advocate suggested that it might be appropriate . . .

mind.[3] Nevertheless I would urge upon your worships that the recommendation made by Mr Silver, the probation officer, in his report is the correct one.

'I do not intend to say very much about the facts of the case following the contested hearing two weeks ago.[4] Your worships will have formed your own view as to what took place on those two nights. What I would seek to remind you, goes to the degree of seriousness of the offences of which you have convicted Mr Blue.

'In relation to the offence in Arbuthnot Street, it was clear on the police officers' evidence that there was no loss to anyone. Otherwise it has to be assumed the officers would have made some effort to identify and contact the owners of the cars concerned. So far as the assault on the officer is concerned, I would ask you to accept that, serious though it undoubtedly was, because any assault on a police officer in the execution of his duty is serious, it is a less serious example of such an offence. The officer suffered no injury and does not appear to have made any complaint of being assaulted when he got to the police station.[5]

'Your worships, Billie Blue does not have a good record. He has been before the courts on a number of occasions. However, he has two features that set him apart from many regular offenders. The first is that he has what appears to be a stable and supportive family around him, together with his own immediate commitments to his girlfriend and baby daughter, and secondly, he has a good regular job that, your worships, he has held for a number of years.[6]

---

4 This form of misleading introduction seems to be a standard technique in the English courts. The declaration, 'I hesitate to interrupt your honour', usually precedes a far from hesitating interruption.

5 These were points Rachel made in her cross-examination closing speech at the end of the trial. She makes them again primarily to remind the magistrates of the shaky basis for their decision to convict Billie. It is often the case that if magistrates are uneasy as to the correctness of the decision to convict they will reflect this in a lenient sentence. The same principle does not tend to apply to Stipendiary Magistrates who may convict on the flimsiest of evidence and then without qualm sentence as if the defendant had committed the offence.

6 The art of mitigation is to emphasise carefully the features in a defendant's background that militate against sending the defendant to prison, thereby making it difficult for the magistrates to overcome the reservations they are likely to have on sending a person to prison. Family commitments and the threat to a person's work are two of the most potent.

'Your worships, perhaps one of the most telling conclusions that Mr Silver has come to during the substantial period he has been able to observe Mr Blue, is that while on probation Billie Blue behaves well.[7] As the purpose of the sentencing process is in substantial measure to find ways of protecting the public from the offender, I would strongly urge your worships to adopt Mr Silver's recommendation of a two-year probation order. Mr Blue is 26 years old with a very young family. Mr Silver seems to be strongly of the view that a two-year order would enable him to bring about substantial changes in Billie Blue's attitude and conduct and it seems to be his view that in addition his attitude will be forced to change by the increasing involvement he is bound to have in the bringing up of his daughter.[8]

'Your worships, I have spoken about Billie Blue's future with his grandfather who employs him. The grandfather has told me that he is thinking about retiring in the next few years. He has told me that Billie is good at his job on the whole, although sometimes he can be somewhat immature. The grandfather has said that provided Billie keeps at the job for another six months he is going to take him in as a partner, with the possible aim of passing the business over to him when he does retire. Your worships, unfortunately the grandfather, Mr Albert Blue, could not come to court today in view of Billie's absence and pressure of work. But he asked me to present his view to the court.

'Of course your worships may well feel that there should in addition be a substantial feature of punishment in any order made. If that was the court's view, may I suggest that this could be reflected by way of compensation for the officer and in costs for the contested hearing.[9]

'I would urge the court that overall the interests of the com-

---

7   It is an effective technique to present points as coming from someone other than the advocate, particularly if the vehicle is a source the court is likely to hold in some regard such as a probation officer.

8   The technique of giving the court a glimpse of how life for the defendant might be under a probation order, makes it that much more attractive for the court.

9   Good advocacy is partly a matter of anticipating the needs of the court. If the advocate provides the court with a realistic course of action, there is a good chance that the court will adopt that course. This applies particularly in mitigation and in applications for bail. The competent and well prepared advocate gives the court the impression of having thought through the problem of disposal. Although the advocate is inevitably partisan, provided the court trusts the advocate and the solution sounds appropriate, there is a good chance that the court will adopt it, at least in part.

munity would best be served by the imposing of the probation order recommended so that Mr Silver can take the necessary steps to ensure that Billie Blue does not offend again.'

Rachel then sat down.[10]

Again the magistrates retired to consider their decision.

The magistrates returned to the court after about ten minutes.

'Stand up please . . . Mr Turquoise and Mr Blue, we have listened carefully to what has been said on your behalf and read the probation reports. You will each serve a sentence of two months' imprisonment. That is all . . . Take them down.'

---

10 In ordering probation and community service reports at the end of the trial, the magistrates had not specifically said that a custodial sentence was what they had in mind. Rachel knew the magistrates and thought that Mrs Yellow and Mr Magenta would probably be following the Lord Chief Justice's guidelines that an assault on the police should normally attract a custodial sentence and that Mrs Beige would not be thinking of a custodial sentence. Rachel also knew the clerk and thought that she would probably not have reminded the magistrates of the guidelines. Rachel had to address the magistrates on the basis that they would be considering a custodial sentence because to do otherwise would have been unrealistic. On the other hand Rachel did not want to show the magistrates that she thought they should be considering imprisonment by specifically referring to a 'custodial sentence', hence the oblique approach.

Index